PRAISE for *The Moved and the Shaken*

"A fascinating book that seeks to understand and illuminate the life of an average Canadian."

The Vancouver Sun

"Dryden's compassion shines through . . ."

The Ottawa Sun

"Chronicles a life of small triumphs, undeserved heartaches, everyday worries, chances missed, and human kindness . . . an unusual book brought to life by Dryden's ability to find subtle shades of meaning."

The Daily News (Halifax)

"Ken Dryden's wonderful portrait of Frank Bloye — middle-aged husband, father, suburbanite, employee of a multi-national company — could be a book about any of us."

The Ottawa Citizen

"Compelling . . . Walking a few miles in the shoes of another is always interesting, and never more so than when we feel a certain kinship; when some of the day-to-day humdrum is our humdrum, too."

Star-Phoenix (Saskatoon)

"Dryden has cut beneath the surface, sometimes exposing raw thoughts and feelings of the ordinary Canadian and his family. . . . We all have the same concerns and worries as Frank Bloye, whether we like it or not."

Winnipeg Free Press

PENGUIN BOOKS

THE MOVED AND THE SHAKEN

Ken Dryden was a goalie for the Montreal Canadiens throughout the 1970s. After obtaining his law degree, he turned to writing, and in 1983 published the phenomenal bestseller *The Game*. He was appointed Youth Commissioner in 1984 by the Ontario Government, and went on to create the CBC series and bestselling book *Home Game* in 1989. Today, he lives in Toronto with his wife and two children.

THE MOVED
AND THE SHAKEN

KEN DRYDEN

Penguin Books

PENGUIN BOOKS

Published by the Penguin Group

Penguin Books Canada Ltd, 10 Alcorn Avenue, Toronto, Ontario, Canada M4V 3B2

Penguin Books Ltd, 27 Wrights Lane, London W8 5TZ, England

Penguin Books USA Inc., 375 Hudson Street, New York, New York 10014, U.S.A.

Penguin Books Australia Ltd, Ringwood, Victoria, Australia

Penguin Books (NZ) Ltd, 182-190 Wairau Road, Auckland 10, New Zealand

Penguin Books Ltd, Registered Offices: Harmondsworth, Middlesex, England

First published in Viking by Penguin Books Canada Limited, 1993

Published in Penguin Books, 1994

10 9 8 7 6 5 4 3 2 1

Copyright © Ken Dryden, 1993

Canadian Cataloguing in Publication Data

Dryden, Ken, 1947 -
  The moved and the shaken

ISBN 0-14-010919-6

1. Bloye, Frank, 1947 -   . 2. Ontario - Biography. I. Title

FC3076.1.B56D79 1994   971.3041092   C93-093825-9
F5526.B56D79 1994

Excerpt from "Musée des Beaux Arts" by W.H. Auden from *Collected Poems* edited by
Edward Mendelson. Reprinted with permission of Faber and Faber Ltd.

Excerpts from Imperial Oil jingles reprinted with permission of Imperial Oil Limited.

Excerpt from "Oh Shucks, Ma'am, I Mean Excuse Me" from *Verses from 1929 On* by
Ogden Nash. Copyright © 1943 Ogden Nash. First appeared in *Ladies' Home
Journal.* By permission of Little, Brown and Company.

To L,

who knows the heart

The Moved

and the Shaken

Part One

1

It is where he most likes to be, the time of day that he likes best. The sun has been up for an hour or two, just long enough to cover the chill of the early June morning, just high enough in the sky to see over the bungalows and shadowless nursery-grown trees of northeast Scarborough, to warm him as he slouches low in a lawn chair on the small brick patio he built for himself a year ago. His leather-tanned hands snuggle around a coffee mug cooling and nearly empty in his lap. "After 40, it's patch, patch, patch," the mug reads, now a little chipped and stained itself, a birthday gift nearly three years ago from his three children, still asleep in their beds behind him.

It is Saturday morning.

I'm tired, or I should be. I don't know why I watch those late movies. I don't even like them. And I can never sleep in. Everyone else can. Why can't I?

He turns his head sideways to the sun, the light painting his thick horn-rimmed glasses opaque gold. He squints a straight-mouthed grin across the brightness, his shapeless, brown-grey moustache curling onto his teeth and almost out of sight.

This sun feels so good. Summer really is coming. 'Course, after all the rain we've had we deserve it. Hope it's not going to be like last year. Couldn't get the patio in until late, the flowers never did come up the way they should. The weatherman says it's going to be good, but you can't believe him. Anyway . . .

He shudders his head to cut off thoughts he no longer wants to think, and searches the sky to see nothing.

. . . and here I've been complaining all week how tired I am, and then I stay up . . .

He shudders his head again.

He has been feeling tired a lot these last few months. Imperial Oil, one of Canada's largest companies, with whom he has worked for nineteen years, has taken over Texaco Canada and there have been complications. Twelve thousand Imperial and three thousand Texaco workers and two startlingly different corporate "cultures" have had to be aligned, the takeover debt paid down; yet business must carry on. Old routines which never had seemed important to him now seem precious. He had been comfortable, had known where everything and everyone was and would be. In the thousand and one gestures, words and messages that pass in a day to make a world understandable, he had known what to expect. Now everything feels out of control.

He has lived so much of his life under the thumbs of others, has worked so hard controlling what he can. Getting up at the same time every day, eating the same breakfast, listening to the same DJ for the same music, weather and traffic reports; leaving his house at the same time, avoiding the expressways, travelling the same slower, more certain route, getting to work, leaving work, arriving home, eating dinner with his wife and children always at the same time. He doesn't go to restaurants, they don't know his habits and tastes; he doesn't go to movies, he may not like what he sees. He has never pushed too hard, never looked too far ahead at what might never be. He has never wanted to change much. He notices, he complains; and he accepts. What is is. He likes to do things over and over until he can almost believe he is good at them. He has found in routine the chance to build and maintain his fragile confidence. In routine, he has found control.

Now he sees trouble around every corner. New names and faces to learn, new styles, manners and expectations to get used to, new systems, terminologies and ways of doing things, not Imperial's or Texaco's, but some new and *better* way he doesn't understand. This and the pressure of time and volume of customers that gets worse. He will get through it. Everything will go back to normal, be comfortable, easy, routine again. He has to believe that, and so he does. Yet as the months pass, angry credit-card holders still fill his collector's ear:

A Texaco customer already has an Esso card but the name on it is different enough from the one on her Texaco card (with a middle initial included perhaps) that the computer sent her a second Esso card to replace the phased-out Texaco card. She kept the new card and cut up the old one, thus obliterating her credit history before the Esso computer could imagine the confusion and send out letters to explain that she should do the reverse. So now she gets two monthly bills from Esso, which makes her angry and causes her to ignore one bill, the wrong one, and receive threatening computer letters about her unpaid account which, so far as she knows, is her only account and which (of course) she *has* paid, which only makes her angrier. But that is nothing compared to the anger she feels this very moment because minutes before, she pulled into an Esso station and tried to use her card, but had it taken from her by a dealer advised by the Esso computer to do just that because of her "unpaid balance," which she paid weeks ago, and because Esso wants her to use the old card which has her full credit history — which card, of course, she has cut up.

And his is the first voice she hears.

It's all going to end soon he and his co-workers tell themselves and each other. They can *almost* see the light at the end of their tunnel. After all, things can't go on like this forever; after all, mergers do end. Then more calls come in, and they wonder.

But here in his own backyard, everything is different. It's more than instinct, more than a mother's voice still pulsing in his head that gets him out of bed on a Saturday morning. Here, he's found something he needs *more* than sleep. Only a few hundred metres from Canada's busiest artery, Highway 401, in the middle of working-class Scarborough in the middle of Canada's biggest city in the middle of his ever more inescapable world, it's as if there is just him. Last night, as neighbours binged in celebration at the end of their week, he watched a late movie he didn't like just to have the house to himself. Now as they binge in sleep, the first battle of the new day is his. Saturday morning, alone in his own backyard with a headstart on the world, it's just the way Frank Bloye likes it.

He opens the screen door on the side of the house, and lets it rattle shut behind him. He takes off his shoes, picks up his brown leather slippers from the second top step of the basement stairs, and puts his shoes carefully in the same spot he found them an hour ago. He glances down the stairs — Matt's door is shut — and strides up the five steps in front of him to the main floor.

Ahead, light through a small window over the sink has given the kitchen a shadowy brightness. He turns, looks down a short hallway to his right, to a bathroom door and three bedroom doors shut tight. Last night's darkness is still shuttered in.

A door pops open. "What's it like out, Dad?" It's Stephanie; always Stephanie. Ten years old and the youngest, she is freckled and fresh-faced; with a ponytail arching from one side of her head, she looks as if she's been up for hours.

His voice ignores the time and slams into the darkness. "It's beautiful," he yells back. "Gonna be a beautiful day. Is —"

"No one else's up," she answers before he can ask. "I heard Mom in the bathroom. She must be getting dressed. Everyone else's asleep. The lazybones."

Frank draws open the living-room curtains. The waiting light pours in through the sheers. He flicks on the stereo and walks back to the kitchen. Elton John's "Yellow Brick Road" fills the front rooms with gentle energy. He looks at his watch. It's still not eight o'clock. He turns on the kitchen light, and, leaning over the sink, again checks the thermometer hanging outside the window, still listening for the weather forecast which precedes the news.

Carolyn, his wife, opens their bedroom door and shuffles out, her slippered feet never leaving the carpet. Her eyes are puffy with sleep. She is a handsome woman, with bristle-short black and grey flecked hair, a long narrow face and the kind of solid good looks little noticed in a girl, more appreciated in someone older. In blue jeans and a plaid shirt, she looks dressed up.

"Matt up yet?"

Carolyn shakes her head no.

"Janine?"

No.

Frank unloads the dishwasher, a towel in his hand, drying the bottoms of the glasses and mugs where water has collected, putting them away in the cupboards directly above. He looks forward to what's coming next. He loves breakfasts, big rollicking family breakfasts with harvests of bacon and eggs, toast and coffee. During the week, everything is such a rush, and today, though it's Saturday, there is no time. Yet, breakfast is still ahead, so things might be different. With a nod and a smile, he steps across the room and leans around the corner to the back hallway.

"Ya-up, Janine?!"

Muffled sounds come from behind Janine's door. He takes one more step and leans in the direction of the basement steps.

"Matt, ya-up?!"

Nothing.

"Matthew!"

Still nothing. He turns back into the room.

"It's gonna be a beautiful day," he sings. Carolyn nods. "I don't know why I watch those late movies, though. I don't enjoy them. I wish I could sleep in. Everybody else can." Carolyn, who stayed up with him as long as she could, sewing, watching, dozing until finally she had to go up to bed, nods again.

He pulls their round, wood-stained table out from its corner of the kitchen where it was pushed after last night's dinner, jiggles it until it sits steady on the floor, straightens three of the table's matching chairs, takes the other two from along one wall and slots them into place, picks up the wicker basket of artificial flowers from the middle of the table and puts it in the dining room on top of a wooden silverware case. One motion dissolves into another; Carolyn joins in.

She gets two cereal bowls, five small juice glasses and three small plates from the cupboard. He gets the quilted floral placemats from the top of the refrigerator where he stacked them after brushing last night's dinner crumbs into the sink; he sets them out one at each place, one for the middle of the table. The placemats, which Carolyn made, match the curtains and quilted seat pads on the chairs. She puts the dishes on top of them. He gets orange juice, milk, raspberry and strawberry jam, peanut butter, granola, brown sugar, honey and margarine from the breakfast shelf on the lower left of the refrigerator; she gets out two big spoons, three small spoons, three knives and the white bread.

"Ma-a-att!!"

Before he can yell her name, Janine stumbles into the light, her long dark hair, T-shirt and oversized blue jeans already drooping under the weight of the day. Puberty has hit Janine. At thirteen, she is taller than Carolyn and Matt, who is two years older and a boy, but her features have not yet taken on their final shape. All that growing has also made her tired, especially in the mornings.

During all this, Stephanie has remained visible enough to avoid attention, absent enough to miss the morning routines and do what she wants.

"Took ya long enough," she says just loud enough to be heard, not looking at anyone in particular, her target clear, her timing perfect.

Janine seems not to hear.

"All right, let's start," he yells, mostly for Matt's benefit. "We can't wait any longer."

Each has a glass of juice. He and Carolyn have granola, his with brown sugar; the girls have toast.

"I thought we weren't getting up until eight-thirty," Janine whines. "You said last night, eight-thirty, and we'd start at nine. That's what you said."

He struggles for a moment, then turns mildly on them. "Oh, but it's a beautiful day. Might as well get up. I've been up since six-thirty. All you lazybones — I told you you should've gone to bed earlier. But no, you had to watch that other movie. Seeee . . ."

There is a sound on the stairs. He and Stephanie stop what they're doing. Matt appears. He has his mother's narrow face and dark, delicate features. Above all, he is breathtakingly thin. His Michael Jordan T-shirt hangs from him everywhere. His eyes focus slightly down, slightly to one side.

"Wellll . . ." Frank cannot resist.

Matt slides into his seat, his eyes still down. He picks up his glass of juice and starts drinking. Frank stares at him, scrolling through all the things he might say, but he's in too good a humour to push too hard, and the mood eases.

Music has gone from the radio, the weather forecaster has just told him what he already knows — the day will be sunny and warm, tomorrow the same — and from across the living room and kitchen, he heard every word. Now a voice is going on about Prime Minister Brian Mulroney and the "Meech Lake Accord," how the deadline for its passage is just three weeks away and time is running out. He hears nothing.

Stephanie, waiting for her toast, is peeling stickers off the jam and peanut butter jars. Matt and Janine are finding it hard eating and sleeping at the same time. Carolyn eats her granola quietly. He is full of his plans for the day.

"I want to get the car washed this afternoon. The pool should be done by then. Oh, and I gotta pay my fine at the library, and we need some milk. We need anything else at the store?" Carolyn shakes her head. "One of these years we gotta start the pool on Friday so I can get the water tested and the chemicals in so we can use it on Sunday. One of these years," he repeats and shakes his head.

His eyes never rest. Spotting Matt and Janine listing over what remains of their breakfasts, they override his thoughts. "Sit up straight; elbows off the table," he snaps. His mood flips back. "We can get that ugly cover off and get most of the pool done, anyway. And Matt, I want you to get at that back hill this afternoon. You've really let that slide."

Matt says nothing. He eats his plain white bread and peanut butter, his eyes down and slightly to one side of his father's gaze.

Stephanie can't wait any longer and walks to the toaster to collect her toast. Frank's eyes follow her slippered feet. "Where're your socks?" he growls. Growing up in Whitby (a small town east of Toronto) to avoid catching his "death of cold," he had to wear slippers *and* socks around the house *all* the time. So now, from the moment his family wakes up to the moment they leave for school or work, from the time they return to the time they go to bed, winter and summer, they wear slippers *and* socks all the time. Except Stephanie, sometimes. "You're gonna get blisters," he warns. "I keep telling you. Wear your slippers without your socks and you'll get blisters." He isn't finished. When Stephanie comes back to the table, he glances at her scarcely darkened bread. "You call that toast," he chides. "It's not even warm."

Stephanie smiles, covers over her toast with margarine and peanut butter and munches it down.

The phone rings. Only Stephanie seems in a rush to answer it, but she's on the far side of the table. Finally, Matt stops the ringing. "It's for you," he mumbles, and hands the receiver to Stephanie. "Not too long now," Frank warns. Stephanie disappears into the dining room, the telephone cord pulled taut behind her.

"Who'd be calling at this hour?" he scowls. No one says anything. Stephanie's absence seems to bring everything to a halt. Seconds turn to a minute and his patience can't hold. "Tell her you'll call back later," he snaps.

Stephanie reappears. "Can I go over to Erin's?" Her voice is soft and coquettish.

"Not before this afternoon. We've got things to do, now you know that."

"Is her mother going to be there?" Carolyn asks.

Stephanie disappears again, and from the table they hear her muffled words.

"And remember we're going to Grandma's tonight," he yells after her. "We gotta leave at six and you gotta get home and get ready, so no later than four-thirty."

Stephanie returns looking pleased. "Can I be excused?" she asks. Expecting her to say something else, he looks down at her mostly eaten toast.

"You haven't finished."

"Matt hasn't finished *his* bread," she retorts, and with that, Matt and Janine who have started to get up, freeze in their tracks.

"All right," Frank relents, "but I want everybody out to do the pool in five minutes."

He has his father's height and mother's weight, he likes to say, though that isn't quite right. His father was an inch or two under six feet but lean and straight, he appeared taller. Generationally taller, Frank appears shorter. His mother was short from any perspective. Forty-one years old with six other kids by the time he was born, she was wide and deep and round like a barrel for all the years he knew her. But she carried her weight in front of her as if with pride, and used it like a battering ram. What in others might have been seen as softness, in her was heft — authority. His fatness came early, and left, but his self-image never changed. As if looking into a side-show mirror, he has always seen himself through convexed eyes. And what he sees is his mother's rounded body others do not notice.

His hair is thin and medium-brown. He normally parts it on the left because his father parted his on the right (a little act of defiance he sees no reason to give up). But on this non-working day he has pushed it carelessly forward over his advancing forehead, more likely by hand than brush. He hasn't shaved since yesterday and wouldn't again until tomorrow, except tonight they are going to Carolyn's mom's for dinner. He always shaves on Sunday. He shaves only to meet the minimum expectations of those he can't avoid. At home, he sets his own expectations. So today he's in blue jeans — dark and indigo-coloured, untapered, unlabelled, unbleached — which hang low on his hips. A wash-shrunken pale blue T-shirt curls over his belly.

Not many months ago he might have passed for someone years younger. There was still in him the look of the boy, eager and fearful, but at some recent moment he crossed a threshold he'll never cross again, and his look changed. He looks middle-aged. Those used to seeing his wispy brown hair now see baldness; they see creeping grey in his sideburns and temples; they see a paunch. Not much is different, but the symbols of age have become his focus.

This causes him no great trauma. Youth for him was no magical time. He was happy because childhoods were happy where he came from. But never "mature" enough to ride his bike across town, wander down to the harbour or up Lynde Creek to hunt for suckers, to get his driver's licence, buy a motorbike, do any of the things that seemed really to matter in a boy's life, youth for him seemed a time of impossibilities. Now he is more "mature." He has reached an age finally where most of the time he can do what he wants, and do fewer things, and doing them again and again year after year, he can do them right more often. His life, more than at any other time, is now his own. And he is content.

He steps out the side-door and back into the morning.

It's going to be a beautiful day. The weatherman was right. For once.

Since Monday, the long-range forecast has been for good weekend weather, and every day on his way to work and home again, he's heard FM 98's Darryl Dahmer and Paul De Courcey deliver the same hopeful news. "It's supposed to be a good weekend," he has assured his co-workers all week. " 'Course, you can't believe the weatherman." In March, he had taken his usual week's holiday to paint and fix things around a house a winter breaks down, and every day it rained despite what the radio promised. He's been trying to catch up ever since, but every weekend it has rained, just as every weekday has been clear and spring-like, or so it seems to him.

Bloye luck, he calls it.

He has never won at lucky draws or raffles. His father and mother never won, nor have any of his brothers or sisters. But no point searching out answers you'll never find, or chancing onto things best avoided. Things are as they are. The "what ifs" and "might have beens" only drive you crazy. In the end you lose most of the time and every time you remember. But that's OK. For what you don't want to have to explain, for what is inexplicable (shrug) *Bloye luck* explains it all.

He begins his weekend rounds.

And how are my little beauties doing today?

In front of him is a small dirt patch with bricks sunk into the ground around its edges. He looks it slowly up and down.

The chives look pretty good, 'course they always do. We're gonna have lots of tomatoes; look at their flowers. That's a lot more than last year.

He shoots a look through his link-metal fence to a parallel garden plot on the other side.

Ho ho, John's in trouble.

Carolyn and their neighbour, John, an aging hippie he likes to call him, compete with their tomatoes. Who gets the plants in first, whose flower first, whose fruit is first on the vine, whose are bigger and redder, anything about tomatoes that can be observed, compared and bragged about. A few years ago, John read in a newspaper that if you bury rocks in your tomato patch, they will keep the ground warm and help your tomatoes grow. Last year, under cover of night, he dug up his ground, planted his rocks and tomato plants, and waited. And his plants came up, and his tomatoes grew, at just the same time, to just the same size as every other year. No room to grow.

He laughs to himself.

This might be Carolyn's year.

He swivels his head around to a nearly leafless twig in the ground.

And how's 'the survivor' doing? Can you believe it?!

Three years ago when he put in the pool, a truck had run it over. He discovered it two or three days later buried under the sand. That winter, Matt, sliding down the back ridge on his toboggan, ran it over again, splitting it in two. Again, he regrafted it, not holding out much hope. But now he sees its tiny leaves where anyone else would see only their absence.

It's gonna make it!

The red maple is still skeletal, but growing; small leaves have pushed out on his apple tree.

I've gotta get that sprayed. I just don't have any luck with apple trees.

As a boy, he had a big, beautiful apple tree outside the window of the small upstairs room he shared with his brothers. It was the perfect climbing tree. As spring turned to summer, big, beautiful apples began growing on it, all of them, every year, filled with worms. Just like this one.

One of these years, I'm gonna spray it myself. Can't do any worse. I gotta remember to call the guy next week, though. Just one more thing to do.

He shuffles about like a farmer in his fields, shoulders hunched, legs swinging forward from the hips, his feet angled out in his old beige Hush Puppies, their suede worn down to bare leather, his hands knifed into the front pockets of his blue jeans, his thumbs, resting on top of his belt, tucked under his belly. He walks up a gentle "hill" which inclines to about two metres higher than the rest of the backyard, then falls steeply on the other side through high shaggy grass to the back fence and street. He sees what he's looking for.

How many times have I told Matt. He's really let it slide. I don't expect him to cut this side every time, but this is no good.

Matt, fifteen, is at that awkward age, old enough to do what he wants, yet young enough to do what *you* want him to, and big enough that he can. So more is expected of him at just the time that with more going on in his life, he wants to do less.

I've gotta do everything around here or it doesn't get done!

One more apparent loss; with right on his side, one more Saturday morning victory.

He rolls his wrist and looks at his watch. The sun fills his backyard. He glances to his right, down the yards backing onto Sheppard Avenue, then to his left down the identical backyards of Neilson. They remain quiet and still. He shakes his head. The neighbourhood has certainly changed in the five years they've been here.

It always had a "stigmatism" about it, as he puts it. The area had been developed by the provincial government principally as low-income housing, and though most of the houses are now privately owned, people remember. A decade ago, radioactive waste was discovered on McClure Crescent, just two or three hundred metres away from where he is standing now. During World War II, an aircraft company had burned rags to reclaim radium, and there had been agricultural experiments with other radioactive materials. The waste had since been removed, they said, and there was never a suggestion that his area was contaminated, still the half-life of a bad name is a long time. Yet it was this bad name that had made their house affordable.

It was what had made *all* the houses around them affordable too, but he didn't think about that then. Now he notices how "ethnic" the neighbourhood has become. Asians,
Indians and Pakistanis, blacks from the Caribbean. He
doesn't think of himself as prejudiced, he always got along
with the Maltese kid who lived across the street in Whitby,
the Chinese who owned the Chinese restaurants, the Jews
who owned the corner store. One of his best friends in high
school was Japanese. And when he gets the feelings that he's
getting more often these days, they surprise him, and
bother him. What he feels has nothing to do with colour, he
says. That's not important. It's the way they live, how they do
things. Their grass always needs cutting, their houses need
paint, their cars rust away in their driveways. Down the street
a bathtub and toilet have been sitting on one front lawn for
weeks. They just don't care the way he does.

He is beginning to feel a stranger in his own country, he
says. It isn't his phrase, he heard the words somewhere, but
what it says is close enough to the way he feels that he's not
unhappy to express it, even if he lowers his voice when he
does.

Yet if his changing neighbourhood bothers him, it's no
preoccupation. It would do him no good. Move to another
neighbourhood? Where? With what money? No, he knows
where he stands. In his house, marriage, job, city, country,
life: he is where he is. He can't get out of here, pack it in,
shove off, move on. He's got to make the best of what he
has. Adapt, cope, accept — do whatever gets him through
his day. So he complains a little, but never so much that he
puts himself so far into his own corner he *has* to be
unhappy, or do what he knows he cannot.

He shudders his head away from his suburban horizon,
and looks down at his pool.

Every winter morning, before he's awake enough to
know better, he draws open his bedroom curtains and
sees "that ugly cover." The black plastic cover he puts over
his pool when summer ends. And every morning, like a

groundhog seeing its shadow, he is reminded that winter is still weeks from over. But today, the cover comes off and summer begins. And he can't wait.

The pool is his pride and joy. Nobody in Whitby ever had a pool, at least nobody he knew. Not Judge MacRae or any of the rich people who lived down by Lynde Creek. His father was a successful businessman, manager of Hobbs Glass in Oshawa, but he didn't have a pool or ever imagined having one. Carolyn was the one who had pushed for it first; many years after they were married and their finances were finally in order. He had bought a small house trailer, it was about ten years old, and on summer weekends and holidays they would go camping. The trailer was his getaway, but Carolyn liked her house. She liked her own bed, her own stove and bath, and all of them were right there under one roof which didn't move, so why should she? What was the point spending all that time driving some place and back just to do what she had to do at home but with implements that were unfamiliar, inconvenient and annoying? Nice getaway.

But a pool. Her younger sister had gone to university, had a good job with the school board, and a husband who made lots of money. She had a pool. Carolyn wasn't working and was home a lot, the kids were young; if she and Frank were going to spend their money why not do it on their house? It made sense to Frank too. And there *was* something about having a pool of his own, he had to admit. None of his brothers and sisters had a real in-ground pool. His youngest sister, Sue, would get one, but "after me," he always added. His dad had never been able to afford one. Wouldn't it be something?! Things *had* gone better for him these last few years. What better way to show it, to them and him, than to put in his own pool?

He sold his trailer for $5,700 and put the money in the bank. A year later, he took it out, cashed some small insurance policies and with money from his savings plan and the credit union at work, put in the pool. It cost him $12,000.

He told his brothers and sisters they were to treat his pool as "everybody's pool." Everybody was welcome; it was there for everybody to use; he wanted, he expected, everybody to use it. All his life he had gotten things from them, hand-me-down clothes, toys; advice, direction, opinions of all kinds. This time, *he* would be the giver.

When he told them about the pool, they seemed happy for him. Then the news settled: "What do you want a pool for?" one of them said. "Isn't that extravagant?" said another. It seemed inappropriate, wrong: Frank, the second youngest, the fat one who had never been good at school or sports or anything else, good-natured, harmless Frank, not John or Jim or any of his older sisters, who in the crush of growing up had always just "been there," who at times they hardly remember, who had had the biggest struggle, Frank, the first of them to get a pool.

Who did he think he was?

Over these last few weekends, item by item, piece by piece, he has gotten himself ready. He knows already the summer will be unusually hot and dry, and with every drop of rain this unusually wet spring, he worries it won't. He has just needed a few sunny days for the cover to dry, but "the weatherman hasn't cooperated." Then earlier this week things began to change. And after several years of rehearsing, he knows exactly what to do.

He knows what lies hidden between the lines of the instructional manuals just waiting to trip him up; he knows now what to do when something goes wrong. He doesn't like manuals. He won't wait for their complicated words to sink in and make themselves clear. As a kid, words stuttered across every page he read. They piled on top of each other, had no rhythm or pattern to them; they made no sense. Sometimes their letters changed order on him, but how could he know? He thought he couldn't read. That's what his mother and teachers thought too.

The boy just can't concentrate, they said. He's got to work harder, learn to apply himself. And his mother's wooden spoon found its new and primary purpose. Words in fictional fantasies never bothered him much. When they piled up, he climbed over them and moved on, and still he would understand. But in a manual, he had to read every word. Now when he tries and his words pile up, he finds himself drifting off just as he did as a boy; he stops reading and starts *doing*. If he gets things wrong, in his own backyard, on his own time, he just tries again. For a pool, a family, work, it's all the same. Life is repetition if you want it to be, if you've made it this far. And once you have, it's gravy time. For the rest of your life, you can do all the things that always got the best of you and never get them wrong again. No one can hurt you. The humiliations are gone.

Now with trial and error in his past, his literate hands know just what to do.

He looks at his watch again.

As he is about to yell, they appear. He walks to the far end of the pool, the kids straggle in behind. He's not entirely looking forward to what is coming next.

"OK, Matt and I'll get the water bags on the end," he says, then glances back to see where the kids are, slows down, bites his tongue and repeats what he's just said. Janine and Stephanie take their positions at the deep end of the pool on either side, Frank and Matt begin hauling up the long flattened plastic bags they filled with water last September, to hold down the cover and give it the buoyancy it needs to keep from sinking with the surface water.

Then the tricky part begins.

"OK, now you girls take up the bags, but slo-owwly," he says, instructing and pleading at the same time. If they bring up the bags too quickly, the cover, losing buoyancy, will sink. He and the kids have done all this before, many times he has taken them through the steps, but he has witnessed a lifetime of their mistakes and at this very moment mistakes are all he can remember.

"And Matt, we gotta roll up the cover, but slowly."

His voice is already angry; Matt nods without looking up.

"If we do it too fast, you know what'll happen." Matt nods again. The water on the cover, pushed ahead too quickly, will puddle up, get too heavy and sink into the clean water. But Matt nods for something else. If they go too fast, somebody will have to wade into the wormy, winter-chilled water to bail the excess. And that will be him.

"Just stay with me, Matt."

Janine and Stephanie gather up the bags, slowly. Matt rolls his end of the cover, his eyes on his dad whose eyes are everywhere.

"That's it, not too fast. Stephanie, not too fast! Stay with me now, Matt. Keep it tight. Don't let it sag. We're sagging! A little faster! Faster!"

They almost make it.

"Ma-a-tt."

He looks at his dad, at Janine and Stephanie. His shoulders sag. "Why do *I* have to do it?" Because you're older, because you're a boy. Just because. His shoulders sag lower. Frank says nothing. Janine breaks into a grin, Stephanie starts to giggle. Matt takes off his shoes and socks, rolls up his pants. "Hurry up, Matt. It's gonna sink." He feels the slimy cold bottom of the pool. Frank holds the blanket, Stephanie hands Matt a pail, he scoops some water from the cover and gives it to Janine who empties it over the fence.

Finally done, he gets out of the pool and dries himself. Frank looks pleased. He walks along one edge. There is the usual pasta-snarl of worms on the bottom, but the water is nearly crystal clear. There are a few stains, but nothing serious, no rust spots he can see. He will check things out more carefully later, but really the pool seems to have wintered well. He looks at Matt who is still drying himself and taking longer than he should, it suddenly seems to him. Janine is beginning to look bored, Stephanie is already looking in other directions. The cover is still in the pool and not rolled up. "OK, Matt. Let's go," and they scramble back to their positions.

He and Matt lift the cover from the pool and carry it to

the back hill where they unroll it again. They wait for Janine and Stephanie to bring some bricks from a small pile beside the vegetable garden to hold the cover down. Stephanie gets to the pile first, and to Frank, before Janine has time to collect hers.

"Janine, she's not helping," Stephanie whines.

Frank shoots a glance at Janine just now beginning to pick up her bricks. "C'mon Janine," he yells to his startled daughter, "you gotta help too."

Matt hoses down the cover, fills a bucket with water, and with a long-handled brush begins pushing at the dirt. His face is mute of expression; his body says everything he wants to say. It is a teenager's body with a teenager's posture. Nothing interests me, this body says, and if something does, there's no energy left in it to let you know in any way you will ever see. Its energy has gone into growing, developing, changing, to complicated internal things you'll never understand. Silhouetted against the black of the pool cover, his body in a deep and infinite mope, he looks like he's melting from the top down.

Janine and Stephanie, on the pool apron, squeezing water from the water bags, eye each other and Matt. Frank puts the hose in the pool so by afternoon's end the water will be high enough to cover the jets and drains.

Here and there he bends down to inspect the walls. Matt soldiers on; Stephanie has gone into the house, to go to the bathroom, she says; Janine wants only to empty the water bags and lay them to dry on the hill and be done with all she has to do by ten-thirty, so she can go downstairs and watch her favourite group, The New Kids on the Block, in their cartoon show. Stephanie saunters back. Janine looks anxious.

"Dad, what time is it?" Janine asks.

He looks at his watch. "Twenty after ten."

"Dad, can I go in and just put on a tape for The New Kids? I'm gonna miss it if I don't."

"Sure, go ahead."

Janine smiles, glances at Stephanie, and walks towards

the house. A few seconds pass. Stephanie looks up from what she is doing. "Long time to put on a tape," she says, and looks back down again.

It has gone like clockwork and he is pleased. He shakes his head.

Oh, they drive me crazy, but I love them. What a happy, loving family. . . . Except when they're whining and complaining which is all the time! But they did pretty well.

He smiles. He likes having his family around him. Years ago, he decided that he would always "be there" for them. And that phrase, perhaps more than any other, explains how he sees family, job, his own priorities, how and why he lives as he does. He doesn't remember any particular moment he decided that. Until he met Carolyn he had made up his mind never to get married, let alone have kids. When his mind changed, he understood completely what he was taking on; that he would live up to it was beyond question. At every breakfast and dinner table, every night as they watched TV and slept, every weekend around the house, around the yard, he would be there.

His father hadn't been there. He would leave for work in the morning and come home as dinner was served, then go back to the office when dinner was done. He never played catch with him, never went to his hockey games the one year he played. And more than any of his brothers and sisters, he had needed him.

He has always been there for his kids. It is his greatest source of pride.

He worries about them. Not whether they will be brain surgeons or rock star millionaires, but whether they will "turn out right." He worries about drugs, about violence in the streets and malls which he hears about every day on his radio on the way to work and home again. About his kids hanging around, getting caught up with the wrong crowd. Not so much Stephanie. She's younger, more for Janine and Matt.

Poor Janine. She has always had trouble reading, and a few years ago tests uncovered a mild dyslexia. He was with her when she was tested, how she confused her p's and b's, her poor spelling and concentration, her inability to comprehend a sound when she hears more than one: they were all problems he had had as a kid, never diagnosed. The school board put her into a special-education class and that hasn't been easy. She goes to a different school, feels the stigma of being singled out, the relentless competition from a precocious younger sister. Her teachers said she would probably be back in a regular school in a year, and now nearing the end of her second year nothing will change for another year at least. Their hope is that when she reaches high school, when streaming is imposed and future options become more circumscribed, she can be back in a regular class.

Then there's Matt. Neither of the girls can get to him the way Matt does, and for such a mess of reasons he can't begin to untangle them. It has to do with fathers and sons and timeless struggles, with memories of his own childhood, mistakes, regrets, with patterns of life he can now see repeating themselves. Matt is older, his personality more developed, his defects more pronounced, Frank's lifelong hopes for him more shaky. He's at an age where what he isn't has become vivid and clear, and more important than what he is. He is the glass half-empty; his sisters, young enough to change, the glass half-full. In him, Frank can see his boyhood self, the same shyness, distance and drift, making the same mistakes with the same imaginable consequences. And so he gets on him before it's too late.

Carolyn tells him to ease up, and he tries. He knows that he goes too far at times. He can feel himself losing control, saying more than he wants, than he means, than does anyone any good, and he can't stop himself. His mother was the same. She angered and loved with the same ferocity. She showed her love by doing; by criticizing, and improving, not touching; by being there. He can only hope Matt knows. His greatest fear is that he will drive him away.

There isn't much more they can do today. The pool has to fill up, and that will take until late afternoon at least. Tomorrow, he'll get an early start and, before anyone else is awake and the girls start arguing about everything two kids can argue about getting their newspapers ready to deliver, he will turn on the pump, vacuum the pool, filter the water and check for leaks. On Monday or Tuesday, he'll get to the pool store for the chemicals he needs; there's no reason they shouldn't be swimming next weekend.

That reminds me. I'll have to give Jim and June a call.

Jim is his brother, June is Jim's wife. He would like to have all his brothers and sisters over. He'd call Sue, but she has a pool of her own, and Trish, but she lives around the corner from Sue, and he and Camille, Trish's husband, "are not seeing eye to eye" these days. Ann, Mary Jean and Lee, his three oldest sisters, have older kids and live far enough away that things hoped for and talked about never seem to happen. John, he just doesn't see much.

But he will call Jim. Jim was the one just older who could do all the things he couldn't, yet was still enough like him that age didn't seem the reason. Jim picked on him the way older brothers do, especially those with older brothers themselves, but whenever Jim gave him a second look, especially the time he beat up the bully who had beaten up him, standing up for *him*, that was truly special. He has never doubted him since. And Jim will try to make it, and when in a few days he calls again and says something has come up, Frank will be disappointed but not surprised.

Carolyn has the third load of laundry in the washer, the second load in the dryer, and is vacuuming outside Matt's room. She has just gotten off the phone with her mother who she talks to every day. The kids come in from the back-yard, take off their shoes, pick up their slippers from the basement steps, and put their shoes in their place. Carolyn is waiting. The regular Saturday chores have still to be done and she needs help. She looks into Matt's room and is not impressed. Her voice soars above the sound of The New

Kids which blasts from a tape in Janine's room upstairs.

"I want your room cleaned up, and that means under the bed too. I want your dirty clothes collected, and when you're done I want the clean clothes brought upstairs. You hear me?"

Matt disappears behind his closed door, saying nothing. Outside, Frank tinkers happily.

I gotta make sure I get to the library to pay that fine. I could get the milk then. Oh, I should see if there're hamburger buns in the freezer; we were a little low the last time. And maybe finally pick up that lumber this afternoon; fix that spot in the fence. That [solar] blanket should be OK another year. It's getting brittle but . . . Maybe I should price them — Oh, and I gotta wash the car, and get some money from Carolyn. Almost forgot . . .

He walks to the pool shed and looks around again to see if he's overlooked anything. Above the top of the aluminum door frame, almost out of sight, is printed: "I HATE THIS." He turns without raising his gaze and looks skyward. Through the vast blue he sees a few billowy white clouds that weren't there before.

I thought it wasn't supposed to rain. Good thing we got the cover up; but now my pool's gonna get cloudy and dirty; and what'll we do tomorrow? It was supposed to be beautiful all weekend. My luck I'll wash the car and it'll rain.

He shakes his head.

It's now late in the afternoon and on this still-beautiful Saturday in June, he is back in his backyard. His library fine has been paid, there is milk in his refrigerator, hamburger buns in the freezer for tomorrow's barbecue. Behind him in the driveway, his car is dripping and gleaming.

It's been a good day. Got a lot done; the weather sure cooperated.

He smiles and turns from his backyard in the direction of the house.

And tomorrow, after I turn on the pump and vacuum the pool, I've got to . . . 'course, that's if the rain stays away . . .

Part Two

"When the tires are humming and the motor purrs,
And your car is eager and the thought occurs,
That it's good to be alive in this land of ours,
Great to drive in this land of ours . . ."

THE HAPPY MOTORING SONG

2

His father, Leo Ernest Bloye, was the seventh of his family's ten children, and the long-awaited first son. "We all thought the world of him," his sister Clara recalls, now in her nineties but tall and straight like her brother, with the thick wavy black hair of someone half a century younger. "Having all those sisters, you'd think he'd be kind of spoilt, but not Leo." She laughs, "He always used to say to my mother, 'I'm going to buy you a fur coat when I get a job.' We used to tease him about that. But he just smiled. He never turned a grey hair on my mother's head."

There is a family portrait. Leo's parents sit on either side of the photo in matching heavy wooden chairs angled towards the middle. His father, Ernest T. Bloye, from Delaware, in his younger years a railroad man like his father and brothers and who, to his grandchildren's endless fascination had lost a thumb to prove it, is broad and blockish, rather short it seems, with a wide, flat Irish face and square Irish jaw. He is wearing, not very comfortably, a three-piece heavy wool suit.

Leo's mother, Bridget (Kate) Feeney, from Omagh, near Londonderry in what is now Northern Ireland, has a face timelessly feminine, its strength almost hidden by a calm, shy resolve. Her nose and cheek bones are sharpish, made more prominent by her small crinkly recessed eyes, but with her luminous skin, posture, white blouse and long dark skirt, her *look* is of abiding softness.

Their ten children are scattered between them. Margaret, the youngest girl, sits on a stool in the foreground in her page-boy haircut and pretty frock; Jack, the youngest, sits near her, uncomfortable in a little boy's sailor suit, a solid, square, five-year-old version of his father. Lillian, the eldest, like her parents, sits in a proper chair. The other six girls stand about in no obvious order of age or height, most in simple white blouses and long dark skirts, slouching comfortably, leaning or propped against something; between them, a look of easy formality. At the picture's middle stands Leo, about twelve or thirteen, in a heavy wool suit and high stiff collar. His body angled slightly, his arms at his sides, his sister Laura, older and taller, stands behind him, her head cocked sweetly to one side, her hands clasped gently around his arm. The family's oldest boy and his doting big sister.

At fifteen, he quit school and was taken on as an office boy by a local London, Ontario company, Hobbs Glass. It was 1920. A few years later, he was transferred to Toronto. Most of his sisters were grown and had families of their own, his father was retired, so his parents decided to move with him. They lived in a duplex at 152 Winchester Street in what is now Cabbagetown, a solid working-class neighbourhood, originally Irish, by this time with a substantial WASPish mix. Our Lady of Lourdes School was on one side of them, on the other, the Lamb family. Daniel Lamb, for many years a city alderman, was the one most responsible for the neighbourhood's signature sight and smell, Riverdale Zoo, now Riverdale Farm, just across and down the street. The area's other great attraction was the Don River. Freezing over in the winter, it would fill with skaters and sliders who hurtled down the toboggan rides across the river and onto the flats. In summer, the kids swam in its still-swimmable waters as trains chugged up and down its banks. A few blocks away, the Don Jail, offering the prospect of hangings or escapes, gave to the neighbourhood an exciting whiff of fantasy and nightmare.

For a few months in the winter and spring of 1927, Leo kept a small pocket diary. In the front of it in his elegant hand, he wrote his name, address and birthdate, his height, "5' 11 1/2," weight, "155," complexion, "dark" and, under "Things Hard to Remember," information apparently considered important at the time: the number on his watch case, size of his tires and, quarterly from his birthday, the dates his life insurance policies fell due, "April 5" and "July 5."

His first entry begins the new year, Saturday, January 1:

At home all day, at Pantages in evening — "The Blonde Saint." Lost 1 silk handkerchief. Same being recovered later. Retired 3 a.m. Very bad cold.

The next day, he goes to mass at "Lourdes," has supper with his sister and brother-in-law, and plays cards in the evening. "Retired at 2 a.m.," his diary reads. After retiring again at 2:00 a.m. the following day, his next entry concludes, "Resolved to retire earlier in the future." It was a resolution he repeated many times the following months, with little success.

January 5th was his birthday:

I am 22 years of age today. Celebrated by attending a bridge by Miss M. Kelly. Had a most enjoyable time.

Two days later, Margaret Kelly appears again:

Spent very quiet day and evening. Met a little nurse on way to hospital. Wrote two letters. Retired early.

From this point on, she is simply "M.K." She and Leo would see each other about once a week, and while he seemed to go out with other girls, his cryptic notes become playfully transparent when she is part of his day. "Had the pleasure of seeing Miss M.K. for a few minutes tonight." "At M.K.'s this evening. Home at 9:45." Indeed, it's only evenings with "M.K.," it seems, that he "retire[s]" before midnight.

For him, week nights seem little different from weekends. One week in February, he spends Monday night at home, not feeling well; Tuesday he skates at Varsity Arena; Wednesday, "dine[s]" at the King Edward Hotel, "played euchre at home in evening. Lost 2 cents. Retired 12 p.m."; on Thursday, he sees John Barrymore in "Don Juan" at the

Regent Theatre, "retired 1:30"; attends a Valentine's Day Party on Friday, "retired at 4 a.m." As for Saturday:

> Late this a.m. — 10:30. Office 11:30. Bowling 12:00 to 2 p.m. Shopping till 5 p.m. Confession and at MK in evening. Very enjoyable.

He makes no other reference to "Confession" in three months of entries. On Sunday, after his usual early night with M.K., he attends ten o'clock mass, also for the only time in three months ("Good sermon," he is well rested enough to notice). As for his last entry of the day, and week: "Snow storm tonight. Wrote a letter."

Nearly every day he comments on the weather: "Snow very heavy, and cold"; "Weather very nice"; "Weather stormy"; "Weather 17 below zero. Do not want to experience it any colder." He writes about his work: "Sold carload of glass to Oakwood Hdwe."; "Drew plans for a store front. My first attempt at drafting"; and more usually, "business rather good today"; "business fair"; "business as usual." Once or twice, he finds some other experience to highlight, "Witnessed a dandy fight between police and gypsies today." And as Easter approaches, weighing instinct, conscience and willpower, he offers himself this bargain:

> Lent begins today — giving up candy and dancing — going to Mass every day.

The diary ends March 27, continues for a few days in September, "Leo H. and I at Nurses' Res in eve. Took A.K. and M.K. to dress makers. Had a very scrappy time," then stops completely. At the back of the diary, he lists his day-to-day expenses for an unspecified time. Small amounts, they are mostly for gas and drinks, candy and "cards." He lists one additional item, his antidote to the high life: "Sal Hepatica $.25."

It wasn't long after, he began taking "M.K." to Winchester Street for dinners with his family. His brother and some of his sisters were still at home, others would drop in with their spouses and children, always there were lots of people, always his mother made them feel there was room for lots more. They would sit around the big dining-room table and talk non-stop. And Margaret loved it. Leo's mother was like Leo, so easygoing and gentle, and she idolized her. Her own family had been so different. Here, the noise and swirling numbers, this wasn't chaos but a real family. And that, she knew, was what she wanted.

Her own life had been hard. Born Frances Margaret Kelly, she was the oldest of five children only two of whom, she and her sister Eileen, lived longer than a year. John and William, twin boys, born when she was two, had died at seven months of "summer complaint," dysentery, ileo colitis or celiac, no one was quite sure what. It was a family story not often retold. A third brother, whose name she never knew, died at birth. The rest of her story she left purposely murky.

They seemed a star-crossed family. They moved from place to place in Toronto's west end when she was young, then her mother became ill with breast cancer. Margaret was thirteen. Her father was preoccupied with problems of his own, and the obligation fell to her to quit school and take care of her mother. The decision was easy: the family had a need and the family came first. She had just finished grade 8. She washed her mother's bandages and did her dressings, took care of the house and looked after her father and little sister. When her mother got no better, she travelled with her parents to California looking for a cure; they may have gone to France, to Lourdes, the story isn't clear. But on September 5, 1923, the day before Margaret's seventeenth birthday, Ann Duggan Kelly died. She was forty-two.

The family was split up. Margaret remained with her father; Eileen, only eight, was taken in by Aunt Margaret and Uncle Eddie, an unmarried sister and brother of her mother's. Margaret returned to St. Joseph's school, but was put back in grade 8 by the nuns because of her two-year absence. Older and more mature, she found little in common with her fellow students. Margaret Kelly, it seems, had begun to take life very seriously.

Her father, William James Kelly, is an indistinct figure in the family story. Nine years older than his wife, he had been considered of dubious character by her family who had tried to prevent their marriage. With a partner, he owned a liquor business, which by the early 1920s was doing well enough that he decided to expand. As usual, his timing was wrong. Prohibition in Ontario was just around the corner. Within months, his store was shut. He began bootlegging. Men were coming to their house at all hours. When they came one more time than Margaret could take, she packed up her things and left, moving in with her aunt and uncle, and never went back.

She had always been the strong one. As a little girl in the Parkdale section of Toronto, her backyard shared a fence with the backyard of the neighbourhood bully. He was a few years older and big for his age; she was short even then and a girl. One day, the bully decided to hand out candy to the neighbourhood kids. This came as a shock, of course, still candy was candy, and they took it. He watched as one by one they bit into it, stopped, and ran spittering and sputtering for the nearby water fountain. He had laced the candy with soap. He laughed and laughed, and thought it was hilarious; she didn't. From the fight that followed, she would carry all her life a slightly blackened tooth, and much satisfaction. The bully was Harold Ballard, later owner of the Toronto Maple Leafs hockey team. It is a Kelly-Bloye family story which Eileen tells; no one knows if it's true. But knowing the public Harold Ballard, and Margaret Bloye, it might be.

She had been born, it seemed, with an instinctive sense of right and wrong, and through the sludge of any circumstance, she made out the difference and *did the right thing*. To those who didn't, she was unforgiving. Her father sold liquor when he shouldn't have, and did it when he promised he wouldn't. From then on, there was no place for him in her life. He would become a peripheral figure, living the rest of his life in the shadows of hers, just a few

miles away in Parkdale in a hotel on money a brother-in-
law had left his late wife. To anyone who wanted to know
more, that was enough. When she and Leo were about to
be married, she let her father know and he came to the
church. When the service ended, he approached a tiny,
black-haired eighteen-year-old girl, not much changed in
the ten years since he had seen her. "You must be little
Eileen," he said. "That's all I remember of him," Eileen
would say later. That night, under the heading, "Married
This Morning," the *Toronto Evening Telegram* ran a picture
of the wedding couple with the caption:

> Mr. and Mrs. Leo Ernest Bloye, whose marriage took
> place this morning in St. Michael's Cathedral. The
> bride was formerly Frances Margaret Kelly, niece of
> Miss Margaret Duggan. Mr. Bloye is the son of Mr. and
> Mrs. E. T. Bloye.

No mention is made of her father.

To Frank and his brothers and sisters, he didn't exist.
They grew up knowing the Duggans, Aunt Margaret and
Uncle Eddie, sharing many Sunday dinners and Christmas
days with them, knowing the story of their grandmother
and her early death by cancer, but left to fill in the rest
themselves, they got the story wrong. They created a grandfather who had also died young, and whose death, with that
of their grandmother's, had left their mother and Eileen
as orphans. His real story came out only after they were
adults, when it seemed to Margaret they were no longer too
young to hear it. "I was thinking of what name to give
Greg," Frank's sister Lee said, recalling a moment with her
mother before her youngest son was born. "I told her we
were thinking of 'William Joseph,' and she said, 'William
was my father's name.' I didn't even know that," Lee said.
She was forty-five years old at the time.

Today, Leo and Margaret Bloye are buried in Mount
Hope Cemetery, a Catholic burial ground in Toronto. Also
at Mount Hope are Aunt Margaret and Uncle Eddie, all the
Duggans and Kellys, and Ann Duggan Kelly as well. The

Duggans lie together in a big plot, Ann lies with them; the Kellys, a much larger family, are spread about the grounds; Leo and Margaret have their own bronze marker lying flat to the earth in a newer shadeless section of the cemetery. Eileen, now in her late seventies, insists her father, William James Kelly, is also buried there, but Frank can't find his gravestone. He's there, Eileen tells him. He's just off somewhere by himself.

It turns out he *is* buried at Mount Hope. Cemetery records state he died of pneumonia in Toronto General Hospital, Valentine's Day, February 14, 1937, at the age of sixty-five. His last known residence was 1214 Queen Street West in Parkdale, the Gladstone Hotel. Built next to the train station, the Gladstone had been a favourite of travellers doing business with the heavy industries in the area, but by Depression times was little more than a "flop house." Records also show he is buried in a plot purchased by a "Mrs. M. Bloye." Frank couldn't find his gravestone because none exists. His grave is unmarked.

It was sometime in these early years, when her mother died and people and circumstances had let her down, when her own world had been sent out of control, that she came to understand that no one else was going to write for her the life she wanted. She'd have to do that herself. If her family was a mess, she would create a new one. If her father dragged her down, he was dead and she was an orphan; it was better that way. She had to get out, and she did.

She began her nurse's training at St. Michael's Hospital in September, 1926. Just turned twenty, she was about to meet Leo Bloye. She moved out of the dark, three-storey Gothic house on George Street, away from her sister, her spinster aunt and reclusive uncle who rarely spoke, and into residence. Many of the young women she met there would become the friends of her life. Adele Knowlton ("A.K.") had been seeing Leo Hickey ("Leo H.") who was great friends with Leo Bloye who played tennis with them at Our Lady of Lourdes Church not far from the hospital.

Margaret would become their fourth. Later, Adele Knowlton would be her maid of honour and marry Leo Hickey,
who was Leo's best man, and whose brother, Father Vin-
cent Hickey, would find the Bloyes their Whitby house and
for more than a decade be their priest at St. John the Evangelist Church.

Margaret was proud to be a nurse. Strong-willed, selfless,
determined, responsible: a nurse embodied exactly what
she wanted to be. And though she would nurse only a short
time, these attitudes and standards remained with her.
One night years later in Whitby, her eldest daughter, Ann,
by this time a St. Mike's graduate herself, had just finished
the evening shift at Oshawa General Hospital. It was about
11:30 at night. She had become engaged a few days before
to Roy Greenaway. Roy had picked her up and was driving
her home when his car broke down (or so they insisted).
They started to walk, tried to hitch a ride but with no success, and walked until they reached home. It was 1:00 a.m.
Margaret was waiting for them. "You're a disgrace to the
uniform!" she yelled. Leo was standing at the top of the
stairs. "Calm down, Marg. Calm down," he kept saying. Ann
never forgot. She shouldn't have said that about the uniform, she thought.

For Margaret, it was the harshest thing she could say.

Most nursing in those years was done privately in
patients' homes, a nurse's job to wait hand and foot on the
sick until they got better, or died. For her twelve-hour shift,
she was paid five dollars a day, six dollars if the patient was
alcoholic. Margaret, graduating in 1929, had as her first
patient an elderly stockbroker. She attended him many
months, until, as the family story goes, she came down with
the flu, another nurse took over temporarily, and the
patient died. While waiting for the next one to come available, Leo and Margaret decided to get married.

These were the early years of the Depression. Leo's commissions had been down for many months; he had made
up his mind they wouldn't be married until the bad times

ended and he could properly provide. But the bad times
wouldn't end. Married women weren't allowed to nurse or
do much of anything in those years, except have children
and raise families. Yet for Margaret, the decision was easy.
She would put away her uniform for an even greater calling. She never went back. It was September, 1933.

When they returned from their honeymoon, Leo and
Margaret found the outside of their duplex plastered with
signs. "Come on Leo," the front door beckoned; "It won't
be long now," read the sign in the upstairs hall window. He
and Margaret had known each other more than six years;
their friends had grown impatient. "No more cold feet,"
read the bay window; "No more cold turkey," read
another. The rest built to a thematic climax: "What ya
doing Leo," "Will ya Whoa" and set rakishly on an angle:
"Whoopee."

They wasted no time re-creating the Bloye family. Ten
months later, Margaret Ann, "Ann," was born, named for
her mother and grandmother, Ann Duggan Kelly. Eleven
months after that, Mary Jean, then another girl two years
later. Fearing perhaps they might never have a boy, they
named her Catherine Lee, the "Lee" for "Leo," and called
her by her middle name. Leo was transferred to Hamilton
and back again; selling remained hard. Several times the
company cut back his salary, but it didn't let him go. That
would be a source of great pride to him all his life, a story
he would tell his children who would later repeat it proudly
themselves. And all this time, he was learning his trade.
When times improved and people started buying again, he
would be ready.

Then in February, 1941, John Joseph, their first son, was
born. Two years later, almost to the day, James Edwin,
followed.

Shortly after John was born, Hobbs held its national
convention in Montreal. To help set the proper tone, the
company published a one-page information sheet in
newspaper form, calling it *The Hobbs Herald*. The *Herald*

welcomed delegates, several of which, it noted, had already "opened unofficial quarters at Club Samovar, Chez Maurice and one or two other educational spots," apparently feeling "the opportunities there for sober(?) deliberation [were] greater." It also offered a disturbing account of a speech made by R.W. Glover, the company's auditor, to the "Association of Glass Widowed Wives." Glover told the women that "definitely" he was "with them in their fight for fidelity," that in the future he would steadfastly refuse to approve certain expense accounts. He cited one company executive's account which had recently crossed his desk:

Nov.	1 — advertising for girl stenographer	$ .50
	2 — violets for stenographer's desk	.65
	8 — week's salary for stenographer	15.00
	9 — roses for stenographer	3.00
	11 — candy for wife	.75
	13 — lunch for stenographer and self	6.23
	15 — salary for stenographer	20.00
	17 — picture show for wife and self	.80
	18 — theater for stenographer and self	7.50
	19 — candy for wife	.75
	20 — Lillian's salary	20.00
	21 — theater and dinner for Lillian	21.75
Dec.	2 — lawyer	100.00
	3 — fur coat for wife	625.00
	4 — advertising for male stenographer	.75

Another submission was from C. F. Wood, the company's leader. Entitled, "Keep on keeping on," he told his salesmen how proud he was of their efforts the year before. Then as they expected his tone to turn hilariously on its ear, it didn't. "Last year is gone forever," he told them in conclusion. "A new year is well on its way. Let us realize that the records we've just made were made to be exceeded."

Only one story had to do with a particular Hobbs's employee, and that was Leo Bloye. "Bloye tells all," the headline blared; "Reveals secrets before Royal Commission."

The story read:

> L. E. Bloye, of Toronto, in the witness stand today unwound the complete web of knowledge which has enabled him for many years to be Top Man of the Hobbs Window Glass Gang.
>
> While Mr. Bloye's evidence was given to a closed court, trained court reporters hinted that his amazing record was made by a careful study of his victim's [customer's] problems, a careful hunt for all prospective outlets for his deeds, and then getting into the back shop to collect evidence. The latter so that his prey could not say he did not need anything when the question was popped.

The article's tone is surprisingly respectful, as if its target was slightly above the audience fray, untouchable, not quite one of them.

Leo Bloye, as the phrase goes, "could sell anybody." Calling on hardware and furniture stores, lumber-yards, house builders and contractors, he made it his business to know as much about their business as they knew themselves. He searched their bins and shelves, then talked to the little guys in the backrooms who few ever bothered with. When later he went to their bosses and told *them* what they needed, he knew the backroom boys would back him up.

But Leo Bloye was no "bullshitter." Bullshit was for the lazy and unprepared, a shortcut from nights at the office, leading nowhere. He began his day when his customers began theirs, an hour before most of his competitors and colleagues had downed their first coffees and eased onto the road. He made calls around the city, got his orders, and from customers' stores and job sites phoned them back to the office.

"Have we got such and such in stock?" he'd ask Bruce Field, the company's sales manager, and Field would tell him. "When can I promise delivery? I don't want to tell him tomorrow if we can't do it." Tomorrow was OK, Field would tell him. "What time tomorrow?" Everything had to be just so.

By three-thirty, he was back in the office writing up his own orders. Others just dumped theirs on Field's desk, "Write these up for me, will ya?" Not Leo. He knew no one had as much interest in his work as he did. He got his own credits approved, wrote his own orders in his own careful hand. He wanted no mistakes. When his colleagues got back from the road, he would be on the phones working on tomorrow. At five, he'd leave the office as the others did, yet never quite leave at all. For Leo Bloye was no nine-to-fiver. If need and trouble cast no eye at the clock, neither would he. If his customers had to reach him, they had only to call. He would be there for them.

But Leo Bloye was beginning to feel his age. He had turned forty-one in January, 1946, less than three months after their sixth child, Patricia Eileen, "Trish," was born. He was able to provide for his family as he always had, meeting their modest expectations, still with eight mouths to feed and the pressure of sales, with more postwar buyers and sellers, and returning servicemen hungry to get going, maybe it was time for a change. Hobbs's salaries had never been very good, so much depended on the commissions he earned which depended on him, which was the way he liked it, except everything seemed riskier now.

The company needed new local branches to keep up with postwar demand, and new managers to run them. There would be commissions on sales and year-end bonuses on branch profits. The more successful he was, the larger the branch he'd get, the greater the profits, the higher his bonuses. He couldn't turn down the chance.

He was given the choice of Oshawa or Vancouver, and he chose Oshawa. It was closer to home, to the area he had lived in all his life, to his brother and sisters and friends. The General Motors plant was booming. Lives that had been put on hold were starting to be lived. Hard times, separation and death had brought a new determination to live family lives, with lots of kids, "baby boomers," in new houses, in new unsoiled suburban spaces, where a family could be a family. For Leo Bloye, there would be lots of glass to sell.

Whatever Canada would be, it wasn't what it was in 1946. A vast land of open spaces, undiscovered or scarcely developed resources, only twelve million people, it was what it *would become*, what its peaceful open spaces and resources would be turned to, what the millions drawn to its shores would make it.

It had seemed always a land to be exploited. Its trees, rocks, fishes and soil, a store of riches to use up; from which to move on. Not a place where roots flourish, where commitment is rewarded, where in the equation of civilization-making one plus one, with human ingenuity, makes six. Too separate, isolated and unforgiving, where one plus one too often made one.

Just south, in a land of incomparable fertility, geography and climate, U.S. movers and shakers had created for themselves a life immensely richer than any they had known before. In gratitude, they had given back their country the energy and vision of "builders," the messianic zeal of a "chosen people." Reaping no similar rewards, much of Canada's élite, living not where they wanted, in the incomparable comforts and glories of England or France or in the action and excitement of the U.S., wanted only to make it and get out. Write common stories, create common myths, build something together: why?

But times were changing. Two world wars in twenty-five years had left the old world broken, exposing wounds that it seemed would never heal. For Europeans, Canada seemed a new possibility. For the first time, it seemed a country to build.

"Today we Live in a Greater Canada."

So began a series of ads for Molson's beer in the mid-1940s, presented "in the interests of a greater Canadian appreciation of Canada's present greatness." One ad, called "Through their Eyes," imagines the perspective of European immigrants.

> Canada is the most desired of countries. It represents hope and opportunity. It is where they want to be.

> The dream of millions overseas is a reality for us.

> "To see ourselves as others see us" strengthens our realization of our country's new importance in the modern world. The Canada that emerged from the war is a far greater country than we ever thought possible — a country of vastly increased and varied productivity, with a million more employed than before the war — with a new wealth of interesting careers awaiting those alive to the opportunities around them.

O'Keefe Brewing Company ran ads telling stories of the country's early missionaries, explorers and of "plain people whose courage rolled back the wilderness and built this nation." "Look back," one ad reads, "see how far Canada has come since the first settlement was founded little more than three centuries ago. Look forward and see how much remains to be done, how far the path to the future leads . . ."

Weston's bakeries focused on the Canadian woman. She is pictured in her kitchen, in a plain dark dress and white apron, her sleeves rolled up to mid-forearm, a smile on her ruddy, slightly fleshy face, her permanent-waved hair in place and looking smart, the very image of Margaret Bloye. "*She* helps build jobs for Canadians," the ad reads. As mother and wife, she helps "make possible the development and progress of modern business," buying manufactured goods from the grocer, preparing these goods for her family, investing her savings in Canadian business.

A simple ad for bread in postwar times is neither simple nor just for bread. "Bread on the table . . . the meal is

ready!" reads an ad "prepared by the makers of Fleisch-
mann's Yeast as a contribution to the advancement of
national health." Everything has been made to seem a
patriotic duty. Everyone has been enlisted in the task of
creation. And advertisers, sensing the country's mood,
have tapped into it. Brewers believe they can sell more
beer, bakers more bread, appealing to this collective aspi-
ration. This is a special place and time, they say. What's
good for you is good for me. Your future is my future.

Born in the first few years of the century, Leo and Margaret Bloye had seen the beginnings of the car and airplane; the development of the assembly line, middle-class
wages for millions of working-class people in working-class
jobs, migration from farms to cities to suburbs; space, newness; motels, drive-in restaurants, travel and credit. They
had also witnessed the mind that changed with them, the
different dreams, freedom, freedom's loss and limits, the
idea of upward mobility, progress, the future as a different
and better place. The rise of hope; the fall of faith.

They had lived through radio, movies, birth control,
atomic bombs, two wars to end all wars and the possibility
of a third that really would. The idea of *total annihilation*.
In the 1940s alone, frozen foods, Mixmasters, paint rollers,
power mowers, picture windows, ballpoint pens, super-
markets, Airwick and wash-and-wear clothes. A time of
science, and the applications of science to daily life; theirs
had been the age of the common man.

They had seen science save time: cars, office equipment,
appliances. With sulfa drugs and antibiotics, they had seen
science extend time. With the bomb, they had seen how
science could end time entirely. It changed the way people
thought, especially those a little younger and about to
become parents of a new generation. Sickness, wellness,
feast or famine, each had always been God's will. Now
science could prevent sickness, or cure it; dams, irrigation
canals, chemical fertilizers could prevent famine. Science
could mitigate or enhance, even reverse God's will. Now

human fate might lie in human hands. In Canada in 1900, God had killed man off at forty-eight; in 1946, science was keeping him alive seventeen years more.

This was the way of the future. What was needed, these soon-to-be parents believed, was to train better this scientific mind. Remove it from the limitations of home and family, put it into schools, expose it to "experts" who could pass on their knowledge. The new family would focus less on its own purposes, more on the development of the individual. New families might be bigger, but few would be truly big like the Bloyes. Once, more hands had made light work; now, they drained money and much-needed time, energy and attention away from the individual. New families would be more manageable. With more labour-saving conveniences and the money to pay for them, they would have fewer chores to do, fewer for its members to do together. There would be more time to do individual things, and more encouragement and reason to do them.

There would be more space. With fewer hands, more kids would have a room of their own, have clothes, toys and books of their own. With fewer chores, they'd have more time to do things of their own choosing. The bus had given way to the car, soon the car would become two cars. There would be television, an instrument of family bonding in its early years, it seemed, parents and kids convening in the same room at the same times to watch the same shows. But soon there would be two TVs in two rooms for two parts of the family to watch two different shows.

This generation about to be born would never learn the skills of compromise, accommodation, consensus, would never learn to live together and share. It never had reason to; it got no practice. Later, when it got to be old enough to take positions of power, it fought to take back the authority and money once entrusted to public institutions, to government and family. We aren't all in on this together, it would say, because together doesn't work. I want to make my own future as I made my own past, as I was trained to do. So from the seeds of the generation about to be born, the yuppie was made.

Leo and Margaret Bloye, however, were a generation out of synch. Their values, attitudes, ways of doing things, and their focus on the family came from a pre-war time. For their pre-war and wartime children, this wouldn't matter much. For those about to be born, one day they would have to face a world that grew up a different way.

Leo commuted from Toronto for a few months, until Father Hickey found them an old farmhouse in Whitby, much in need of repair, across the street from his church. This was summer, 1946. Margaret was now nearly forty and well on the way to her Bloye-sized family, from Ann the oldest at twelve to Trish just fifteen months, six kids in all. Not thinking of biological clocks or worrying much about the size of Leo's pay-cheque, she would have as many children as God gave her. With a little sewing and mending, clothes handed down from one to the next could be handed down to one more; another bunk bed wouldn't overcrowd an already overcrowded bedroom. Leo had a good job; God would provide.

Having all those kids, however, was harder than she had thought it would be. But she loved the dinner-table conversations, the energy and clockwork efficiencies of a family working together. She loved everyone *being* together, under the same roof, knowing where they all were, safe, clean, warm and cared for. She had a need to do things for others, for them, mending holes in their socks, knitting their sweaters, washing, ironing, making sure Leo had a fresh white shirt and handerkerchief, pressed and folded, at least once a day; cleaning, dusting, helping the girls with their homework, baking a pie, a cake or cookies, something special each night to fill the house with the smell of home, to welcome Leo and the kids through the front door and back into the family. It was doing things, more than by hugs and kisses and kind, gentle words, that Margaret showed her affection.

It's what she also expected of her kids. There is a lot to do in a big family; everyone is needed, everyone depends on each other. Making your own bed, scrubbing the bathroom floor every Saturday are necessities. They are also acts of love to be done without question, complaint or exception, not to be put off for track meets or football games, for love is not a sometime thing. She just couldn't be like Leo's mother, she realized. Kate Bloye was so calm, nothing bothered or upset her. If one of her kids was late or spilled something all over a freshly washed blouse, that was the way kids were, the way life was. It didn't seem that important.

She wasn't like that. She had never been able to stand silent when something was wrong. She had to notice everything, had a *need* to correct. A soiled blouse, a tardy arrival *did not* have to happen. Each was an act of carelessness, thoughtlessness, worst of all, selfishness, putting yourself ahead of others, ahead of your own family. That wasn't love. And who paid for this? Not the selfish wrongdoer but those who did right, who *were* on time and ate properly and who now have to rush to make up lost time, wash and iron clothes that were just washed and ironed and hang them to dry. She paid the price. Later on, it would be a spouse, some other children, some new family, some new generation on into the future, and why should that be? She wouldn't let that happen.

For her, the gentle, free-flowing chaos of Leo's family, no matter how appealing, was too messy and uncertain. She needed control, twenty-four-hour-a-day, seven-day-a-week vigilance. And now since moving to Whitby, she had that much more to do. Leo was opening a new store, he had a community to get to know. Much of his day he had to be out meeting contractors and lumber-yard operators, and especially the plant engineer, architects and maintenance workers at General Motors. He had to be open on Saturdays. His paperwork could only be done at night, so every week-night after dinner he'd drive the eight kilometres from their Palace Street house back to his office.

The girls had gotten to an age where now they seemed more in need of her than him, "the boys," John and Jim, had each other, Trish was a baby. He was losing his "feel." He didn't know them as he once had. Put in more time than the other guy, he always told the young salesmen, and you get the "feel" for how things are. Then act on that feel, because you are right. That's what had made him the best glassman in Toronto. Now at home *he* didn't have the time. He could catch up on the highlights of the day with Margaret, late at night when he got home and the kids were in bed, but in the morning, he couldn't predict any more what they'd say, how they'd react to what he was saying. If they asked to go to a friend's, "Why don't you ask your mother?" he'd say, knowing the next time they'd bypass him completely, cutting him off further. It was becoming easier just to say nothing, not to be around. A genial, easy-going presence at dinners, Margaret more and more ran the show.

He had joined the Knights of Columbus, she joined the Catholic Women's League. They didn't go out much any more. The Hickeys, Leo and Adele, drove from Toronto for the Friday-night poker games, the kids hanging around the upstairs landing, out of sight or so they thought, watching their father laugh loudly, their mother the happy, serene host; ghosts from the past. On Sundays, they still went to Aunt Margaret's and Uncle Eddie's for dinner, but not as often as before. It was harder to keep up with friends. They all had their own families, Leo worked Saturdays, the distance to Toronto on 1940s' roads was formidable.

When September came, Ann was in grade 7 at St. Bernard's School, Mary Jean in grade 6, Lee grade 4, John, Jim and Trish were home. Ann was sturdy and strong, a dependable first child mature beyond her years; more was asked of her by her mother, more was expected, and with great pride and pleasure she delivered, often with too much enthusiasm her brothers and sisters thought. Mary

Jean was waif-like and shy. Eleven months younger, she and Ann were close; Lee was their tag-along. Two years younger than Mary Jean, three years younger than Ann, she didn't quite fit in, but in a big busy family, she *was* fit in, with no little resentment. "Ann, Mary Jean, when you go to the store/post office/movies, take Lee along too!"

In her first communion picture, Mary Jean, in a long white dress and veil, glances down at John, about one, in the middle of the photo, being held up by the armpits by a shy, demure Ann who is behind him, John dangling like a puppet, his tongue sticking out. Opposite Mary Jean is Lee, angling away from the scene, her hands folded, her eyes raised to heaven. If she was going to be made to fit in, determined and contrary, Lee would do it on her terms.

Then came "the boys," six and four, then chubby, pretty, good-natured Trish, the baby. Being the first two boys, only two years apart in age and close enough by birthdates to share the same parties, with John, the older, a little small for his age, and Jim a little big for his, with the two of them able to wear the same clothes, play on the same teams, do the same things, be treated the same way, John and Jim would grow up linked in their own minds, even more so in the minds of others. "John and Jim," "Jim and John," "Johnny and Jimmy," their names ran rhythmically together. They were "the boys" — "Ann, Mary Jean, call 'the boys' for supper" — and always would be.

They settled into their new lives through the fall and early winter. Then in January, 1947, as Ann, Mary Jean and Lee went back to school after their first Christmas in the new house, Margaret found out she was pregnant. The world couldn't stop or even slow down. She was forty, Leo nearly forty-two, in a new community, new job, in a more exciting, demanding postwar time. They were old to be still having children, their routines were set; the circumstances of their lives, where they lived, Leo's job and health, the money he earned, the company he worked for would keep them where they were for years to come. What mattered to them, what they valued, was clear and unchangeable. Also set were many of the family roles, its relationships, connections. Ann and John were responsible, Mary Jean a good helper, Lee strong-minded, Jim the emerging clown, Trish the adorable baby. There wasn't much left.

It was into this world, on July 29, 1947, that Francis Leo Bloye was born.

3

"Mom and Dad couldn't decide what to call me. This went on for days. It got to the point where they'd brought me to church to be baptized and Father Hickey had me in his arms. He said, 'What name have you chosen?' and they said, 'We don't know.' So he said, 'I baptize you, Francis Leo Bloye; Francis for [Frances] Margaret, and Leo for Leo.' I don't know if it's true, but that's the story Mom told me."

It is the opening story of his life.

When he thinks of his childhood, he thinks of his family, and when he thinks of his family, it is mostly of his mother. A story about Jim or Trish or Mr. Wilson, the egg man who lived down the street, no matter how it twists and turns somehow always ends up back at Margaret Bloye. Through authority, personality and presence, through the sheer volume of time she spent with her kids, she dominated their inside worlds and was gatekeeper to the world outside.

She has been dead more than nine years, Leo more than twenty. Their possessions have been spread among their kids and now dot their personal landscapes. On a table in his living room Frank has a picture of them when they are much older. He gave copies to his kids to hang in their rooms and amid Janine's and Stephanie's shrines to The New Kids, they are there. One of the living-room chairs is "Mom's chair," at least to him; some of their silver is "Mom's silver"; their good pearl-handled knife and fork set "Mom's knife and fork set"; a fake diamond brooch she always wore, which he's put away for safekeeping, is

"Mom's brooch." On the little finger of his right hand he wears the ring his mother gave him after his father died, "Dad's ring," though it was really his grandfather's. In the basement, "Dad's encyclopedia" and "Dad's dictionary" fill most of the bookcases on either side of the TV.

Yet most of his living past resides in a gesture, a tone or phrase — "sit up straight, get your elbows off the table" — in family stories and attitudes, experiences and lessons learned which from the kitchen table on Palace Street to the kitchen table on Blackwater Crescent have echoed across time. And in him this past lives powerfully on.

He doesn't have many "treasures" of his own from his childhood years, to prod his memories and keep them in line. His parents didn't keep much for any of them. Maybe with so many kids there wasn't the room, or maybe they didn't have the money or the different ways of capturing a moment; maybe people didn't do so much of that then. Maybe individual lives didn't seem so be-all and end-all, requiring an urgent moment-by-moment chronicle of photos, home movies, report cards, birthday, Christmas and Easter cards, to evidence existence. Maybe life to them seemed more a continuum, evidence of importance coming more from a nose or eyes which generation after generation stared back from yellowing photos. Maybe holding onto a person didn't seem so important when people believed that not many years hence they would all be together again; when everlasting life awaited.

He has from his earliest years only one report card and one class picture, no Boy Scout badges, team photos, school projects or scrapbooks. He has a stamp album, his first communion certificate when he was not quite eight, some first communion cards, one "To Frankie" from "Dad and Mother." He has a Christmas card he must have made in school. On pale green construction paper "To Mother and Father," it reads at the top, "At Christmas," it reads below. Inside, it is signed "Frankie Bloye," but neither the signature nor the writing on the front is his. What is his is the Christmas message to his parents, printed carefully in pencil on faint pencil lines not quite erased:

My Offering
Masses 20
Communions 20
Rosaries 12
Ejaculatians [sic] 13

Below his offering and above the "Frankie Bloye" signature is the paper imprint of his own, sloppier, little boy's signature, erased.

He has a confirmation certificate, his Red Cross "Senior Swimmer" card, his certificate of promotion from grade 8 to grade 9 from St. John the Evangelist School. He has some first communion pictures, one with his whole class on the lawn in front of the church, fourteen boys and twenty-five girls, the boys kneeling in the front row, most with their hands folded carefully in front, most, like Frank, in black double-breasted blazers, black shorts, black knee socks, white shirts, round high collars and big white ribbons tied in big bows around their necks, white ribbons tied around their left sleeves. The girls stand behind them in their pretty white dresses, white tights and veils, many with their hands held prayerfully together; and behind them is Father Hickey. Frank's hair is neat and greased into place; he is a handsome, sturdy-looking boy.

He has a picture of himself on Santa's knee, wide-eyed and uncertain; another with Sue when he was nine, at her first communion. There is a picture one Christmas morning, he is kneeling on the floor in his pyjamas distracted by something away from the camera, smiling and bright-eyed. Filling most of the picture behind him is a Christmas tree lush with Christmas balls, lights, candy canes, tinsel garlands, bells and numberless other decorations. Some presents lie opened under the tree. Father Hickey sits to his right bent forward in a chair. Intent on a big white box in front of him, the directions for which he is apparently reading, he pays no attention to the commotion which has caught Frank's eye. On the side of the box are the words, "Heavy Duty Bulldog Tractor and Road Scraper." Margaret stands to Frank's left, all dressed up in a plain dark dress, her favourite white imitation pearl earrings and favourite brooch, the one Frank now has in his drawer. Her fists are clenched and firmly on her hips, her head is tilted forward, her chin tucked into her neck. But it's her eyes; they are two small piercing black holes. She is not amused. It's what her kids call, "that look."

He has a few other pictures from when he was older, divvied up from the family collection and given to him when his mother died. Occasionally it is his turn to have the family home movies. They begin in the early 1950s. They were taken of special occasions only, mostly of family events: Christmases, birthdays, weddings, baptisms, first communions and picnics. One movie shows brush-cutted young men in convertibles with big chromed fins, parading down a highway and through town with floats and marchers, the day the Whitby Dunlops came home as world hockey champions. There are movies of trips: Mary Jean and Lee at Martyrs' Shrine in Midland, Ontario; Lee and her cousin in Bermuda, where they panned back and forth and forth and back, every inch of coastline, every boat and beachfront villa, no single image bigger than a fly; John's trip out west after he had graduated from Ryerson when unsteadily he panned every mountain and cable car that climbed it. It was as if whoever went away did so as the family's eyes, for they were the chosen ones. And when they got back, everyone gathered to see what they had seen.

The movies capture the family as it wants to be captured, as home movies do. Every Christmas table groans with serving platters and bowls and white linen tablecloths and mounds of food, and lots of dressed-up people, smiling and happy in their party hats around it. Every scene groans with kids, Frank, his brothers and sisters, later the grand-kids, the boys slicked and scrubbed, the girls in their puff-ball best dresses, crinolines and lacy pants. Every inside scene is in the living room or dining room, every outside scene in the front yard, for these are a family's public places, what a family allows a world to see.

And in every frame, Margaret looks like a mother. Old-ish, dressed up and looking smart, her hair curled and always in place, still dark even in her fifties. She is standing to the side, serving or picking up, doing whatever needs to be done; blushing, waving the camera away when she knows it is on her, her apron always on. Leo looks just like a father. Always old, never in less than a white shirt and tie, his dark grey pants held high by suspenders, his black, grey-ing hair slicked back and parted slightly to the right of mid-dle. We see him carving the Christmas turkey, sharing his bounty, beaming and proud, or in his favourite chair, a child or grandchild cozy in his lap, a book in his hand, reading a story.

When the camera moves outside, we see a house and yard like every house and yard of childhood memory is supposed to look. The big welcoming front lawn, white picket fence, chestnut trees, the old verandah stretching across the entire front of the house, its rocking chairs and lawn chairs for musing, snoozing and chatting away sum-mer nights. We see kids running through a sprinkler, brother Jim with Frank in a headlock, Jim making faces, Frank laughing. Margaret in a summer dress snipping lilacs and cherry blossoms for the coffee table in the living room.

And in all the movies, the young kids look like kids, the older ones like fine young adults. They had been teenagers just after the war, before the movies begin, before there was money enough for marketers to take a timeless attitude and create from it the teenage *identity*. We first see Ann in sensible skirts and sweaters, so mature and serious, then suddenly with her own children, the first grandkids to appear, a matron at twenty-four. We see Mary Jean and Lee in sensible coats and pillbox hats; John, no matter what his age, always with the same solid, upright look. Then Jim, two years younger, even as a little boy with a body attitude waiting to be expressed. He was the family's first teenager.

We see Trish, Frank and Sue, "the little ones," almost from the first days of their lives. Trish, a little shy and in the background, Frank either nowhere to be seen or mugging too hard into the camera. Both have about them a slightly fleshy cuteness and the sweet vulnerable faces that go with it. Then Trish, because she is two years older and a girl, then Frank, get chubby. It's when they were about eleven. Trish also grows tall; Frank, in glasses, has his hair cut short in a brushcut. Their sweet, soft vulnerable looks remain.

Movie years pass. Trish becomes a mismatch of body parts, the same cute face on an older body that doesn't belong to her. Then suddenly her parts fit. Then suddenly Frank's Adam's apple pops out, his cheeks shrink and ears shoot out from behind them. *He's a string bean.* It wasn't that sudden, yet was so dramatic it seems overnight. He was fourteen.

In these movies, everything looks so normal, so routine, so much as it should be. A life selected and told, reinforced and remembered in the telling; and lived. The way it seemed to be, and so the way it was. But what about the rest, what happened when no camera was there?

"I was in an old red snowsuit, I had boots and mitts on, a scarf and hat and long johns, the kind with the trap door in back. I must've been four or five, pre-school anyways. It was in the middle of winter and I was standing on the verandah in front, banging on the door, crying my eyes out because I was cold and wanted to come in. I banged and banged, but she wouldn't let me in. Mom had this thing about fresh air; rain or shine she made us go outside at least an hour a day. She knew that would make us sleepy. She used to try everything to get me to stay in bed for my nap.

I remember more than once she took one of Dad's old ties and tied my foot to the bed frame. I never dreamed of untying it."

It is his first memory.

By this time, "everybody else was grown up." Ann was seventeen, Mary Jean a year younger, Lee was fourteen and in high school as well. His father was forty-seven with a smoker's cough, about to cross the line into chronic bronchitis on the way to something worse; his mother, eight children borne and to bear, was forty-six. "I can still see our kitchen table," he says. "Dad was at the end nearest the front of the house by himself. John and Jim were together, against the wall on his left, Mom and Sue opposite Dad, though Mom was usually up serving and whatnot. Trish and I were on Dad's right. Never can I picture Ann, Mary Jean or Lee sitting at that table."

It's a different family, one of five and not eight. In this family, John is the oldest, everybody's big brother. Quiet and patient, reasonable and fair, solid and reliable, he was the pivotal child in the family, perhaps the only one who truly grew up in a family of eight kids, the only one who related and felt connected to everyone above and everyone below.

It was John who allowed Jim to be Jim. He did for Jim what David Nelson did for his brother, Ricky. He protected him, never told on him, stood up for him, most important, he *explained* him to their mother who couldn't understand why he'd do what he did. The "responsible" role already taken, Jim could let out his own personal leash and take chances. And his brothers and sisters loved him doing it. He was their *alter ego*. Every time he stood up to his mother, ignored her, talked back to her, came home when he wanted and not when he was told, they were right there doing it with him.

He was a rebel with *their* cause, and outside the house he was the same. Remember the time, his brothers and sisters say, when Jim's teacher was trying to teach his class to dance and Jim got fed up, opened the window and jumped out of the classroom — right into Father Austin's arms! Or the time he and Donny Antstey were horsing around and Donny fell into a ditch and hurt himself, and Jim jumped down to help him. A car comes by and this lady rolls down her window, "Are you hurt?" And Jim says, "Hey lady, mind your own beeswax." And Donny, now *really* in pain, whispers to him, "Hey Jim, that's my teacher."

And even if Jim mumbles that it really didn't happen that way, it doesn't matter, because that was Jim.

With John, they were "the boys." "Hey, what am I?" Frank would come to ask. But the everyday language of the house had been set, the family's way of seeing things ingrained. Today, even when he tells a story about John and Jim, his speech pattern is unchanged. "I remember one time we all rode our bikes down to the harbour, but 'the boys' —" and there he'll catch himself. "Ahem, yes, 'the boys,' " he repeats. "Anyway, 'the boys' had to come back early to do their papers."

He was never one of "the boys."

There is a little more space when the family is five, more room to take on family roles, though not so much for "the little ones." With only a few kids in a family, with each new birth the focus of attention shifts to the youngest. His or her demands come first, he or she sets the pace for the house, the way he or she lives is the way they live. With more kids, especially when they come quickly, a house gets busier. Lots of people are now moving at different speeds, and accustomed to things certain ways, young kids just get in the way. There isn't the time now to give the same attention, for them to monopolize the pace and routine of the house. So the balance shifts. Now older kids set the tone and kids born later must fit into that older world. When they struggle to keep up, they now find mothers and fathers, brothers and sisters, with less time and much less patience. The younger one fumbles, the others fidget, he fumbles again, their patience runs out. They find him his words, finish his sentences, put together his toys, for him, for them, anything to get things done, to go back to what they were doing.

Still, he fit easily into that world. He was an easygoing kid, always smiling, didn't talk a lot; wasn't loud. As a baby he didn't keep the house awake with colicky cries, didn't wet his bed any longer than the others. He wasn't any sicker. He had tantrums, but his "terrible twos" were not so terrible. He did battle his mother at nap time, but everyone did, and most nights went to bed without any fuss. It gave him no particular pleasure making life miserable for everyone else just to get his own way. In a full-up house where everything was in short supply, he didn't insist on more than his share; of time, energy or attention. If anything, he asked for, and got, less. He just wanted to fit into the routine of their days.

For him each day began with the sound of his mother's voice, and the smell of coffee. Margaret was always the first up, about 6:45, and was soon down in the kitchen getting things ready. Leo was still in the bedroom in his pyjamas, sitting by the side of their bed, hunched over, coughing until his lungs were clear and he was out of breath:

cougha cougha cough, wheeze, Cougha Cougha cougha cgha cgha cgha ca, Wheeeeeze

The abruptness of the sound shook them from their shallow morning sleep, but not for long. *It's just Dad,* they all knew, and they slept through the rest. Then Leo put on his slippers and shuffled to the upstairs bathroom, the only one in the house.

The kids took their baths at night, Margaret took hers in the lull of the afternoon after the washing and cleaning were done, after the kids and Leo had finished lunch, the kids were back at school and Leo at work. Only Leo took his shower in the morning. She waited for the pipes to stop groaning, then yelled upstairs to awaken the kids. By the time they were out of bed, into their slippers and on their

way to the bathroom, she knew Leo would be back in their
bedroom at her dressing table, shaving.

He'd be in his white boxer shorts and hod carrier's
undershirt. The night before, he had hung up his dark
grey pants (he had only dark pants) by their suspenders,
over the corner of his clothes-closet door, placed his dark
grey suitcoat (ditto) on the back of Aunt Margaret and
Uncle Eddie's chair, put into his closet his black shoes
(ditto), polished to a spit-shine gloss by John, or Jim, or
Frank, whoever was old enough to do the job and young
enough to be stuck with it. Tight on his head was a plain
white handkerchief tied in little knots at each corner that
trained his straight black hair to stay in place while it dried.
Why it still needed training after forty-seven years, no one
wondered.

First up was first to the bathroom and first out before the
next voice hurried him or her downstairs. The bathroom
hummed. If there was some special reason to go to morning mass (and there was always a special reason), the early-
risers went before breakfast. September was the start of
school so September was special, October was the Rosary,
November All Souls', December Advent. The church was
just down the street, Father Hickey was a friend of the family. Every morning in school the nuns asked those who had
gone to mass to stand up, and gold stars were put on a classroom chart beside their names. During Lent, whoever got
the most stars received an award, and word of victory was
sure to follow home.

Margaret and Leo would be talking and listening to the
radio as the kids straggled down, Leo eating, puffing on a
cigarette, Margaret moving about. "Dad always talked
about his business," Frank recalls. "And Mom always listened. With interest; nothing pretend." She knew the people at work from the Christmas parties they had each year,
knew those at head office from conventions and the day-
to-day news Leo brought home. He had his white shirt on,
his sleeves not rolled up but folded over, three times, to just

below his elbows, his tie now tight to his neck, his wine-coloured suspenders pulled up and in place. He wore suspenders so his pants would hang straight, a belt, of the same dark grey cloth as his suit, to complete the look. His handkerchief was still on his head.

Margaret was in a housedress, pale blue or pale green, they all looked the same, loose and shapeless, with buttons down the front; an apron tied around her. She *never* wore slacks, never wore a skirt and blouse, she only wore dresses. She had on a pair of comfortable old mesh shoes with a wedge heel, her stockings were rolled nearly to her knees, to just above the hem of her dress, the rolls out of sight except when she sat down, which wasn't often. Her curly permed hair was freshly brushed.

Another voice drifted into consciousness and out. It was morning-man Wally Crouter on Toronto's CFRB. He had been in their Whitby kitchen since three months after Frank was born. (In November, 1993, he would complete his forty-sixth year, in the same time slot, on the same station.) His voice was deep and crackling, and when *he* talked about the weather, *they* talked about the weather. When he gave last night's scores, even sometimes for John's beloved Whitby Dunlops, "the boys" listened. He sounded like one of the family, rambling and friendly, so sometimes they listened and sometimes they didn't. At eight o'clock, his voice stopped and for five minutes the table went silent as Jack Dennett read the news. "Shush," Margaret or Leo would say if they had to, which wasn't often. Authoritative and untouchable, Dennett was treated like a guest. When he talked, they had to listen.

Margaret made porridge every winter morning, hot porridge, toast and coffee; she administered cod liver oil, with orange juice to wash it down. Bacon and eggs were for weekends; shelves of cold cereals for the summer. On the floor beside Leo was the newspaper. Frank began delivering Toronto's *Globe and Mail* when he was twelve, and as long as he delivered it the family had a morning paper, but it wasn't for the breakfast table. School began earlier for the older ones, soon they were rushing about. When "the little ones," finally done, were off playing, Margaret and Leo would open the paper and share their morning coffee.

At lunch the kids came home, except when it rained. Margaret had soup on the stove, sandwiches or hot dogs and tea; on Shrove Tuesdays she made pancakes with quarters and dimes and buttons in them. The radio was always on. Any unmade beds got made at noon. Trish practised her piano. All of them had taken lessons, but year after year only Trish kept at them. When they all had left for school, Leo arrived home for *his* lunch.

Frank never thought much about that then. He does now. Then, he didn't know his father came home, and later when he did, he didn't think about it because he was his father and fathers did no wrong. His dad was busy at work, customers came in on their lunch hours and, being store manager, he had to be there. He felt no need to explain, Frank felt no need to question. Until later, long after Leo had died and Margaret was dead; though he couldn't have asked her anyway, and he wouldn't have asked him either. So now with questions and no answers, he makes up his own.

Maybe there were just too many of us, he thinks now. Maybe he wanted to get away. At the office every night, every Saturday and much of every Sunday, no one *needed* to be there all that time. It wasn't just work. He didn't want to be around us, around Mom, around me. The only year I played hockey, he never came. We never played catch. When I struggled at school, he was never there.

And now in Frank's head, there is no other voice that says: Hey, hold on. That's not the way it was. I wasn't gone *every* night, it wasn't *every* Sunday. I *was* there. We *did* do things. Those car rides, those Sundays in the country? Don't you remember? What about the Ex each year? And the movies we went to? There were lots of things.

Besides, fathers weren't supposed to be around. Mothers were. Mothers were supposed to stay at home, create a family, be there when their kids needed them. That was their job; that's why they stayed home! My job was to put food on the table, clothes on your body, put something over your head. And I did. I ate dinner with you, I gave you advice when you needed it, lived with your mom and you and was part of your life all your boyhood life. I wasn't there all the time, I know that, but who was? Ward Cleaver, Ozzie Nelson, Jim Anderson and all the TV fathers? Sure, but for them it was *always* dinner or night-time or weekends and the camera was there *only* when they were there. They never had to think about work or health or money or career, but that's not how people live.

What about being forty-one years old when you were born, and having six other kids? Do you think that was easy? What about having lungs so filled with crap that whenever I climbed the stairs they took my breath away? Doesn't that tell you something? You saw me. I worked my whole life, I was *fifteen years old* when I started. I worked through the Depression, I never missed a pay-cheque. I worked for *fifty* years, never stopped. I had no family fortune to live on, no big bank account. What about the heart attack I had when you were eight, every year the trips down south after that? I *had* to take those trips. They *were* for the good of my health. I know, the first year we took Sue and not you and you were hurt; I understand that. But Sue was too young, we couldn't leave her, and if we took both of you what kind of rest would I have had? But is this *all* you remember about that time, about me having a heart attack, that Sue went and you didn't?

And when we got back, do you think you just get over a heart attack, go to Arizona and *snap* everything's fine? Your life is changed. There're lots of things you can't do. I know, you were too young to think about that, but what about now?

Is this all I am to you, now, after all this time? Twenty-three years together, all the birthdays and Christmases, all the laughs we had at dinner. Don't they mean anything? Is this how it turns out for me? *I was never there?* Is that the legacy of my life in your life, in the lives of your children and their children, I'm some object lesson, some caution-ary tale, a family story that gets passed on and on?

Noise. It's all just noise. He needed him.

When lunch was over, Leo would sometimes shuffle upstairs for a nap, to get himself through the day.

Margaret was always there. It was her duty and her job; it was what her church had taught her and with every bone in her body what she knew was right. She knew what it was like when a mother wasn't there, when siblings died, when nothing was certain, when a family broke apart. That wouldn't happen to her. Her aunt and uncle had been there to take her in, but that wasn't the way it was supposed to be. She had had no real family life, no childhood. Later she had seen her own sister's life unravel, an alcoholic husband, unexplained absences, tension, separation. Who knew what Eileen's children had seen and heard and had to bear? She had always tried to guide her, direct her. When she had gone out with the wrong kind of men, she had let her know as only a bossy big sister can; when she found out she was seeing a divorced man, she was unforgiving. Eileen didn't under-stand. Life is hard; there are consequences. You must make the right choices, do the right thing. Family must never be taken for granted. Husbands can die, kids can die. You must take care of the present for the present can do you in. The future will take care of itself. God will see to it.

She seemed always to be working. John had allergies, she had her own impeccable standards, there was always vacu-uming and dusting to do. Being clean mattered a lot then. Polio was the greatest threat; measles, mumps, chicken pox, TB, whooping cough, scarlet fever; there weren't many vaccines. Most parents carried on their arms a crater-like smallpox scar, and memories of the flu epidemic and the millions who had died a generation before. Cleanliness to them *was* very nearly "next to Godliness." When disease hit a house like theirs, it laid waste. One after another they would fall sick. It might be weeks before regular routines could be resumed. And whose life would be affected? Not Leo's. In sickness and in health, he was at the office.

There was also the garden to care for, its bounty of flowers and fruits to use properly, neighbourhood expectations and pride to satisfy. She picked raspberries, gooseberries and black currants which grew beside the driveway, canned them, picked the wormy apples from the apple tree outside the boys' window, cut out the worms and turned wormy apples into applesauce. Leo brought home bushels of fruits and vegetables from the market and she canned them too. When Mr. Bedding, the man next door, went fishing at the harbour, he'd bring her back hundreds of tiny smelt, and she stood at the sink, cut off their heads, sliced them open and cooked them. The smelt, the berries and wormy apples, they were all God's blessings given to her to be used. Waste not, want not. Eat up, there are kids starving in China. See a pin and let it lie, you'll want a pin before you die. Or a smelt or wormy apple . . . take *nothing* for granted.

After breakfast and lunch the kids hurried to school, and she was left to clean up. Neighbours were always dropping by. She was older, had nice, polite kids, she had been a nurse. She was on the CWL executive, was friends with Father Hickey; good company, she was a good person to know. Mrs. Morrison from across the street, Mr. Wilson the egg man, it might be almost anyone. Once every spring and once every fall, an old guy would knock on the door and ask for clothes. "You got any nice clothes for me," he'd rasp, " 'cause if you don't gimme them now, I'll come back later and take 'em off your clothesline." And every year she gave him one of Leo's old suits. But before he went, she'd take him into the backyard, sit him in a lawn chair and bring him a tray of soup, coffee and a sandwich. She'd sit with him as he ate and when he got up and left, bring the tray into the kitchen and in a great big pot on the stove, boil all his dishes. She washed everything he touched in disinfectant.

One spring, the old guy looked sick to her. He was coughing and sweating, and she thought he might have pneumonia. The nights were still cold and after she had fed him his usual hot meal, she told him he should see somebody, that he was sick. He offered no protest but as she got up to go in the house, he yelled after her, "Don't call the police." Inside, she called the police. "Look, I don't want to turn him in or anything," she said, "but he's sick. He needs a warm bed." A few minutes later, the police arrived, picked him up and took him down to the new jail to a new warm bed. As they tried to wrestle him into their police car, he cursed her.

The next day, she took him a carton of cigarettes and talked to him on a phone through a plate-glass window at the jail. "I'm really sorry," she told him, "*but it was for your own good.*"

She didn't go out much or go too far when she did. Overweight, she didn't like walking. "I walked all over Whitby," she'd complain at the dinner table. But not even Whitby was that small. The milkman came to the door, the breadman, Mr. Wilson the egg man; freezers were small, there was little fresh produce in the stores except in summer; in winter they ate mostly food from the pantry which was just off the kitchen by the basement steps — canned everything from the store, canned fruits and vegetables from her garden. The rest of her grocery shopping she did late Saturday afternoons with Leo and the car. It was only meat she needed each day and that the girls brought home on their way from school.

One time of the day she reserved for herself. It wasn't every day because of errands or appointments, but it came right after lunch. The cleaning and dusting were done, the baking and fixing of dinner was for later, Leo was back at work, the kids were in school, she had an hour, maybe

more. She would take off her apron, climb the stairs and
have a bath. In a locked bathroom with no one else around,
she'd wash her hair and then just lie there. Reading, thinking, dreaming, who knew? When finally she was done, she
wrapped herself in a big beach towel and sat in the chair
in her room by the window. There she would watch the
street, the vendors and housewives coming and going;
she'd read, *LIFE, Time, Maclean's, Reader's Digest,* they sub-
scribed to them all. Then, before Leo got home, she would
freshen herself up. The frumpy housedresses, the stockings rolled down to her knees, were put away. She put on
her make-up, took a fresh dress from her closet, then went
back to her chair. With her head back, she listened. When
in the distance she could hear the sound of kids, she knew
her time was up.

The moment they opened the front door, they knew
what day it was. Damp and clean-smelling, it was Monday
or Tuesday, wash day. The dining-room table covered in
fresh-washed clothes, wrung out and slightly dry; their
mother, a sprinkler bottle in her hand, dampening Leo's
white shirts and handkerchiefs, as wet as the clothes, her
hands freezing and red from the rinse water of the ringer
washer in the basement. They dropped their books, gathered the sheets and hung them up, outside on the line in
summer, down in the basement in four long rows in the
wintertime. Leo had wanted to buy her a dryer, but she
wasn't interested. When finally she relented, she still put
her clothes on the line. A dryer only dried clothes, she said.
Sunshine killed germs, in winter the basement's cold
would freeze them out.

Beside her was a laundry basket with a bedsheet tucked
into its bottom, spilling over its sides. After each shirt, pil-
lowcase and handkerchief was dampened, she rolled and
piled it in the basket, one on top of the others, until the
dining-room table was clear and the basket full. Then she
folded the sheet over top of the pile to keep the dampness
in, for Wednesday was ironing day.

It smelled like nuts gently toasting. And there they were, Margaret and Mrs. Smythe, their two ironing boards side by side in the dining room, the radio on, talking and laughing as their irons flew. They knew each other from the CWL, Mr. Smythe ran the lumber-yard downtown, the Smythes had older children and two young foster kids, both girls, one year apart. The ironing helped Mrs. Smythe make ends meet. Both the girls were in Frank's class at school and every Wednesday, the three of them walked home together. Mr. Smythe would arrive from the lumber-yard about four-thirty and take them all home. Mrs. Smythe wasn't a very good ironer and Margaret gave her the things that didn't matter much. She did Leo's clothes herself.

Leo liked to look right. It was the salesman in him. Wear the right clothes, drive the right car, and everyone thinks you're the guy for the job. Look like the man you want to be and no one wonders if you are. He wore a white shirt and dark suit pants weekday and weekend. Outside the house, he wore a tie and suitcoat as well. But there was no better symbol of his ways than that pile of shirts every Wednesday. To the kids, the girls especially, no better symbol of their mother's burden. Ironing does that. A fresh shirt each day, sometimes two; she starched his collars and cuffs, ironed his handkerchiefs and folded them the way he liked them folded. She ironed his boxer shorts as well.

Every second Friday when they got home, the smell was light and clean, as if all the windows had been opened and all the crud in the air had been driven away. The pied piper was Mrs. Hendriks, "the Dutch lady." Every two weeks, she helped Margaret with the big jobs, the windows one time, a bedroom or the bathroom the next. At Christmas, the two of them moved the furniture from the living room and dining room into the halls and Mrs. Hendriks waxed the hardwood floors. It was that Friday in December, when they opened their front door, the kids knew Christmas was really coming.

Thursdays and every other day, the house smelled of baking. When the front door opened, the odour swarmed over them and took them in. "Mom is at the counter," Frank says, his memory still fresh. "I can see her in a pale blue housedress and flowered apron, the one with the torn pocket. She is at the pull-out breadboard, rolling out cookie dough, or pie dough. I smell oatmeal cookies baking. There's a pot of stew on the stove. She gives me a bowl of stew broth and some bread to warm me up. She has a pot of coffee on. We sip our coffee and eat fresh-baked cookies. Everything smells so good."

And if she was always there, she expected *them* to be there too. She needed the older girls to come home after school. They had to collect the mail at the post office, and pick up the meat. There were all the little ones to cope with as she got dinner ready. Besides, there wasn't much else for them to do; not many sports for girls, no Girl Guide troop for Catholic girls because their church didn't have one. There was more for the little ones as they got older, skating lessons and ballet, "elocution" lessons when they were the rage, but what they started they would rarely finish. Somebody would get the measles, then everybody got the measles. Besides, the family had its needs and the family came first.

The boys broke the after-school pattern because they were boys. They got a paper route, together, then separately. They came home from school, had a snack with the others, then as their sisters started into their homework, or peeled potatoes, set the table and did all that needed to get done for dinner, John and Jim went out into the world to learn about money, responsibility and all the things boys needed to learn.

Still, there was always some free time. To read or listen to the radio, to "Dick Tracy," "Terry and the Pirates," "Sky King," shows which soon would follow their audiences to television. Later, to watch Gene Autry, "Children's Theatre" and "Queen for a Day" on their own TV. But most of these free minutes they spent with neighbourhood friends, outside, but not far away.

Frank's first and favourite play spot was the verandah. Big and open, it looked like a ship's bridge and ran across the whole front of the house. It had no screens to rip or glass to break, no rugs to dirty or wear out. There, he could run and jump to his heart's content, bump into anything, scream, laugh and never once worry about the voice in the house. He liked to watch the street from there. When the kids went by on their bikes, he'd scrunch his neck down into his shoulders and watch through the slots of the white picket fence, the grey blur of their spokes turning *backwards,* when he knew they were not. One more thing he didn't understand.

He liked to watch the rain. Especially in summer, when the day turned suddenly to a dark amber dusk, the air growing heavy and cool; then feeling that air drawing away from him, sucked away as if to fill up the sky for one gigantic blow; and then the explosion. He used to be frightened by thunderstorms, especially at night. His mother would walk around the house with her little bottle of holy water, sprinkling it on them. "A few drops will make us safe," she'd say. On the verandah, he could get close enough to the storm's rage, and still feel protected.

It was also a place of exile. His mother's washing and cleaning took no holiday, he seemed always in her way. Why not a nice game of tag, or blind man's bluff, on the *verandah?* Immediately, it was his fort or pirate ship. Perfect for cowboys and Indians, just high enough above the lawn for him to jump from one stampeding horse to another, from a saloon roof to a bad guy's shoulders, from a careening stagecoach as it raced towards a cliff and certain oblivion. Perfect to slither low behind and out of sight, to whisper, hatch plans, *tzing tzing,* to duck and dive from ricocheting bullets that always just missed. And when the time was right, a perfect prop to the throes of death, a bullet in the chest, arrow in the back, a body draped upside down, dying, dying, dead, like in the movies.

His "best buddy," Gerald Lynch, lived a few houses down
on the other side of John Street, a block away. Two girls,
the other members of their "gang of four," Judy Heffering
and Joey Bryant, lived almost as near — Judy across the
road from Gerald, Joey one block over on Euclid. Gerald's
mother had died, his father was a labourer on a construction crew. Mr. Lynch seemed always in blue jeans, plaid
flannel shirts and workboots. Their white stucco bungalow
smelled, and to Frank seemed not very much like a home.
The Lynches were Catholics, as were the Hefferings and
Bryants. Al Heffering ran the Esso station in town, Margaret and Mrs. Heffering were on the CWL together, and
when they weren't helping everyone in the neighbourhood as Catholic women were supposed to do, they took
care of Father Hickey, who for meals and cleaning up, especially before periodic visits from the diocese, needed all the
help he could get.

Joey Bryant was different. "She was the smart one," Judy
recalls. "Gerald, Frank and I were always the slowest, always
behind, quiet, always on the sidelines. I liked having Joey
with us because she was popular." Mr. Bryant owned the
Studebaker dealership in town, Bryant's Garage. The
Bryants were Catholics, but not "good Catholics," the
neighbourhood knew. They didn't go to church very often,
Mrs. Bryant wasn't in the CWL, nor Mr. Bryant in the
Knights of Columbus, and there had been a "scandal," as
the kids called it, as well. One of Joey's unmarried sisters
had had a baby, and had given it up to be taken care of by
an aunt. Good Catholics didn't have babies out of wedlock,
and didn't give them up once they were born. So in the
Whitby parish, the Bryants were on the other side.

The four of them seemed a strange combination, yet in
ways they didn't quite understand they needed each other,
and for most of their elementary school years, stuck
together. They would climb the Bryants' apple tree and in
a makeshift fort pass a salt shaker from hand to hand and

eat green apples. They would walk over to Lynde Creek to catch suckers and frogs, searching the shiny rocks and bits of glass for treasure. They sat and tore weeds from its banks, rolled the weeds into long tight cylinders, lit them, then shoved candies in their mouths to hide their smoker's breath. If Sen-Sen worked for tobacco, surely candies were good for weeds. Saturday afternoons, they might go to "the show," to the Brock Theatre just north of the Four Corners. It cost fifteen cents, they would take twenty-five. They went to Turansky's first, across from the theatre, bought ten cents' worth of candy and took it with them into the show. Then one day, unknown to them, the Goodmans, who owned the theatre, had upped the price to twenty-five cents. When they arrived from Turansky's with their candy, they didn't have enough money to get in. "Just this time," Mrs. Goodman let them pass.

In winter, they would walk up to Hillcrest School, mount a slow, gentle rise to a patch of polished ice, turn their toboggans around and career down the "hill." Sometimes, they went all the way to "Whiteface Mountain." Everybody in town called it that, and even if it was no mountain, it was a pretty good hill for prairie-like Whitby. They trudged in a line like robots, mummified against the cold, along Walnut until the houses stopped, up a dirt path, across wide-open fields, the snow swirling about them, the knee-high grass squeaking under their boots. Then just before the railway tracks was Lynde Creek, and rising above it on the other side, Whiteface Mountain. "It was about a two-mile walk," Frank recalls, measuring with childhood legs; it would be half a mile today. They crossed the creek, climbed the mountain and slid down on their toboggans, shedding kids at every bump until the last big jump from the bank onto the sometimes-not-so-frozen creek.

There was so much space then. "I remember our house and feeling I lived on a hundred-acre farm," Frank says. Their street was the town line and everything behind them was open fields all the way to Toronto, fifty kilometres away.

That didn't begin to change until Dunlop Tire opened a factory in 1955 and modest development followed. Behind their house, where High Street is now, was a dirt pathway that led to a farm and a rickety old building, the House of Refuge, built for the "poor and the friendless." To Frank everyone who lived in that awful place looked old, so to him it was an "old folks' home." It had a big barn and apple orchard, cows which grazed along the fence near the path, and one huge and monstrous mad-eyed bull. They threw apples at it, chased it, teased it, got it all excited and laughed as it charged stupidly against the fence. When they managed the nerve, they would climb the fence and, like cartoon spies, tiptoe through the "bull patch" towards the apple trees, the bull snoozing in the distance. At the first swish of its tail, they'd be running for their lives.

The House of Refuge closed, its land was sold, its orchards and fields turned into 1950s-style houses as Whitby began its slow creep towards Toronto. The smell of farm, so powerful when they first moved from Leaside, disappeared for good. Down the path that became High Street, a new home for the elderly, Fairview Lodge, was built. But the "poor and the friendless" kept coming back. One old man the kids called "Skunky." He was small and bent and had no teeth, and so when he screamed at them, which was often, he whistled. Every night, summer and winter, he walked by their houses in his old soiled coat and make-believe shepherd's staff, the fur flaps of his hat curled and hanging down. He'd go up Palace Street, along Walnut and down the dirt path to collect the herd of cows he had always collected, then walk back again, his make-believe herd obediently trailing behind him.

There were always plenty of characters around. Bill Bandel was Judy Heffering's uncle and had the "mind of a six-year-old," it was said. Frank would see him coming down the street, and walk with him; Bill Bandel always knew the weather and the baseball scores. Leo would bring him home old business forms and pencils from the office because he loved to draw and write his name. He wore a floppy, plaid tam-o'-shanter hat, and at every funeral he was there. Somehow he got word of the service and as Frank walked his walk of freedom from the school to the church, let out to serve "on the altar," he'd see him there, his solemn face and tam-o'-shanter hat, holding open the doors to the church so the casket could be carried in and out. That was his duty and no one would take it from him.

There were lots of other kids in the neighbourhood, but only the four who were the same age, and who as Catholics went to the same school. That was the way their world divided. Not so much by age, gender and income as by religion and neighbourhood. The dirt and gravel roads, ditches, big front lawns and backyards, the trees that had been there since who-knows-when, all ran together like so much connected space, safe and secure, and all of it they treated as their own. There were fewer, bigger families then, in fewer, smaller houses, older kids were used to younger kids. They shared the same bedrooms, were needed for the same family chores, took the same family drives for Sunday dinners; they needed each other to make up sides for after-dinner softball games, for the town's hockey and baseball teams; in pre-war built schools, they shared the same multi-grade classrooms. As models and mentors and baby-sitters and second-mothers and second-fathers, they were responsible for each other whether they liked it or not. The family came first. The older ones dragged around the younger ones, the younger ones were dragged around by the older ones, each had little chance to escape the other. It was why Frank's gang of four was so important. Frank and Judy and Joey and Gerald were among the youngest in each of their large families. But together, with no one else around, each could be the biggest, strongest, smartest and funniest, each could talk the most, be listened to and heard, do the craziest and bravest things, be the most respected, be the leader. They knew that when they climbed down from the Bryants' apple tree and stepped back through each of their front doors, they would be hidden in the pack again.

Frank's memories of Gerald, Judy and Joey come easily. When he thinks of his childhood and not of his family, he thinks of them. They seemed to fill much of each other's childhood lives, the after-schools, weekends, the summer days and nights. But they didn't, or not for long. Except for Joey, they were loners. They liked each other's company but company isn't easy. They were good to each other, didn't test and expose and put each other down. They didn't do unto each other what others were doing unto them. But in a group, risk is always there, so those times when nothing specific drew them together, their way was to drift and fade from view. To a bedroom, a favourite private spot, as out of sight, as out of mind as possible, so others would forget their existence, and they could do what *they* wanted.

Not long after, Joey skipped a grade and they hardly saw her again.

4

"Whenever I try to draw up a memory, I always visualize a lad of eight or ten years old," he says now. A puzzled look crosses his face. "Why? Surely not everything happened to me between eight and ten."

Memories of time alone do not come so easily or vividly. Not much happens when you're alone except inside your head, no words get expressed, there is little for memory to grab hold of, to shape and manipulate and turn into rememberable story, to retrieve years later and tell. There isn't so much that seems of interest to others. And though his stories might suggest otherwise, time alone filled much of the volume of his childhood, if little of his memory.

He remembers most vividly that "lad of eight or ten" because few memories stick in anyone younger, because after he was ten, after Gerald and Judy and Joey, he spent more of his time alone. Something happened at just that time that changed a lot of things. He got fat. He had been a little chubby before, but this was different, and the change was sudden. He has a picture of his grade 5 class at St. Bernard's School. It is May, 1958, two months before his eleventh birthday. Whoever took the picture is standing in a front corner of the room, most of the students are seated at their desks, a few, him included, stand at the back with Father Marco and Mrs. Davies, their teacher. He is round-faced, slightly more so than the other thirty-six kids in the picture, but not significantly, and is one of three boys and one girl wearing glasses.

The next picture is less than two months later. It is late June, school is out, it's Mary Jean's wedding day. He is standing with Trish and Sue near the front steps to their house, flowers and bushes in bloom all around them. He has had his hair cut nearly to the scalp and in the sun it shines almost white-blond. He is wearing a white shirt, grey slacks and a tie, but it's his blue double-breasted blazer that gives him away. He appears stuffed into it.

He may only be five pounds heavier, but his look has changed. He had struggled in school the years before. In grade 3, he had so much trouble reading that his mother arranged private lessons with Mrs. McGee, the mother of one of his friends. At about the same time, he also began wearing glasses. He recalls that first morning, "the proud, *hey, look at me*, feeling I had when I walked into class, which lasted about five minutes. Then somebody yelled, 'Hey, four-eyes.'" He had always been able to keep most of his failures private. Hating the times he had to stand and read in front of the class, he had learned to become as invisible as an empty wooden desk, and was rarely called upon. But the glasses, now the fatness, he couldn't hide. And with them came an unmissable *look*. This kid can be picked on, it said. Test him, push him, take advantage anyway you want. You can hurt him and he can't hurt you.

Returning to school that fall, everything was different. More and more of his after-school time was now spent alone.

Much of it he spent in his room. He had a fascination with cars. As a little boy, he'd crawl under the back stoop with his Dinky toys and pretend he was a stock-car driver. He'd lie in the upstairs hall, using his mother's Indian throw rug as his infield, the walls as his crash barriers, and race his cars down a slick and perfect hardwood floor racetrack. When he was a little older, his mom and dad brought him back a model car each year from their trips to Florida. Always an Oldsmobile, it was the same model as his Dad's, and he painted it the same colour. He would take it with him under the back stoop, gather some bricks and pile them to make a house, stick some grass and tiny branches into the ground for a garden and trees, put down a few stones for a driveway, and drive his big Olds off to work and home again.

But what he liked best was building his own plastic models. "Jim got me my first one," he recalls. "A Chrysler Imperial, I was eight or nine, and I took that great big limousine and turned it into a hot rod. I painted it a weird colour, put fender skirts and aerials on it, put spinners and everything on it I could." A few years later, with money from his paper route, he bought his own models. He had only six or seven by the time he was a teenager, but for him that was enough. He got little pleasure from the finished cars themselves. He wanted only enough parts from enough different models to assemble his own creations.

He used to sit alone at his desk in "the big room" he shared with John and Jim, spread out a newspaper, and lay on it his shoeboxful of pieces. Tires, engines, fenders, hoods, seats, lights; he kept the "trees" the parts came attached to, shaved them down and made them into frames. But first he imagined the car he wanted to build. "I used to dream of what it would look like," he says. "Just sitting there on my dresser, maybe racing down a track, a stock-car, maybe a long-nosed dragster. But you know how it is," he shrugs, "it never quite ends up looking the way you imagine, so the picture in my mind kept changing." He laughs. "Sometimes, I'd never even finish it. But that was OK. I'd put it up on my dresser and just look at it, and a few days later imagine something else, tear it apart and build it again." He used as little glue as he could. Whatever was done had to be easily undone.

"There was a model shop in town that always had contests. I never entered any. My models would never pass muster. But I was happy the way they were." "I had a '52 Merc, and an old '32 Ford Coupe, a hot rod and a '59 Olds, a '60 Corvair and a '64 Chev Super Sport. And I had a truck too." The names gush out. One day when he was nineteen, he gathered his models, cut out pictures of country scenes from magazines, set the pictures behind the models, got up close and took some pictures of his own. Though the backdrops are blurry, he could almost see what he'd been imagining all along.

When he wasn't building models or poring over his stamps, he dreamed what boys of the time dreamed of. Being a cowboy, owning a ranch, being a train engineer, being tall. But different from other kids, he held his every dream in check. Each one came with a solid earthbound "yes, but . . ."; each he put into deadening perspective. "At one time I wanted to be a train engineer," he recalls. "But I found out with my eyesight I couldn't qualify. I considered being a policeman in high school, size wasn't a problem, but my cowardice was, and again my glasses. The same with being a fireman. I used to think of being a farmer, because of the farm behind us, I guess. Being independent, growing your own vegetables, *but . . .*"

Never once did he dream of hitting the game-winning home run in the seventh game of the World Series. "I didn't play baseball much," he might say. Or, "whenever they picked teams, they'd always pick me last." As if he never deserved the dream, as if dreaming anything like that would be just too stupid. When he ran home from school, never once did he see a finish line, a wall of people, a victory podium, a shiny gold medal around his neck. Never once was he the hero of his own stories. He may have liked to drift from everyone's sight, but never would he lose sight of himself. He had worked too hard to avoid the mockery of others, why mock himself? Who did he think he was?

It was with cars he came closest to losing control. "I used to dream I got ahold of an old '52 Merc," he says, his voice and body springing to life, "a blue one, just like the model I had. And that I had this great big barn where I worked on it, and in the back I had this track . . . And that I got hold of a '64 Ford Fairlane, powder blue, and fixed it up . . . And the car Dad was supposed to buy too, but Mom

wouldn't let him, a '64 Chev Super Sport, two-door hard-
top. 'No, no,' his voice suddenly mocks, his mother's voice
ever-present in his head, 'he needs a four-door sedan for
his family.'

"Just silly dreams."

Outside that room, everything happened *to* him.

"I got stuck in the mud in the backyard once, and my
foot began sinking. I started crying, 'Mom, help! Help!!'
Then, trying to get out I got my other foot stuck, and sunk
up to my knees. She couldn't pull me out. The milkman
was coming down the street with his horse and wagon, and
she yelled to him. Together, they got me out but I lost my
boots. I remember Mom yapping at me. I learned early
not to listen but I could still see her mouth going, how
she'd told me a thousand times never to play out there.
On and on. She hauled me into the basement, stripped
off my clothes, turned on the hose and soaped me down.
Then she gave me a good whack on the rear and sent me
upstairs for a bath."

And again. "I had this fascination with thin ice. I loved
to pick it up and look through it. It was like looking
through a window — then I'd throw it and smash it, and it
would break like glass. One day, I was bending over a ditch
trying to pick up this big piece and some smartass pushed
me, and I went headlong into the icy water.

"He took off, but I knew who it was. He was younger than
me, but a bully and lived down the street across from Gerald Lynch. The next day, Gerald and I cornered him and
washed his face with snow to teach him a lesson. I mean,
I'm not a fighter, actually I'm kind of a chicken, so maybe
he thought I wouldn't do anything. But I was just mad
enough. It was the indignity of it. The next Saturday, I went
to confession."

These stories come from a time when he still had stories
to tell. Outside his room, escaping danger, surviving, was
as far as his fantasies would stretch. If he could stretch
them that far, that was his gold medal. And he was happy.

Leo got home from work about six, hung his suit coat over the back of "Grandad's chair," and got himself a beer from the refrigerator. He always drank O'Keefe and always from a glass. "I don't think he'd ever drink out of a bottle," Ann recollects, not quite sure and sure just the same, and sometimes he lined up little glasses and poured some into each for each of the kids. Every month, a beer truck backed into their driveway to pick up the empties. A few days before, Father Hickey would call up Margaret, and one of the kids would wheel the little red wagon over to the rectory, load it up and wheel it home. Father Hickey, the kids were told, found his empties a nuisance to return.

Leo untied his shiny black shoes. "Frank, on your way down, would you bring me my slippers?" "I'm not going up, Dad." "Well, on your way up, will you take my shoes." Every night it was the same, just as it had been with the older ones, later it was Sue's turn. "I used to wait for him to come home," she remembers. "I just loved doing that for him."

The table was set, "properly," with serviettes beside each place, a bread basket with bread, a tablecloth, a jug of ice water in the middle of the table. If any of the kids brought home a friend, a little white table was pulled out from the wall and set properly for the youngest there, usually Frank and Sue. Somehow there was always enough.

CFRB's Gordon Sinclair was just finished "Show Business with Sinclair," and was reading the news. They said no grace, that was kept special for Sunday dinners and Leo always said it: "Bless us O Lord for these thy gifts which we are about to receive from thy bounty. Through Jesus Christ our Lord. Amen." If Sinclair wasn't done, they were quiet until he was. They might talk a little about the news, something the infectiously blood-boiling Sinclair had said. One Christmas, he had talked about how there was no Santa Claus, and that parents should level with their kids and stop pretending there was. This at six o'clock, as thousands of kids were sitting at dinner with their now apoplectic parents. "The bugger was ruining Christmas for a lot of kids," they decided.

They talked mostly about their days. Leo about the office, Joe So-and-so did this, Tony got a contract for that, and knowing everyone, Margaret listened and some of the kids did too. She would tell him what Mrs. Smythe or Mrs. Hendriks had said, about her CWL meeting, what Clara or Lillian or Jack or Eileen had said in their letters, and Leo listened too. The older kids, especially, talked about school. It was all very noisy, spirited and not at all formal.

When the kids got to be old enough to eat *properly* what was in front of them, when they had learned when to talk and when not, the focus of dinner could turn from basic priorities, and them, to conversation, to being a family. But always there were lessons of manners to be learned, lapses to be fingered, and Margaret was the cop and the family her beat. *Semper vigilate.* At dinnertime it was easier for her to go about her appointed rounds. Everyone arrived at the same time, there was no coming and going, for her more time to sit down. And notice. Everything. "Use your serviette. Put it on. Put it on! . . . Don't reach for things, ask for them . . . Eat with your mouth closed . . . Sit up straight, elbows off the table. Francis Leo Bloye, get your elbows off the table!!"

"Francis Leo Bloye," the name seemed to run together, like Johnny and Jimmy and Jimmy and Johnny, and she ran it together so often all its bumps smoothed out. She may not have known what to call him when he was born, but she never forgot after that. It wasn't the first thing she'd say, she would build up to it, but the build-up came quickly. First was simple correction, spontaneous, reflexive, from eyes to tongue, no thinking or feeling, no passage through brain or heart, quick, stern, atonal, nothing personal, an order barked out, a reminder to *everyone* not just the perpetrator that she was watching. Stage two. No change of behaviour evident: eyes to brain to heart to tongue, angry, deliberate, multitonal, personal. And if still nothing, if insolent, dumb, brain dead or all three: stage three. Monotonal, full volume, full names only — FrancisLeoBloye!!! It was a voice that penetrated flesh and time. As Roy Greenaway, Ann's husband, once put it, "When she yelled, every kid within six blocks ran home."

At the other end of the table, with a side to himself, Leo *presided*. He didn't say much and didn't have to. He was genial, kind, reasonable, slightly above every fray and always to be left there. He was someone to be respected. If he decided to speak, everyone went quiet and listened. He was their father. For her, tall-short, young-old, boy-girl, rich-poor, strong-weak, likeable-unlikeable, needy or not, everyone was treated the same, except for Leo. He was special. The roast beef would be done medium rare because Leo liked his roast beef medium rare. The newspapers were his newspapers and not to be read until he had read them. On Saturday, if she bought hamburger meat for dinner (it's not hamburger, she'd insist, it's "ground round"), she bought two steaks as well. One cube steak for Leo, one for her; hamburger for the kids. Then fittingly, Leo would cut a piece of his steak for Sue, one for Frank and pretty soon they all had a piece, and his wasn't much bigger than theirs. He was the family breadwinner. He worked hard. Whatever he earned was his, whatever fruits his earnings purchased were his too. It was out of generosity not duty that he shared his bounty with them. Whatever time or goods he gave to them was a family blessing. No one had a right to expect more. He could not to be criticized. He was the good cop.

Margaret was judge, jury, executioner and the only witness that mattered. Leo came into the picture, when he came into the picture, somewhere after that. His punishment was a lecture and a straight gaze, and if things went that far you knew you were in trouble. If he disagreed with the way she had done things, he never said. Whenever they felt a fight coming on, they got in the car and went for a drive. In front of the kids, he backed her up, with silence if nothing else.

None of the kids remembers him disciplining them more than once or twice in their lives. She was there when things happened, he was not. In a big, complicated family, what went wrong had to be quickly set right. Anger to be expressed and forgotten, life to go on, which suited her temperament exactly. Her justice was swift, impatient, often harsh, and if sometimes blind, was followed as swiftly by heartfelt apology. Her favourite instrument was a wooden spoon, sometimes she used a hair brush, once or twice an electric cord.

"One Sunday, we were out in the backyard and got filthy dirty," he says, "and she called us all in the house. She was livid. The only way was in through the back door and up the back stairs. She stood at the bottom of the stairs with an electric cord, and not one of us got by without being beaten.

"Another time I stayed at school to play with Patrick Watters. His parents cleaned the building at night. It was late in the afternoon and I wasn't home, so Mom called Dad and told him to pick me up on his way. 'Come on, you're supposed to be home,' he said to me. And I said, 'I promised Mr. Watters I'd help him. I'll be home in a few minutes.' Well, I forgot, and when I did get home, she was livid. 'You told your dad you'd be coming right home.' I said, 'No, I didn't,' and she said, 'That's what your dad said, and I believe your dad.' Oh, did I get a whipping for that one."

"She was livid." Again and again he uses the phrase to describe that moment before the storm breaks. The look in her eyes. Her mouth tight, her chin unmoveable, everything on the outside of her body squeezing tighter, everything on the inside swelling, the explosion a breath away. In her eyes anger, hatred and unbreakable resolve. She would set that look on them, hold it and hold it and, unable to match her anger and resolve, they had finally to jerk their heads away. The pain of losing was easier than the pain it would take to win.

He got strapped at school; it was the accepted discipline of the time, especially for Catholic children. "He that spareth his rod hateth his son," the good book said. And Margaret Bloye, they knew, loved them all.

"I wonder if she'd be arrested today for what she did," he thinks. He has heard the reports on radio. They don't sound much different from the stories he has in his head. Yet, they are different, he is certain. They are hateful stories of hateful people, and she was loving. "I only got spanked if I did wrong, you know. Not if she was having a bad day or couldn't stand my silliness. If we did bad, we got severely punished, that's all. We'd go up to our rooms and cry for an hour, she'd call us down for dinner and there wouldn't be another word said. She never held a grudge, and we would forget." Now, he holds no grudge himself.

It was a dinner table that might have worked for everyone. It worked for Ann, she was the oldest. When she was young and unable to bear all her load, her parents were there, with time, to help her and teach her how, and imbue her with the desire to do it herself. It was the same for Mary Jean, a little harder for Lee who was just enough younger to make across-the-board treatment and expectations unworkable. But Lee was like her mother, she wouldn't be ignored. If she didn't get her proper due, as *she* defined it, with wit, wile, wilfulness or stubbornness, she'd take it, whether that made her a nice little girl or not. She would even stand up to her mother, which Margaret seemed to like.

It worked for John and Jim because they were the first boys. They did different things, got out into the world to deliver papers, played on hockey and football teams; they had different stories to tell. For John, his older sisters weren't so impossibly older that if he struggled he couldn't connect with them. And the more he tried, the more he was able to hold his own, the more others wanted to help him, the more worthy of their attention and delight he seemed. It worked for Jim because Jim was Jim. He was Lee with a sense of humour. He didn't care who was talking about what. What he had to say was more important; besides, he was going to say it anyway. And because he said what the others only dreamed of, they were happy for his interruptions. It worked for Trish because she was so pleasant and nice. She did so many things well, piano, sports, school, she was the best student in the family, so whenever she spoke they would stop and listen. It worked for Sue and their cousin Michael Northcott, Eileen's son, who lived with them in the early 1950s, because they were the family pets, little, giggly, spunky and cute.

It might have worked for Frank too, but it didn't. He would have been the cute one for awhile, until Sue and Michael. Then he had to be something else. Would he be the smart one, the athletic one, the funny or quirky one? The kid with style, who loved to build things, read newspapers or write nonsense songs? Maybe. He was for a time as everyone is, all promise and possibilities. No door was closed, what he wasn't he might be tomorrow. Then tomorrow came.

And with it expectations, standards. Suddenly he was old enough to be *something*, and to be seen and treated as what he seemed to be. What happens when just being one of the family is no longer enough? When the others feel no further duty to draw you into the goings-on at the table, when you're old enough to be on your own, when it's up to you? When in the free-for-all of the family, you have to compete for the table's time and attention? What would he do and say? How would he fit in?

It was as if every story had started without him. All but Sue were older, there were so many of them. They talked of things he had never heard about, talked faster than his brain and tongue would function. They laughed when nothing seemed funny, got angry and he didn't know why. It is the mystifying early life of anyone younger. Ann had gone through it, so had Mary Jean, Lee, all his brothers and sisters, his mother and father. They had to adapt; now it was his turn. But how does someone find his way into a dinner-table's stories? How does he learn enough to begin to understand, so things can become interesting or funny enough that he *wants* to listen, take part and learn some more? So he can catch up and be at the centre of some of his own stories? What must he, what must those around him, do?

They both must try. It is not so easy or automatic as it sounds. He may be a brother and son, he may love his sisters and brothers, his mother and father, he may spend hours of every day and years of his life in their presence. He may have every reason to want to make that time good time. They may love him, may be family, may have obligations to him. But they are people: if the task is too hard they will look for another.

It was easy for Ann and Mary Jean, they were the first. Easy for John and Jim, Sue and Michael, they had each other; harder for Lee and Trish, they didn't fit in and had no natural allies or soul mates. But it was hardest for Frank. Cut off from "the boys" by age, interests and personality, with two girls, Trish and Sue, on either side, he had no one to bring him along, guide him, stand up for him and ease his path. And when he needed them most — when he fell behind and got fat, his mother had a hysterectomy, his father a heart attack — it was harder for them.

Still, everything might have turned out differently. Against circumstance, against the momentum of instinct, personality and routine. Leo was a nice man. He loved his kids. When everyone at work talked of hockey or TV shows, he talked of his family. "Leo Bloye? He's a great family man." They all said that. One night, he might have come home from work and stayed home. Not feeling well perhaps, sensing something was wrong. With dinner over and Margaret and the others with reasons to be somewhere else, he might have found himself in the living room alone with his youngest son. The newspaper read, the TV off, with no other escape, they might have begun to talk. Awkwardly, at first. It seems they have nothing to say, that maybe they had never talked, never had any separate existence in each other's worlds, Leo just husband to Margaret, father to them all; Frank just one out of many. One of them mentions the weather just to stop the silence. Other words follow. The details of each other's lives begin to fill in. The stories, unknown for so long, fascinate, and as they listen, looking into each other's faces, they like what they see. Good faces, the image of each other they had always held inside them. Eyes fix on eyes, but this is no contest of wills. They welcome each other in, causing an intimacy suddenly too naked, that trusts too much, that frightens and repels. Then trusts again. They come to no resolution, she returns before they are done, but they know now that things will be different.

Or maybe with Margaret. He spent so much time with her. At breakfast, at lunch, the coffee they shared after school. She saw everything. Surely she had noticed, and just as surely she would never let something pass without comment and reproach, making the wrong right. It begins one night at dinner. Noise and laughter pinball around the table; in and out of her chair, serving and eating, she takes everything in. Her third, all-seeing eye hovers above them. Again and again, she notices Frank. He sits as the others sit, his face carries a look of engagement; his eyes are somewhere else.

It's too much. She can't take it any more. From here on things will be different. He will listen and understand and take part in the life of the table. He will try harder, and she will make sure he does. Every time she catches him drifting off, she'll give him a verbal slap. "What do you think, Frank? No, that's not good enough. Pay attention. What do you really think? We all want to know, don't we kids, and we're all going to wait until you tell us. Now, what is it, Frank?" And she'll interrupt dinner and keep on interrupting dinner and draw attention to him and embarrass him if she has to, until he starts interrupting dinner himself. He is a member of this family. He *will* carry his share of the load like everyone else.

He did struggle for a time but he couldn't keep up, and no one intervened. The gap between him and the rest of the table widened, and he began to lose contact. Trying became harder and less fruitful, then harder and less fruitful still, until for the most part it stopped. "He was like a lost soul," his cousin Michael Northcott said. And whenever he did feel the need to talk, not quite listening, he'd squeeze, not ease, himself into the conversation. Too serious, too loud, too off-topic, too annoying, too ignorable; nothing fit. Everything seemed just beyond him. The more you know, the more you are able to learn; the less you know, the wider the gap and, like runners in a race, the less energy, less hope, less instinct to try. The wider the gap still.

He talks of it matter-of-factly. "I didn't read the papers or care about the news. I'd shut off my ears when the news came on. I was only a kid, eh? My older sisters and brothers probably read the papers and talked about them with Dad and Mom. I'd just sit there and every so often pipe up, 'Oh, so-an-so at school was talking about that.' Like, 'Hey, I'm still here,' you know. Look, I'm the seventh of eight kids and a lot younger. They're talking about things at a high-school level, about careers or voting. I mean, who cares? So I'd eat my dinner, maybe I'd mess around with Sue or Trish, hit them in the elbow, tell them to move over, make a big fuss, that sort of thing. Generally, though, I'd tune out."

They were all members of the same family, they were all on his side, except that's not how a family works. Before people are family members, they are people. Everybody has to find his or her own way. You love your brother but the cookie he gets is one you don't, the hug from your father, kind word from your mother, are time, attention and good, warm feelings that don't come your way. You love your sister, but you want what's best for you. You fight every outside threat together, inside you scratch and claw for everything. Identities are at stake, personalities and outlooks. A family may be a refuge from the outside world, but it's also where the lessons of that world are learned and practised. It's where you learn to fight.

You don't have to beat everyone. Some lives run almost in parallel, never after the same things at the same time, never colliding. He wasn't rivals with Ann, Mary Jean and Lee, with John or Trish. He was too young and unthreatening. He was rivals with Jim and Sue. She was the baby of the family with one mother, four mothers-in-waiting, one father and two big brothers to look after her. To him, she was spoiled. To her, he was a "goody goody," doing what he was told to do because everything else was too hard to live with. The time he had stood up for her, when the bully in her class was giving her a hard time, "It was the kindest thing I ever did," he remembers. He made such a thing of it, she remembers, making sure everyone knew, and the kid was two years younger.

Jim, with an older brother, needed to win too. He needed to show *his* superiority, *his* specialness. He did it with his tongue, standing up to his mother, and he did it with him. "It was the joy of his life to make me cry," Frank says. "It wasn't physical, it was the teasing, getting me mad, knowing I wouldn't do anything." They were like two boxers, Jim, nimble and quick, *jab jab jab*, he the plodding target. His head snaps back, his nose bloodies, *jab jab*. Jim grows bored. He stands in the middle of the ring, arms at his sides, letting him come closer. And closer. One arm still at his side, he raises the other, resting his hand against Frank's forehead, Frank swings and swings, Jim laughs and laughs. He can't lay a glove on him.

Two more video images from his childhood: he is in his bathing suit on the front lawn. He is about eleven, in the middle of his "fat stage," and the only one on the screen. The image is jerky, then steady. Unseen, Jim has placed the movie camera on the car, put the camera on automatic and left it running. Frank looks off-camera towards Jim, self-conscious, laughing, shy, not knowing quite what to do. Jim enters, slick, self-assured and fifteen. He gets him in a headlock, they pretend to wrestle. Jim mugs to the camera, stress and strain on his face. Frank, his head turned sideways, laughs.

A family get-together. A picnic or backyard birthday party, and it's time for a picture. Family members drift slowly together into whatever spots are open. The photo is taken, they go back to what they were doing. The picture, one of several, shows lots of smiling faces, his and Jim's side by side. "He had this favourite pose in our pictures," he recalls. "He'd make sure he was beside me so he could rest his elbow on my head. Which to me sums it up: here's the bully, and there's the sucker that took it."

He tells a story that John told him not long ago. John had come home from school crying one day. His dad asked him what was wrong. A bully had done this or that to him, he said. Leo listened. When John was done, Leo told him to go back out that door, find the bully and get even. He wouldn't let him back in the house, he said, until he had made him cry. And so John did.

He told Frank how later Leo had sat him down for a talk. He told him the same thing had happened to him as a boy. Someone had taken his baseball, he had come home crying, his dad had met him at the door and said, "You're not coming into this house until you get your ball back." So Leo went out and won back his ball.

John never forgot his father's story; Frank never heard it.

Why didn't Leo and Margaret try harder? Leo left the house and the kids to her. She knew far better than him how things were. He wasn't well and was feeling his age, his business demanded always more of him. The kids kept coming, then Michael came, then the girls got married, there were weddings to be paid for. Everything was fine, or wasn't bad. Everything had to be. Maybe he didn't notice.

She couldn't have not noticed. She had helped him when he'd needed help with his homework, had arranged for Mrs. McGee to tutor him. She was always correcting him, what more could she do? She had seven other kids and a husband. They had needs too. In a big family there's only so much time you can give one person. Everyone is equal, no one deserves special treatment. You have to help yourself, and what's wrong with that? That's the way it had been in her life, and Leo's life. Her mother had died, her father let her down, she had to step in and take control herself. She had to move out, set her own course, leave behind her own disastrous family and create a family of her own. Where would she be now if she hadn't, if she'd let things go, let those in control of her ruin her life? What the Creator hadn't done, she had to do herself. She was a self-made person, and if she could do it, why couldn't everyone? Why couldn't her own kids? Why couldn't he? And why *shouldn't* he? God helps those who help themselves. And to the extent anyone does, so does everyone else.

What Frank needed was Frank's help. She resented all his special needs, not that she ever said so. It wasn't even that he asked more. He probably asked less. But he needed more and she knew that, but every one of her kids was equal and would get equal treatment, but it bothered her that she couldn't give him more, and bothered her that she should feel that way. So she took it out on him. I'm sorry if it hasn't been easy for you. I'm sorry you don't feel part of the dinner table, that other kids pick on you, that I pick on you. But I can't help it and they can't help it and if you don't fight back, none of us will stop. That's the way it is. That's how people are. The more you take it, the more you get it. The more you fight back, the less you need to fight. God helps those who help themselves because they're more fun to help. Because they deserve it; because it's easier.

She didn't try harder because trying is hard, because life was tough as it was, because she didn't want to. She had a stake in Frank being Frank, just as Leo, Ann, Mary Jean, Lee, John, Jim, Trish, Sue, Michael, all the kids at school, all the kids in the neighbourhood, just as everyone did.

Everybody needs a whipping boy. Everyone needs to win some time.

He might have fought back, he might have emerged tougher and stronger from the whole experience. He might have come to understand his mother. She had to control her own show, she needed compliance to run a crowded house the way it had to be run. She seemed to encourage weakness, yet really she despised it and trampled it. The other kids understood, and fought back. He was the dutiful one. What she said, he did. He thought he was supposed to be nice, he thought that's what she wanted. "Everyone else had a quality about them which made her back off eventually," Michael recalls. "He just stood there and took it. And he never really did anything wrong. I mean, he'd put his elbows on the table. 'FrancisLeoBloye, get your elbows off the table! What's wrong with you? How many times do I have to tell you?!' "

There might have been a moment. When he got older perhaps, when there weren't so many at the table to take conversation where he didn't want it to go. Some trigger: OK, enough's enough. I've had it. You want fight, I'll give you fight. It nearly happened one night after dinner. "I was about twelve or thirteen," he recalls. "We were in the kitchen drying the dishes, and Jim did something. I got really mad. This had been building up. I mean, I'd been thinking about this a long time. 'I'm gonna get that guy, I'm gonna get him.' And now he does this. I just looked at him, 'Jesus, when I grow up,' I said, 'I'm gonna kill you.' I guess everybody stopped dead in their tracks. But not Jim. He thought it was the funniest thing he'd ever heard. Mom turned around and made me apologize."

Nothing did change. He had his moments of rebellion, but for each one a put-down quickly followed. He got too old for the wooden spoon, but he couldn't outlast "that look." Whenever she fixed it on him, as Michael recalls, "He'd melt." "I tried to stand up to her a couple of times," he says, looking back. "When I was a kid, she'd spank me.

As a teenager, she just stared me down. I'd leave the room so mad, 'I'm going to smash her bedroom window.' But you couldn't cross her. With Mom, you did what you were told."

It would have taken something extraordinary for things to have been different, and he was an ordinary kid. He needed desperately to fight back, to win, not all the time, just sometimes. Once. She loved him and cared for him. She never let him win.

With dinner over, the family dispersed. When the kids were younger, Margaret and some of the older ones did the dishes, Margaret washed; the others bathed the babies. In. Out. The water never changing. Exempt from kitchen work, Leo sat on the verandah in summer, in his favourite chair in the living room the rest of the year, reading the newspaper, "every line, every page." He was still in his white shirt and tie. Weekday or weekend, day or night, he was either at the office or on his way.

He had a Player's cigarette in his hand, several butts littered the ashtray on the coffee table next to him, wisps of smoke rising gently from it. When the kids were done their chores, the girls did their homework in the dining room, the boys went upstairs to their bedroom where each had his own desk. Until he was old enough, Frank stayed behind in the living room to watch TV. "We were one of the first on the street to get a set," he says, the pride of a seven-year-old frozen in time. He sat across from his dad, sideways in a big brown chair that matched the sofa, his legs dangling over one of its arms, the TV set, a big wood-veneer box on a swivel table, swivelled towards him. He watched as if absorbed into it, his face on the edge of every emotion. Margaret, finished in the kitchen and her apron still on, was in her favourite chair near Leo. The chair was nubby and worn, and like the rest of the furniture needed recovering but, first things first, it never was.

She read some of his paper, knitted or mended, and talked. TV noise bothered her, she insisted she could read lips, so the sound was turned low. Frank, who claimed no such skill, couldn't sit close enough. "Frank, you're too close." "I can't hear if I move back." Their phrases rebounded as one. Parents in the 1950s feared that TV, more than rotting their children's brains, would ruin their children's eyes. When he and his mother were done their nightly ritual, Sue, sitting next to her mom, moved to the floor next to him, close enough to hear.

Leo might doze for a few minutes, unnoticed behind his paper, but before eight o'clock he gathered up his suit coat and was on his way to the office. He would be back about eleven, after the kids were in bed and asleep. When he had gone, Margaret shut off the TV so the girls could concentrate, Frank went upstairs for his bath and she soon followed, bringing her knitting with her. There were devotions on Wednesday nights at the church for an hour after dinner. One night a week, "the knitting ladies" of the Catholic Church Extension met in a member's home to talk and knit. They served little cakes and cookies, tea and coffee from silver trays and services, knit mitts and scarves for the missions, turning their night into an evening out. There were CWL meetings as well.

It made for a busy life for Margaret, her duty to her church, her duty to her husband and each of her kids; there was only so much time. She was too much of a perfectionist to live with the kind of uncontrolled order Leo's mother accepted. Things should be a certain way, anything else offended her. Love was *doing*. It was her doing things for others, and them doing things for her. So no matter how old and tired she got, no matter how much she had to do, she had to keep on doing. And they had to keep on doing back, because that was love, and that's what family was. Love could take no rest.

None of the kids remembers sitting on her knee. They sat on their dad's knee sometimes, when he was around. They weren't a family that hugged or kissed or touched a lot. If the kids were crying, she might give them a hug.

Returning from a trip, Leo would shake their hands, the boys at least. Between Margaret and him, there were good-bye and hello kisses. No one remembers them cuddling or holding hands.

What the kids do remember are a few special, quirky, now golden moments: the Friday-night poker games with Uncle Gen and Uncle Jim, two of their dad's brothers-in-law, with Leo Hickey and especially Father Hickey, their very own parish priest, his suit coat off, his vest and collar off, down to his white T-shirt, a big stogie in his mouth, looking very unpriestly. From their bedrooms they could hear the laughing, the jokes, the whoops and hollers. "Dad would get so excited," Frank says. "That was a side of him I didn't know he had much of. I mean, he always had his hat on and walked perfectly straight. Being silly was beneath his vision of what a proper businessman should be."

They remember the office parties at the house just before Christmas, the time their dad was dancing with his young secretary and she was "all over him." Their mom, watching from the sidelines, missing nothing, talking to a woman who suddenly laughed, "Hey Marg, looks like she's stealing your husband." And still they can hear her voice, "Over my dead body," and the way she looked as she marched onto that dance floor and stopped their music.

The older ones remember the nights the Hickeys, Halls and Killingsworths, their mom's friends from nursing and their husbands, drove down from Toronto. The girls would sneak into their parents' bedroom and pick up the fur coats, try on the hats and smell every perfume smell. Mostly they remember sitting on the steps in their pyjamas, and through the posts of the bannister seeing their dad do the Charleston, crossing his knees and hands, a big grin on his face.

They remember the home movies of their parents' trip to Florida. It was 1959, Leo had just turned fifty-four, he had had his heart attack a few years earlier, his lungs were getting worse. Margaret was fifty-two. The camera pans the beach, the skyline of hotels and apartments. It follows some seagulls, highlights another middle-aged couple they had apparently met on the trip. And then there's their mom. In shorts! They had never seen her even in pants. The camera moves up her legs, slowly, and they know who's running the camera! She tries to hide behind a door, and she's laughing. She's out on the beach and they can read her lips, "Don't Leo. Stop that," and she's laughing. They see their dad, so relaxed, years younger than a few weeks before. She walks into the water, stands in the waves and plays with them, once she almost stumbles then sets herself right and laughs. Her hair feathers from her head in the breeze. She looks like a young girl.

They share one more memory, one that each thought was his or hers alone. It happened whenever they got sick, which was often, after the well ones had gone on to school and Leo was at work. Margaret would take the one left behind and put him or her into the bath, into clean pyjamas, then into her and Leo's bed. "It smelled wonderful," Trish says, the fresh clean sheets, the scent of her mother still in her nostrils. She would turn on the radio, later the TV, then leave and return with a pitcher of fresh-squeezed orange juice. The pitcher was silver and covered in frost, on a tray with silver handles, with a glass and lots of ice. She talked with them, made them comfortable, and when she was sure they were, she went out and came back with a colouring book and crayons, and when Leo came home at lunch he'd bring them ice cream in Dixie cups.

She was the good nurse, attentive, caring, but at these moments much more. It was as if there was no one else in her world. She didn't have to worry about sharing herself around, what it would look like, how the others would feel. It could be their little secret. Her chance to make them special in her life, to make them feel special themselves. Then she had time, to give them all the attention they needed, all she had wanted to give. She could make each of them her favourite. In the rest of her life, for the control she felt a big family needed, she needed to distance herself. No hugging, no touching, no special time, and if her temper was instinct, it was frustration too. Theirs was a good family, a family that worked, but it didn't have about it the feeling she had wanted so much to duplicate. Except when the kids were sick and everything slowed down. Then so calm and loving, she enjoyed those moments as much as they did.

Every night before they went to bed, they said the rosary. One year it had been the Catholic church's "year of the rosary," its slogan, "The family that prays together, stays together." She never forgot that. They sometimes said it in the kitchen. One of them, exempted from dishes for the night, would kneel at a chair and recite, Leo in the living room at his favourite chair, the others doing the dishes, answering back. Other times, she knelt at the top of the stairs, the kids at their beds. Whoever happened by at the time, joined in. If Leo had already returned to the office, he and Margaret said their own rosary in their bedroom when he got back.

The kids said their own private prayers in their bedrooms. Margaret would sit in the upstairs hall, knitting, listening to her radio, later in their bedroom in front of the upstairs TV. She knitted mitts or scarves, her eyes on the box in front of her, and when the action drew to its climax, her hands stopped. Just outside her door, he and Sue were watching. They had sneaked out of bed, crept down the hall and were peeking through the crack in the door. Margaret never closed the door so she could listen for the coughs and rustled sheets that if unattended would mean trouble the next day. They watched Red Skelton or Dick Van Dyke until the sheer daring of what they were doing made everything too funny, or until they hit that one board in the hallway they insisted their mother had loosened intentionally. "Go back to bed," she'd yell, her eyes still on the screen, as if she'd been expecting them. Giggling, they scampered back to bed.

There is another end-of-day image they all share. It is

from a time before their second TV has arrived, their mom is still using the open space in the upstairs hall between the stairs and her bedroom as her sewing room. The hallway is in darkness, a tall floor lamp from over her shoulder casts a yellow-gold aura around her. She is in her chair, in semi-profile to the scene, beside the window that leads to the balcony above the front verandah. Next to her on the floor is her sewing basket, and next to it, along a short wall and section of bannister, are two big round-top trunks filled with old clothes and pictures. An old black phone is perched on the bannister post, its long extension wire running down the stairs under the wooden stand in the front hall where the phone sits all day. A pile of dirty laundry is on the floor ready to be wrapped in a big sheet to be carried to the basement. Her sewing table and Singer sewing machine are beside the pile, and on top of the table is a radio.

She has her housedress on, the one with the ripped pocket. She is knitting or darning socks or the knees of the breeks the boys wore. On the radio is "The Lux Theater," and down the hallway, around the jog of the stairs, out of sight in their darkened rooms, the kids lie quiet and still. They are listening and she knows it. Here, now, she has the time to do what she needs to do, and the respite of peace and quiet that will get her through another day. It's her chance too to let the kids feel they have put one over on her, while she is putting another over on them.

There are no whispers in the rooms, no one is sure who's asleep and who isn't; everyone is trying to listen. It is his last memory of his childhood day. Lying in bed, "I remember the theme song coming on," he says, "I can never remember the story. I was asleep before it began."

The Perfect Day

"I'd be about fourteen, I think. It would be summer. I was never a winter person. I liked snow, and making forts and snowmen, but I didn't care for skating much. So it would be hot. But first of all, I'd sleep in, until ten or eleven at least. Mom would never have let me sleep in. I'd fix my own breakfast, toast and jam, maybe a poached egg, and go sit on the verandah. I'd take a coffee with me. I loved the verandah. You could see the street and everything that was going on in the neighbourhood. I'd sit out there with my coffee and think to myself, what should I do today? I could go and see what Peter Millar was up to, or ride down to the beach, or up to the canning factories, or down by the railroad tracks. But if I went to see Peter, we'd probably end up doing what he wanted to do. So maybe I'd just wander around by myself, with Mom not worrying about me, and me not worrying about checking in or what she'd do to me if I was late.

"A perfect day is me not getting into trouble," he laughs, "that's what a perfect day was." He returns to his story. "I didn't have to be with people. I didn't have to have special things to do. I could live quite happily in my own imagination.

"I'd probably go down to the lake on my bike. There was an industrial area, I didn't go there often, it was quite a bit farther, but I'd go down there and see what ships were in. Maybe later I'd go for a swim. I'd make a sandwich, ham and cheese, Kraft sliced cheese, bring an apple, and some of Mom's homemade cookies, oatmeal or chocolate chip. I'd wash out one of Dad's beer bottles and pour some orange juice in it, and get one of Dad's old beer caps, straighten it out and snap it on. Or maybe I'd stop at the corner store to get some pop, a Coke, then go down to the beach.

"Or maybe I'd head the other way. Go north up the concession roads. There was an old wooden railroad bridge, I could go up there and watch the trains. I was fascinated with trains. There was a creek there, near Whiteface Mountain, maybe I'd go wading in it. You didn't have to worry about your bike getting stolen, so I'd drop it by the creek.

I'd look for fish and frogs, I wouldn't catch them; I'd see if there were any treasures around, you never know what you might find. The creek was never deep enough for swimming, and often was full of broken glass, so I'd have to go in in my shoes. I'd roll up my pants, then go for a wander up and down the creek, lose track of time and — Oh my gosh, I gotta get back!!" He laughs.

"I'd go back to my bike, sit down and eat my lunch. Then, probably head home and go up to my room and work on my models or stamp collection, or lie down and read a book.

"For dinner, it would just be me and Mom. Maybe Dad, to be fair, because I always complained he wasn't around. I'd have a steak. A cube steak medium rare. Mom would fry it in the frying pan then pour water in the pan to make gravy. I like french fries but not the way she did them, so I'd have home-fries, and no vegetables. I'd have a salad or celery sticks or carrot sticks, maybe I'd have beets. And for dessert, stewed rhubarb right from the garden. I loved stewed rhubarb.

"And to end the perfect day, I'd get them to go for a car ride. Just the three of us. We'd go out in the country, I don't know where. Not to relatives. We'd visit a model home, one of the furnished ones. One of those very expensive, rich homes. And then we'd come home and that would be it."

5

"The church used to be just down the street from us. It was one of those old-fashioned, dark, high-ceilinged churches with a big fancy altar at the front and statues on the side. It was always jammed with little kids like me sitting behind all these people who were a mile high, and you couldn't see a darned thing. We'd be fidgeting and told to sit still and be quiet; the kneeling benches didn't have pads and the pews were hard and uncomfortable. It was just the way it was on Sundays."

He doesn't go to church much now. Carolyn is a Protestant and hasn't attended her own church in years, Matt and Janine have lost interest and he's tired of pushing them, it's just one more thing to fight about that none of them needs. Only Stephanie shows interest sometimes and when she does, he goes with her. Otherwise on Sunday mornings he just putters around his quiet, night-darkened house and garden. But if it seems his mother would roll over in her grave if she knew, maybe she wouldn't. He questions more than before, believes the church is wrong about many things, abortion and birth control included. He may believe in his own free will to decide most things himself, still, with the church as his counsel, he is as embued with religion now as he was as an altar boy thirty years ago.

He sees life, and *his* life, the way his church has taught him; the rest are details. He has learned that while *hope* gets him into trouble, *faith* never does. Hope has to do with him. Something he must generate himself, something only he can realize and fulfil. It comes from reason, thought and the scientific mind, from a rational, controllable universe capable of being understood, where every question has an answer, where for every desire there is a way. And it's up to him to find them. Never satisfied, hope requires always more hope. And more of him.

Faith doesn't. Faith happens to him. It is everything that isn't him and can't be him. It has to do with all the things he doesn't understand and can't control and never will; with questions which have no answers or none he will ever find. Things happen; no need to look too hard, to wonder, examine or doubt, there *is* a reason. That's all the answer he needs. He never has to search tomorrow's horizons where hope wails its siren song, horizons take care of themselves. And while those without faith see a universe anxious to punish them for what they don't know and cannot control, his universe is different. One of pain and tribulation, a constant test, but one ultimately, fundamentally good. Where everything will work out, where somehow, someplace, sometime, the hard-working and just will be rewarded. With faith he has put himself into hands that know and control and will watch out for him; into hands he trusts.

Faith makes his every today fine.

He learned early about right and wrong. Before First Confession at six, he learned about mortal sin, killing and stealing. About obedience and little white lies and not taking pennies from the collection box. He learned that his mom and dad had been given a job by God to raise him, and he had to do as they said. If he disobeyed, that was a sin. Fighting with his brothers and sisters, that was a sin. Stealing his friend's marbles or baseball cards, convincing him a card he had given him was rare when he knew it wasn't, that was a sin.

Confession loomed every second Saturday. "It was such a dark place," he remembers. "The priest wasn't supposed to see who you were. There was a compartment with a scary little hole in the side. You'd hear this screen door open, you didn't see anything, and this voice, 'Start your confession.' " Like the voice of God Himself. "I was sure he knew if I was lying or not."

Father Hickey was looking for sins. Confessing none, he knew, would focus God's gaze far more unblinkingly on him than spilling out a fortnight's rampage of wrongdoing. Guilt was presumed, so he always confessed. If no sins came to mind, he confessed old ones, and Father Hickey was satisfied and he felt cleansed, and their ritual was over for two more weeks. But if he had done something truly wrong, it wasn't so easy.

It was Easter Sunday before mass, Easter eggs were everywhere. He was ten. "I knew Mom expected me to go to communion and, before communion, you had to fast for an hour. Well, I picked up this candy . . . I was just playing with it. I opened my mouth and put it in, then took it out, then put it back in. I didn't bite down on it — Maybe I licked it a little. Anyway I was just standing there, and Mom was heading off somewhere and bumped into me — and I came down on it."

It was as if the world had stopped. All breathing, all sound, all movement; everyone disappeared. Suddenly his head filled with an incredible screaming match of explanation, accusation and panic.

He was young to face such a test of character. It was Easter Sunday, Margaret Bloye was his mother: was it better to lie to God and take communion, or tell the truth to his mother?

He quickly put down the candy, rinsed out his mouth; and took communion.

For a week he suffered; for a week he went over his story. It began to seem like an accident. An unlikely trail of events, with no intent, yes, it was truly an act of God. It was his mother's fault. On Saturday, he went to confession. Father Austin was their new priest. He pulled back the tiny screen door. "Start your confession."

"I burst into tears, then told him the story. He didn't say anything at first, then in that soft, slow voice, he said,

'Wellll . . . I'm sure you didn't mean to. You didn't actually take a bite and eat it. You just put a little in your mouth then rinsed it out. *God knows,*' he said finally, 'you were only fooling around.' "

His mother's justice would have been harsher.

Saying the rosary was a family ritual, saying his own prayers mattered to him more. He could do that at his own pace, by himself, and between him and his God he could say what he wanted. He would kneel beside his bed, his hands folded, and close his eyes tight so as not to be distracted. "God bless Mom and God bless Dad," he began, "God bless Ann and Mary Jean" and he went through the whole family. Then he said, "God bless me, and may my Guardian Angel watch over me."

After that, he would change around the order of his prayers. An "Our Father," sometimes a few "Hail Marys" for something that had happened at school, or a famine his teacher had told them about. The "Act of Contrition," and when he was really in need, the "Apostles' Creed." He didn't say his prayers out loud, but listened to his words inside his head. Prayers were a comfort to him. There was something quite unfinished about a day if he went to bed without saying them. One time at camp he was too embarrassed to kneel at his cot so he crawled into his sleeping bag and said them there. He found no shame in that. He didn't think he had insulted God, though he had always been taught not to hide his faith. But he knew boys could be boys, and he felt no comfort in ridicule.

He would take the rosary to bed with him, running through its prayers instead of counting sheep. His mother had told him that if he fell asleep and hadn't finished, his Guardian Angel would finish it for him. And each night he went to bed, it was with "the utmost confidence" his Guardian Angel would do its job.

He was nine years old. It was the scariest moment of his life. "We had an old mountain maple at the side of our house. I built a little platform in it, and wedged it between some branches. It was two storeys high. And one day I fell. It was a long fall. In my mind it was free-fall, but I must've slid down the trunk. Because about four feet from the ground, there was a branch that had been cut off, and it caught my shorts and stopped me." To the child, it *had been* free-fall, there was nothing between him and the cold, hard ground, except suddenly, somehow, there was, and his life was saved. Every night he had asked his Guardian Angel to watch over him, and now when he needed him, he had been there. For the rest of his life he would have a memory of faith rewarded and destiny explained.

"It was my Guardian Angel that caught me," he says today with a nod. He goes on without pause. "He certainly didn't catch me when I fell over the bannister though, because I went flat on my back." With faith, he knows, everything may be OK but it's not always great. "Probably because I was too heavy at the time."

He has thought a lot about religion, and when he talks of it it's in complete sentences, with a flow of certainty, as if this time he's not waiting to be interrupted and corrected, as if he knows he's right or that no one can prove him wrong. He talks about nothing else quite the same way. He is comfortable. His mother may have influenced him too profoundly in some ways, but in religion he was her beneficiary. The God he learned of was gentle and comforting, wrathful and stern, yet always forgiving, and there were few so attuned to His ways as Margaret Bloye. In her household, she was nearly as all-seeing and all-powerful as He was, and if he could please her, he could please Him.

Everyone needs to be good at something, everyone needs something that gives him pleasure and pride, brings status and reward. Other boys were good at baseball, building models or fixing things. He was good at religion.

He was especially good at being an altar boy, though the story doesn't begin well. The new church in Whitby was about to open, it was midnight mass on Christmas Eve. He was ten. John and Jim were still altar boys, and "did all the important things"; he was one of six torch bearers. "We had to carry this great big thing with a long handle and a big red globe on top with a candle in it, and walk in a procession." When the procession was done, the six of them came forward with their torches and knelt in front of the altar.

"Father Austin had told us to hold onto these things so they were nice and straight and didn't sway back and forth. Well, we finished this part of the mass . . . and I guess it was mostly from tiredness —" While kneeling at the altar, he discovered if he set his torch on the floor and let go of it, it would balance by itself. This he found fascinating. His fascination went on for some time, his eyes on the torch, the torch solid and unmoving. In fact, the torch never did move. He did. "I fainted or fell asleep," he says, "I don't know which. Then someone carried me off the altar, I think it was John. They had to bring in one of the other guys to finish the ceremony."

Things didn't go much better for some time. "There was one Latin phrase I could never memorize. I'd always just mumble through it. After one mass, Father Austin called me back to the altar. People were still there [in the pews]. He said, 'I didn't hear that response. Say it to me loud and clear.' I couldn't bring myself to tell him I didn't know it, so I mumbled it again. 'I can't hear you,' he said. Finally, I said to him, 'Father, I don't know it.' 'I didn't think so,' he said. 'But before you go on the altar again, you *will* have it down pat, won't you?' "

Then his story turns. Mr. Mills arrived at St. John's school. Frank was twelve, in grade 7, and Mr. Mills was the first man teacher he had ever had. Father Hickey or Father Austin had trained the altar boys until then, but mostly they had left it to the new boys to learn by watching the older ones. Not Mr. Mills. They practised every Monday night at the church. "He drilled us in the proper way of walking. We'd be slouching around and he'd yell, 'No, no, you can't do that. Straight and tight, elbows in, hands folded, pointing towards the sky. Now, slowly, *with* the priest, solemnly, ceremoniously.' "

"I'd never seen things done like that before. We knew exactly where to go, we didn't have to read the cards, our responses were clear and precise. We were a proud group. A lot of us won a special sash, the Archbishop awarded it to us. There was a big ceremony. We used to wear it at every mass." He has no scrapbooks or trophies from that time, but in the bottom drawer of his dresser, he still has that sash.

There were about twenty altar boys in all, but only five on his special "team." Two were needed for weekday morning masses at eight, so they rotated. On Sundays, regular masses were nine and noon, high mass at ten-thirty. They did high mass and all the funerals.

Before each service they helped the priest with his vestments. They had to make sure the robes came out of the cupboard in the right order and were laid on the counter as Father Austin needed them. A long white over-vest, the alb, had to be put face down and rolled up in back, then came the rope to cinch the alb, a stole which Father Austin kissed as he put it around his neck, finally a long robe which also had to be rolled up so Father could slide his hands easily into it.

They prepared the water and wine. The holy water was in a special reservoir and he pumped it into a carafe. The wine was locked in a cabinet. He got the key from Father Austin and poured it into a matching carafe, then made sure he locked the cabinet and returned the key to Father when he was done.

High mass lasted a full hour. The priest used incense to bless the altar, then just before the consecration of the host as the body of Christ, it was his job "to go down and bow to the people and incense them all, that was great, then bow again."

For funerals, they were the ones let out of school. Two acolytes, a cross-bearer, and the "Master," his friend Pat

Watters, who assisted the priest; as "Theuifer," he assisted him. Hidden by the altar, he put incense into a dish and made sure at least one small coal was burning in the incense-burner. Then at just the right moment he brought the burner and dish to Father Austin, who sprinkled the incense on the coals, smoke and fumes filling the air. When the funeral was done, they cleaned up and put things away, then "dilly-dallied getting back to school," arriving in time for lunch. He liked doing funerals. "It put us one notch above the other altar boys."

In high school, he had to bus to Ajax and could no longer do morning masses. His time as an altar boy came to an end. "I enjoyed being on the altar," he says. "We were an important part of the mass. Our parents were proud. There was real responsibility, adult responsibility, we had to be mature, and that made us feel good."

"John and Jim were altar boys before me," he also says. "But they never got the sash."

Sometime in his boyhood years he began to sort out the place of God in his life. It was only years later he had the words to express what he believed, but his outlooks and attitudes were evident even then. He believes in God; he needs God. He had learned not to trust his own hands. He has seen all his life how frail they can be. He needs a partner in his life's successes and failures if only as an explanation for both, to keep him from trying to explain what he can't; and so to get on with his life.

But he is no puppet of God. God has set for him no predestined course. He has given him free will, the power to set for himself his own path and He will not interfere unless he asks His guidance. And if he does ask that guidance, he knows he has only to stop and feel what he is feeling, and he will know.

"If I think things out and make the wrong decision, if I'm unhappy, there's a message there. God's trying to tell me something. If my employers aren't satisfied, if I'm not doing my job and my life is miserable, I've made the wrong choice. God's giving me a sign, and maybe I should try something else. It's only faith, and that's the difficult part. Faith is unexplainable. It's something you have or you don't. And if you have it, it answers all your questions. To a non-believer, that seems a cop-out, you can't answer the question so you say God did it and that's the only answer. God won't make me go the right way, but He *will* show me there's a choice. Then He'll leave it up to me to make the choice, and if I make the wrong one, He'll make my life miserable. So I try again."

He doesn't resent those to whom God has given the long straws. It's a matter of free will, he says. They did more with theirs, that's all. He is more impatient with the chronically unhappy, who see only what they haven't got. " 'I never get anything,' they complain, but they never *do* anything. They never go to school, never take courses to achieve their goals, they just complain. They're the selfish ones. They're the ones who don't believe in God. And they're the ones who push into line and cut me off on 401. I deal with people like that on the phone all the time. They've got no inner peace."

The symptoms of a faithless life he sees all around him. If you don't believe in God and in eternal life, in hell for those who sin and heaven for those who don't, no one has anything to lose. "I'm going to do what I want to do and take what I want and push to the front of every line and fulfil every hope and wish and dream and what's going to stop me? Who's going to punish me?"

In his life, God has always provided. Everything he needed, everything he was taught was important, he had. Food in his belly, a roof over his head, a shirt on his back. He had a mother and father, and a mother and father and family who loved him, and not everyone did. He had a God who loved him. Kids were starving in China; he was lucky, no doubt about it. If he didn't have something he didn't know anyone was supposed to have it, and didn't miss it.

Once when Ann's husband, Roy, was on strike at GM, Margaret sat her daughter down for a talk. "She told me she and Dad didn't have health coverage when she was having all her babies. 'But you know,' she said, 'I never worried about money because every time another baby was on the way, Dad got a promotion.' Everything just sort of looked after itself. I remember her saying that." When Leo suddenly got sick and every year they had to go south on vacation, there was money to do it. When the girls were old enough to get married, Dunlop Tire had moved to Whitby, other businesses were following, new housing was needed and they had their big back garden to sell. Everything worked out somehow.

"I remember somebody falling off a bunk bed, bleeding all over," Trish says. "Mom was holding a cloth to the cut and she couldn't get a hold of Dad. She said, 'Let's start saying the rosary. If we do, Dad will call.' So we're all kneeling at the chesterfield in front of the window on Palace Street saying the rosary, and Dad drives into the driveway. It wasn't five minutes later! I thought to myself, *she prays to God and he drives into the driveway*. I tell you, my belief in God was sealed that day."

Only at Christmas did they have more than they needed, because Christmas was special. Margaret started her baking weeks ahead; Mrs. Hendriks came in to wax the floors and leave behind her forever smell of the season. The weekend before, the tree went up. Everyone helped in the decorating, Leo and the boys always put up the lights, and at the top went a big red ball with long translucent spikes, and a light inside. This was the late 1950s, so this was "the Sputnik." It broke and was fixed many times until it was finally glued permanently together, which was fine until the light burned out. Then, like its namesake, it fell into disuse. More than thirty years later, Sue still has it.

On Christmas Eve, presents began appearing. One wrapped gift from each brother and sister, one wrapped gift from his mom and dad, the presents piling so high "you couldn't see the first layer of branches." Each kid had a special place in the living room as well. His was his mother's chair, Sue's the chair by the TV, John, Jim and Trish shared the sofa, and on Christmas morning at each special place, beside their stockings full of fruits and candy canes, were lots of *unwrapped* gifts. These were from Santa.

"We weren't allowed downstairs until Dad checked to make sure Santa had been there," he recalls. Leo and Margaret would still be in their bedroom. "He'd hear us up, and yell, 'Oh, go back to sleep. It's too early. I just got to bed.'" And they would coax, and he would tease, he'd go to the bathroom and blow his nose, one of his slippers would go missing, then he'd shuffle down the hall mumbling and grumbling, and finally down the steps with the speed of the dead. Following him with their eyes, they closed in around the upstairs bannister and watched him turn into the living room; then he was gone from sight. They waited. And waited. Then the lights sprang on. "That was the signal," and they all came racing down.

They went straight for the unwrapped gifts. Soon Margaret would slip into the kitchen and begin her work, and for the next hour or so move back and forth from kitchen to living room as the rest of the gifts were opened. She had the turkey in the oven from the night before, and while fixing and serving breakfast, she'd be fixing other things for their Christmas dinner.

After mass, as the kids played with their toys, the neighbours would drop in, the Morrisons, Foys and McKays, Father Hickey and his housekeeper, Rose Coffey. Margaret had tea ready, she passed out her Christmas cookies and cake, and just glowed, her kids recall, just as she did every social occasion.

Margaret's sister, Eileen, and husband, Mel, their kids Michael and Mary Liz, arrived later in the afternoon, sometimes one of Leo's sisters and her husband, and more presents were opened. The toy train that wasn't used much the rest of the year was always put together for Christmas. He and Michael would disappear downstairs to play with it or with Aunt Margaret's old things that had been stored in a big dusty trunk.

Leo carved the Christmas turkey, the plates were passed down the line to Margaret who dished up the vegetables, and back again, the big people cutting up the meat for the little ones beside them. After dinner, the dryers took assembly-line positions and the Christmas dishes, piled hopelessly high, soon disappeared. Later, they watched a Christmas special or listened to Christmas records, until the kids fell asleep and the adults began gathering their things for home. Yet for all of them, Christmas had really ended an hour or two earlier, when after the last bite of dinner, Leo had cleared his throat, and as he did each year, announced, "Only 365 more days until Christmas."

When Margaret was in the hospital to have each baby, those already born were sent to various relatives. By the time the youngest, Sue, was born, with five already in school, the kids stayed and Ann, the oldest, took two weeks off from school to care for them. When Margaret had her hysterectomy, Ann was in nursing, Mary Jean in her last year of high school, so it was Lee who took care of her. Lee was at home for a year. When Leo had his heart attack and he and Margaret went south, Ann took a month's leave of absence from nursing. The next year, it was Mary Jean's turn, even if later that summer she would need to take time off without pay for her honeymoon. If the family had a need, its need came first.

To Leo and Margaret, family and faith were central. It was a belief in and love of both they wanted most to pass on to their kids. Beyond that, "they never pushed," he says, as they all say. They wanted for their kids only to get through grade 13, to have enough education to take care of themselves.

To them and to their parents, university had seemed only for the monied and academic élite. With grade 13, they could teach or nurse or be businessmen, except for medicine or law, they could do almost anything that rewarded hard work. Grade 13 was the ticket to a life where a man could provide and a woman could stay home, where all that was really important was possible, where family and faith wouldn't be threatened and need not be compromised.

Indeed, anything more was *personal* ambition. For his or her *own* benefit, a personal indulgence. It meant tuition, books, room and board, a cost on all of them, Leo and Margaret included, and that wasn't right. Everyone was loved and cared for equally, everyone would be treated alike. Personal ambition was fine, but the expense was your own. That was only fair.

Only one of them had a special gift, and that was Trish. She was different, something different was expected of her. When she brought home a 92 in history, Leo joked about the eight marks she didn't get; Margaret didn't. But why should Trish have been surprised? What did a 92 in history matter except you could do it, and could do it again and maybe better the next time, but only if you didn't get a big head. Life isn't a 92 on a history test. It's 92 on every test, doing things *right*, now and forever. Grade 13, marriage, family, home, working hard, being a good person, they are what matter, and they are every day and always ahead. Why should I be pleased, why should you? Just keep on going and doing and when my job is done and your job is done, when some day we meet in eternity, then we'll both know how we did, and then it will matter. Until then, you can do better.

So if education mattered, character mattered more. What saw a child through to the right kind of future wasn't education or job, even love. It was character, the gift that kept on giving, that came from raising kids right. Character was her obligation to her children and to her children's children, and theirs to theirs and so on and so on. In the great chain letter of humankind, she would not be the weak link. The rest, the future, what jobs her children did was out of her hands unless the lessons of childhood had been made so indelible that the memory of them would continue to zap them, like Pavlov's dogs, into the straight and narrow and never go away.

Younger parents, baby-boomer parents whose *first* kids came after World War II, parents who believed in science and learning and progress, in hope more than faith, whose kids he and his brothers and sisters would one day compete against for jobs and promotions, they pushed. To them, grade 13, hard work and God's will were not enough.

6

After World War II, new schools, new parks and roads were built, it was a time when public services seemed a benefit to all, and taxpayers were willing to pay for them. Schools were bigger, brighter, with gyms and auditoriums, libraries and science labs, with more, bigger windows, fluorescent lighting, acoustic-tile ceilings and sound-absorbing floors, with moveable desks and pastel-coloured walls in learning-enhancing configurations and tones. These were community centres, and this was extravagance in the service of the future. What each building said to its own community was that living here and now was a privilege, that going to school and learning mattered. But this was a time too when the gap between public schools and the more poorly funded Catholic ones grew. In a few years, new Catholic schools would also be built, teacher salaries and the quality of instruction would improve, but not so soon and not in time for him.

He remembers little about grades 1 and 2. In the early fall of grade 3, he was still in St. Bernard's school, but over-crowding meant two grade 3 classes were sharing one room and when St. John's school opened, he was moved. Miss Norris, a friend of Mary Jean's, was his teacher. "It was in grade 3," he recalls, "I began to feel inadequate."

He'd had trouble reading right from the start, but so had lots of kids. People learn at different times in different ways, sometimes the pieces take longer to fit. By grade 2, he was further behind, but only a year into school, how far behind could he be? The words in the reader still seemed recognizable and within his grasp, at any moment, the light would go on, he'd leap ahead and all his troubles would be past. But in grade 3, he fell still further back. Like a runner in a race, stay close and those ahead pull you on with them, they fill you with energy, hope and strength, and make you go faster and longer than you ever thought you could go. Fall back and contact is broken, the forces that drive you are cut, energy and hope disappear, you grow weaker, fall back further, and you're out of the race. In grade 3, he lost contact.

A lot of things were happening at just this time. He was chubby now, and his classmates were beginning to notice. They were interested in sports and, soft and slow, he wasn't. He also wasn't seeing well. Maybe that was why he wasn't good at sports, why there seemed so many things going on he didn't quite "get" when the other kids did. But that's not how it seemed to him. He didn't know he wasn't seeing well. He was seeing what everyone else saw, he thought. He was just slow.

It turned out he had more than myopia, but it would take thirty more years for him to find out. It happened by accident. His daughter Janine was having trouble reading and her grade 2 teacher decided she should have some tests. He went with her. "They put these earphones on her. She got a series of instructions and in the background were faint noises. They asked her to repeat the instructions, and she couldn't. She hadn't taken any of them in. Then they gave her more instructions, this time without the noises. She could repeat only the last instruction they gave." He was astonished. "That's exactly the way it had been with me."

Janine has dyslexia. Recent studies, more recent than her tests, indicate it can be more than a reading disorder. It has to do with the circuits of the body's visual system and their failure to keep proper timing. The system has two pathways, one for fast processes like motion, depth perception and three-dimensional vision, the other for slow processes like colour, stationary images, detail, etc. Dyslexics respond much better to the latter. It can be the same with sound. Many can pick up longer tones, the "ah" in "ba" and "da," but can't distinguish shorter ones, like "b" and "d," so "ba" and "da" will sound the same.

They may also have difficulty with their sense of touch, and appear clumsy. If they put a hand under a table and one of their fingers is touched, they can feel the contact and identify the finger. Touch two fingers in rapid succession, they feel only a single touch. Again, whether for sight, sound or touch, when everything is slowed down, dyslexics may respond the same as anyone else. Speed things up, and they are lost. Like him and Janine, they must make sense of the world without being aware of great amounts of fast-moving information. They must rely instead on the context of things, on facial expressions, repetition, etc., to know what's going on.

He remembers vividly the times with his mom in the kitchen trying to read the most basic passages from his school books, and not being able to do it. He can still hear his mother's frustration, "That's a 'p' not a 'b.' A 'p,' the tail goes down, not up. See!" And no matter how many times he felt the wooden spoon, the tail still went up.

Lots of kids overcome dyslexia and become stronger for it. Virginia Woolf, General George Patton, Nelson Rockefeller, Tom Cruise, Olympic diver Greg Louganis, Thomas Edison, Cher, Rodin, Albert Einstein, all were or are dyslexic. They fought back and succeeded. But most don't.

In his world, there were too many sounds, too many things moving too fast, too much he couldn't take in. But no one knew. He didn't know. He looked normal. When he had a problem with his eyes, he got glasses and could see as well as anyone. Why can't he read now? Why does he stumble and drop every pass that's thrown his way? He's lazy, that's his problem. He doesn't concentrate, doesn't try, looks for every easy way out, and with seven other kids in the family, with thirty-seven others in a dark, over-crowded classroom, what's a teacher, what's a mother to do? Help him out, make the extra effort, give him that last bit of energy you're not sure you have? Why? And why to him? Why should *you* give what he doesn't? God helps those who help themselves.

Lee remembers him in grade 4. His teacher was sick, Lee had just finished teachers' college and was called in to substitute. "I remember this adorable little guy with big eyes who could wrap any teacher around his finger. But he just sat there. I said to Mom, 'That kid doesn't do a thing in school all day long. He just sits there day-dreaming.'"

The school stories he tells involve a litany of cruel misunderstandings. "I was in grade 3," he recalls. "I needed a new pencil and the principal, Sister Enid, ran the tuck shop. She also taught grade 8, and Jim was in her class. My teacher gave me permission to see her.

"I knocked on her door. I was scared. I'd heard stories about her from Jim, how mean she was. She wasn't very happy to see me. I told her what I wanted, in front of the whole class, and she could see the state I was in. 'I've had enough of people like you coming in here, interrupting my class,' she yelled. 'You should have your pencil with you. If you lose it, see me at lunch time. Not before.' She got madder as she spoke. She said how she'd heard bad things about me, and was planning to call me into her office anyway, and that once and for all she should teach me a lesson. 'I might as well give you the strap before I sell you the pencil,' she said. So she grabbed my arm and reached for her strap. I burst into tears. She threw her arms around me and gave me a big hug. 'I wasn't going to strap you,' she laughed. 'I was only going to hit my leg.'" Across the room, Jim was roaring.

A year later, his teacher was handing out holy cards for Easter. "I tapped my friend on the shoulder and said, 'Let's play cards.' You know, toss them, see who can come closest to the wall. I was only joking. I went as if to throw one, then stopped, but the card slipped out of my hand onto the floor. So this other guy yells, 'Hey teacher, Frankie threw his card on the floor.' She turned and glared at me, 'That's terrible,' she said. 'That's a holy card. Get down on your knees and kiss the floor.' "

He told her he didn't mean to drop it, but she wouldn't believe him. He stood beside his desk, he couldn't move. She dismissed class and still he stood there. And stood there. He realized the only way he was going to get out of that room was to do what she said. So he kissed the floor.

He could never pick up the little clues. Always he was missing something. Because he couldn't take in things others could, his world always surprised him, turned on him when he didn't expect it. He could never feel certain, never be confident of his own place in it. Always he had to be passive, wait for things to happen to him and hope against hope if he made himself invisible, it would leave him alone. He couldn't try to direct it, or take control himself. It moved to a different, shifting rhythm. He couldn't see through its jokes, pick up its subtleties. He'd take in something as serious which everyone else thought was funny, which only made it funnier for everyone but him. When he heard others talk loud, he talked loud, except he was louder. He'd interrupt, interject, bring up something new just as everyone else was getting to the heart of something old. He was just enough out of synch to make others think the problem was him, not enough to make them think it was beyond him and not his fault. So everyone picked on him — parents, brothers, sisters, friends, classmates — not out of any extraordinary meanness, out of the routine meanness of human nature.

It was God shooting him down again.

That's why home was so nice. His room, his model cars and stamps, his time alone. There he could set everything to his own pace, do it all in his own time, do things over and over. There were no surprises. There were continuities and consistencies; there was his mother. With her he knew exactly what to do and when, what was wrong and right and expected. And she was always there.

But he also needed to find some way to deal in this

other, exterior world. His way might have been to pick on others as they picked on him, to become the toughest, meanest kid on the block. To see all his problems as *their* fault, not his, not God's. If the world was to make him its victim, angry, hostile, with nothing to lose, he'd fight back, take control, get even. In prisons, four in every five have learning disabilities. That could have been his way too.

But he was too nice. Too fat, too stupid, any problem was his fault, and what wasn't was the way things were. In Whitby in the 1950s, you were either smart enough to go on, or you weren't and didn't. No big deal. No heroic measures were called for, no great interventions by parents or teachers; there was a place in God's world for everyone. No point frustrating yourself or your parents, trying to be what you aren't and cannot be. One kid in two who kills himself has learning disabilities. That could have been him, but that wasn't his way.

On his grade 5 report card, his teacher, Mrs. Davies, wrote: "Got through by the skin of your teeth." The same might have been said almost any year by almost any of his teachers, except the two years in high school he didn't get through at all. One was grade 10, the other grade 11, both after big changes in his life. He had spent his first year of high school at a Catholic school in Ajax. The next September, he was on his way home from the first day of school. When the bus driver reached the Whitby town limits, he announced he'd go no farther. He would no longer pick up and drop off at the public high school. When the matter couldn't be resolved, Frank and the other local kids transferred to Henry Street High School in Whitby.

He was going back home, to where he had wanted to be all along, but it was too late. He couldn't take "shop" because he hadn't taken it in Ajax, he was one year out of touch. New friendships had been made, new roles were set, new routines were comfortably in place without him. Teachers, classrooms, books, all the surroundings had become familiar to everyone but him. Without the summer to get himself ready, it had all been too sudden.

Instantly he was behind. His body showed up each day to class and sat where it always sat; at home, his eyes still scanned the pages of his books, but no one was there. Within a few weeks, there was nothing left for him to do but put in time. He needed the year to pass and end, a summer to prepare, a new year to begin. But this time on the same day, at the same starting place, even.

He failed the year, passed the next year, then in the fall of 1965, he began grade 11. Life was pretty good. He was settled and comfortable at school. He was skinny. Now he could slide more easily into the background, be ignored, and be allowed to stay there. He had become more "mature." He could do more things, with most of his brothers and sisters gone he was needed around the house. He felt more important.

The boys were in college at Ryerson and living in Toronto, the three older girls were married, already Ann and Mary Jean had four kids of their own, Lee had one. Trish was in Toronto, in residence at St. Michael's Hospital. Only he and Sue were left. His dad was sixty, his mom fifty-nine, their long hours and vigilant ways had left them worn out. Margaret was still the cop on the beat of his life, but even she didn't press fights very much now. He knew the rules, he accepted and lived by them as if they were his own, there was less to fight about. With four girls graduated, three married and in their own homes with kids, John and Jim without their grade 13 but in college, with him and Sue coming along, for Margaret and Leo, their jobs were almost done.

This was a good time for him, the happiest in his life he thinks now. Many see their high-school years the same. As teenagers, they've seen and done and read many things, they are old enough to know more of what the world has to offer and are not yet old enough to know its terms and conditions. One day, they still might be handsome or ravishingly beautiful, a movie star, big-league slugger, president or prime minister. They might make a million dollars, drive a big car or two, live in a big house with a big pool, live lives much different and better than their parents'. But for him, it was something else. For the first time in his life, he wasn't so dependent on others; for the last time, they weren't so dependent on him.

He had had his first taste of independence when he got his first bike, a year after his friends got theirs. For boys, a bike meant the chance for a paper route and licence to be in parts of town that had always been off-limits. John and Jim had had routes, together and separately; he got his first when he was twelve, seventy-eight papers, Toronto's *Globe and Mail*. Later, he would have two other routes. Never good at collecting, on two of the routes he went "bankrupt."

To him and the rest of the family, this was another predictable chapter in the predictable story of his life. John and Jim had earned lots of money on their routes, never had problems, never did anything wrong: that was *their* story. He goes bankrupt: that was his. Typical Frank. A few years before, Jim had had his route taken away too, but the rest of the family wasn't told. Jim had to be Jim; Frank had to be Frank.

Jim would land on his feet at Dominion Stores, where John had been working since giving up his route a few years before. There were five or six hundred kids in the high school, part-time jobs were hard to come by and more important as each year passed. For even in Whitby, by the mid-1950s, the teenager had become an important consumer being. If cars had become more plentiful in postwar years, old ones would be too, and to have your own jalopy and keep it filled and on the road, you needed a job. The Bloye family had one important edge. With ten mouths to feed, it meant a lot of groceries. Dominion Stores owed them one, then two, then three.

So Jim followed John, and he followed Jim. If his paper

route represented the old Frank, his job at Dominion was the new, improved, mature Frank. Indeed, when he talks of his childhood, he does so with pleasure, confidence and pride about just three things, being an altar boy, being manager of the Don Mills high-school football team, and his job at Dominion.

He started when he was fifteen, lying about his age to get the job. He earned fifty cents an hour, worked Thursdays and Fridays after school from 5:00 to 9:30, Saturdays from 7:00 a.m. to 6:00 p.m., twenty hours in all, ten dollars a week. A lot more than he had earned delivering papers even those weeks he had managed to collect. John and Jim were stock boys, Jim in frozen foods, John in baking goods. He was a packer. "In those days, the store took time to teach you how to pack bags properly," he says. The head cashier's name was Florence. "Call me Flossie," she said, so he did. She showed him the proper technique, and he became "quite good at it," he says. "I even had cashiers and customers ask me to pack for them. They knew I wouldn't damage anything."

Speed was very important. There was just one packer per stall, per cashier. "She'd wing the groceries at you and you had to move fast. The big thing to remember was, 'heavy on the bottom,' so cans went in first. You wanted bags to have a tight square bottom so they'd stand by themselves, so I packed them so solid I could throw them on the wagon and they'd never flop over. After the cans came boxes or celery stalks, then the soft stuff on top. Eggs were always in a separate bag, I'd put them to the side and ask if the customer wanted to carry them herself. Any detergents went in separate bags too.

"I had this one lady, she asked me specifically to do her packing. I took her things out to her car. It was a big Olds. She wanted the stuff in the back seat. I had just these two big glass jugs of milk left, one in each hand. As I swung them into the car, they banged together." He apologized, ran into the store and grabbed some aprons. "I dumped them on the floor of her car and wrung them out. I got everything dry, then ran back in the store and got her some more milk. I remembered what Mom had said, and told her she should soak the carpet in vinegar to get the smell out. I never heard a complaint from her."

He soon became second in command. "Whenever the head packer was absent, I assumed control. I had to see there was a packer at every cash, doubling up on big orders. See that we didn't run out of bags, that the floor was kept clean of the bottle returns. I assigned lunches and breaks, and clean-up duties after the store was closed."

One summer, with someone on holidays, he was put behind the meat counter. Besides his regular duties, he had to sweep the sawdust from the floor and lay down fresh each day; he had to scrub the walls in the meat freezer. One Saturday near closing, he was scrubbing away, sides of beef hanging all around him. He had drifted off into his own little world as he liked to do, when a voice came into his head. "It was asking me how I was doing, how I liked the job, not to miss the spot to my right, or the one to my left," and all around him were only dead cows. It took some time before he realized where the voice was coming from. It was his boss.

But what he really wanted was to go "on the aisles" and be a stock boy. His brothers were stock boys, there was more responsibility. You had your own aisle to take care of. One day a senior person called in sick, and he was given the produce aisle. "It was a Thursday night, I was all by myself, and with all the packaging, weighing, pricing and delivering to the floor, I couldn't keep up." The produce and meat managers both said they would try to get him transferred, but nothing happened, and he remained a packer.

He wouldn't get another chance in Whitby, but soon he'd be running the baking goods aisle at the Dominion in Don Mills. That was for him an even better time.

If the last few years in Whitby were good ones for Frank,

they weren't for his dad. Leo was sick. Bruce Field was manager of the company's Ottawa store at the time. Each year, he and the other managers received annual sales figures from the stores across the country. From big branches in Toronto, Montreal, Winnipeg, Edmonton and Vancouver, slightly smaller ones in Ottawa, Calgary and London, from mid-sized branches in cities like Oshawa. In its category, Oshawa was always at the top. It was 1961, Field thinks, when he first began to notice. "I looked at the sheets and was stunned. Oshawa was going downhill. Their sales were down, their profits were down. You knew something had to be wrong. And knowing Leo, I said to myself, there's only one explanation. His health."

It wasn't an easy company to deal with in bad times. Nobody made much money unless they sold lots of glass. Commissions might triple if targets were met; bonuses might represent one-third of a manager's income. There was pride as well. Everyone knew each other, they had worked together for years. They competed against the big guys in the industry, and just as hard against each other. And they loved it, and hated it. They complained of the pressure, and couldn't live without it. They were "sales jocks," always and in every way trying to outdo each other. Who's the best "glassman" around, who runs the best shop? And who doesn't have it any more, because everyone knows that too. Who's on the booze, who's not putting in the hours, who doesn't want it any more? "You just didn't want to be seen as the guy who couldn't produce," Bruce Field said. Like reading every obituary that isn't yours, too bad Harry died; it's great to be alive.

Leo was failing. He had had two minor heart attacks, was in and out of the hospital, he wasn't up to the job any more. All his life, he had lived and worked on the outer margins; he had nothing in reserve. The cigarettes he smoked for forty-five years, his cough and emphysema, his early-morning head starts on his competition and nights at the office, the vacations he took to keep himself working, his attitude to work and family, his need to do things right, his eight kids. Six days a week he worked and on the seventh day there was church, big Sunday dinners and at night Ann, Trish or one of the boys to drive back to Toronto. There was no rest. He needed every hour and every penny and every bit of strength just to make his considerable ends meet. But now he couldn't square the circle. To do the job physically, he had to cut back; if he cut back he couldn't do the job. His only way out was out. In 1964 the company moved him to headquarters in Toronto. No more nights at the office, no more weekends.

He commuted for a year. John had graduated from Ryerson and was back at home. Working with an architectural firm in Toronto, he and his dad drove together. Trish was in residence at St. Mike's and Friday afternoons she met her dad at the office with her dirty laundry and drove back with him to Whitby for the weekends. "Oh, this is my daughter," he'd say to people in the office, being sure to introduce her. "I always felt so special when I went there," she said. He had had so little time, there were always so many of them, it was so rare for the two of them, any two of them, to be alone. This was Leo's chance.

But commuting was too much for him. He wasn't yet sixty years old, he and Margaret had no real savings or investments, there were weddings ahead to be paid for, Lee that summer, then Trish and Sue, their only car was the company's car, Margaret hadn't worked for a salary in over thirty years and nearing sixty had no job prospects, his pension would be modest at best. He was too vulnerable to retire, too sick to work. So he kept on working, but now they needed to move. On Hallowe'en day, 1965, they left the house that had been their home for nineteen years and moved back to Toronto, to Don Mills.

It was just Margaret and Leo, Frank and Sue; John and Jim for a while. The house was a small three-bedroom bungalow, 3 Talwood Drive, one bedroom for Margaret and Leo, another for Sue and Trish when she was home, the third for the three boys, now twenty-four, twenty-two and eighteen, together again and too old to be sharing a room. Leo decided to finish part of the basement as a bedroom for John and Jim. They did all the work themselves. Leo had no detectable skill as a handyman; Frank, with no experience at all, was the go-fer; John and Jim had taken high-school shop so they were the bosses. They were one boss too many.

Don Mills was what *Maclean's* magazine in 1961 called "the most suburban of Toronto suburbs." It was what the postwar world had come to more than a decade after, when two TVs, two cars, the values, ambitions and affluence of the rich had made their way down to the middle and upper-middle classes. Everything about it was new, planned and purposeful. *Omnia per scientiam*, "everything through knowledge" read the motto of Don Mills Collegiate Institute, his new school. Just five years old, bright and clean, there was about it a sense of possibility and excitement; the feeling of importance and self-importance was everywhere.

"The gentlemen at the U. of T. are sure to prefer blondes when they see Barb next year," read the *Orbit*, the school's yearbook. "Brian hopes to attend Western in a phys-ed course," Marvin and Paul, the Hersh twins, the U. of T. for Maths, Physics and Chemistry, Sharylee for Medicine, Karin to York for Modern History, for Dave "it's McMaster and Dentistry." This was the first suburban-raised, university-bound generation. One hundred and forty-seven had made it to grade 13 the year he arrived in grade 11; according to the next year's *Orbit*, 119 passed, 77 were in university, including Barb, Marvin and Paul, Sharylee, Karin and Dave. Busy with hockey, it took Brian a year longer. There were 8 more in teachers' college, 8 in nursing, 4 at Ryerson. It was a high-flying group in the classroom, on playing fields, in its clubs and organizations, and still overwhelmingly WASP. All the girls still wore blouses and skirts, no slacks, but that was about to change.

"I thought the teachers were working from the back of the bloody book," he says of the shock of his first few days. "Right away, I was two months behind. And somehow they put me in a brain class too. So how the heck was I going to catch up?" At Christmas, he passed only English, geography and math; in June, only English.

He spent his school year drifting, smiling, being pleasant and agreeable; the happier he looked, the more things had to be fine, the more everyone would leave him alone. In dress, manner and posture he learned the ways of his new school, ridding himself of exaggerations, smoothing out every edge, blending in, fading, disappearing from view. When someone did notice him, he tried humour. He wrote funny stories, about his family building the bedroom in the basement. About a turtle who wanted to fly so badly he killed himself trying; getting his wings in turtle heaven.

On one exam he had to answer the question, "Do you see yourself as others see you?" something he had thought a lot about. What he tried to say, what the pressure of time and occasion didn't quite allow, was this: I am eighteen. To others I look older and more mature than I ever have. I don't look stupid or fat, which is good except that inside I feel as I always have. So I feel I'm tricking them, fooling them, which makes me feel worse and makes *them* expect more; which makes me more insecure and more desperate to hide what I've hidden; which gives me more to hide. "A pleasant change from your usual comical efforts," his teacher wrote.

"Recent arrival to 11F oasis," wrote the *Orbit* his first year. "Likes a good joke. Particularly his own." The next year, "Half of his laugh is for his own laugh." The year after, "Have yet to see him in a bad mood."

In January he got a job at the local Dominion. Once again, he had money in his pockets. Knowing he was about to fail his year, he bought a little Honda motorbike "before Mom got my report card." He had been a long time getting "wheels" of any kind. For a sixteen-year-old boy, a driver's licence and car meant status and an easier time gaining and keeping friends and girlfriends, in feeling you belonged. "Back then, you lived for your sixteenth birthday," he remembers. But as good as having a licence or car was, having none was many times worse.

He got his learner's permit just after his sixteenth birthday. A few days later, he told his mom he was going over to Peter Millar's to show it to him. "I rode over on my bike, this was in the morning, and we got to goofing off and I never came home for lunch. We bicycled all over Whitby, went down to the beach. I finally got home about three-thirty, just to check in and say, 'Hey, Mom, I think Pete and I are going to the show.' She was livid. 'Where have you been all day?! Why didn't you phone?! I was all set to call the police!'

"Then she said, 'Give me your licence.' So I pulled it out of my wallet. I thought she was just going to hold it or something . . . She ripped it up. 'What're you doing?!' I yelled. 'Get up to your room!' All this time I'm saying to myself, can she really do that? Does she have the right?

"So I went up to my room. I could hear her in the kitchen and she's yelling and Trish's saying, 'Mom, calm down, you're going to kill yourself.' The next thing I know she's coming up the stairs with an electric cord in her hand. She told me to take my shirt off. I said, 'Listen to Trish.' 'Bend over the bed,' she said, so I bent over and she started whacking me. I didn't make a sound."

It would take a whole year. Never once did they talk of what had happened. Her anger passed quickly. "Mom was very forgiving," he explains, "She'd get mad and when it was over, it was over." But not always for others; and this time not for him.

Once more, he'd be a year older than everyone else, just what he didn't need.

His new job at Dominion was on the aisles. The baking goods aisle — cake mixes, sugar, flour, spices and Jello — and it's here he met Dave Turner. Turner was a year younger but a grade ahead of him at Don Mills C.I. He had also been a packer, but had recently been promoted to the same aisle. He remembers Frank as thin, with a short brush cut and black-frame glasses, and wearing the uniform they all wore: black pants, white shirt and apron, and a little green bow tie. Together, he says, "we made a good team."

"We practically ran the aisle on the weekends," Frank says with pride. "The full-time guy did it during the week but Saturdays he'd have to be upstairs unloading the trucks. Dave and I would walk up and down the aisle, one of us reading off a list, 'Do we need Jello,' and the other would climb the shelves, 'Yeah, lime and lemon.' 'Do we need cake mix?' 'Yeah, Robin Hood and Duncan Hines.' We had the shelves full all the time, which wasn't easy. It was a fast-turnover section."

The store closed at nine on Thursdays and Fridays, but Fridays they had to stay until ten to load stock onto a dolly and have it in position for Saturday morning at seven-thirty, when they came in and filled their shelves for the opening at nine. At day's end, "We'd bring the stuff from the back of the shelves up to the front, so the manager would see full-looking shelves and tell us we could go." Dave Turner had a girlfriend, he didn't, so at six-thirty they went their separate ways. Sometimes they saw each other outside work, but not often.

Turner hasn't seen him in more than twenty years, only a few disconnected images remain in his mind. "Frank was always hard-working and conscientious," he says, "and very friendly to customers. Today in a supermarket, if you ask for salt, if you can find anyone to help you at all, he'll point, 'Four rows over,' and keep on going. He would take you there, and really enjoy doing it. It was always 'Yes, Mrs. Jones. You might like to try this, Mrs. Jones.' "

Once he saw a puzzled-looking woman searching through the cake mixes, and asked if he could help. She wanted a new pudding cake mix, she said. He didn't have it, but "I told her my mom makes a real nice pudding cake.

'I don't know the measurements,' I said, 'but being a real good baker, I'm sure you could figure it out.' I gave her all the ingredients I knew and she started buying all this stuff. I don't know if she ever made it." He wishes he knew.

"He was a Catholic," Turner recalls, "and he used to talk louder than most people. And he didn't used to swear. He'd say, 'friggin.'

"I don't think he was very good in school, and maybe this job was his first real experience at doing something well. I don't know whether he told me that or whether it was just something I knew. But he did his job well. You didn't need a college degree to do it, but you did need personality and dedication, and he had that.

"He was just a nice guy. A little shy, to others at least, and a good friend, not a close friend, because we didn't spend that much time together, but a good friend."

Years later, Frank was trying to pinpoint the best day in his life. If his mood or the circumstances had been different, he might have said something else. But this is what came to mind: "Birthdays were always good days, the Exhibition was fun, but one of the most meaningful days in my life was when Dave Turner's marriage broke up and his mom asked me to visit him."

Turner was at Ryerson by this time, no longer working at Dominion, and he had moved back home. "I figured something must be wrong, we were kind of strangers at first. Then he said, do you want to go to the driving range and hit some balls. I said OK. I didn't want to talk an awful lot. I brought up work, and school, then we hit some balls and I got in the car to go home. Then he says, 'I guess you want to know what happened,' and he told me. I didn't give him any advice. I wasn't mature enough. But I guess his mom thought he needed somebody. It made me feel grown up."

He also got great pleasure being manager of the Don Mills senior football team. He had tried out for football himself at Henry Street in grade 10, but had his nose broken in a pre-season practice and that was enough for his mother, and him. At Don Mills, the team had lost all its games the year before, but a new teacher named Mike Lavelle had arrived at the school and taken over as coach. Young and strong-willed, from a Catholic tradition himself, he believed that sport built character and character won championships. After several early season run-ins with his players, the discipline problems of the year before diminished, and diminished further when they won their first few games.

A football manager's job isn't glamorous. It's usually filled by someone not good enough to play who wants to press his nose against the glass of the action and get as close as he can. For that privilege, he accepts the abuse of his superiors, the players, kids his own age, in his own class, who may have no one else in their lives but little brothers and sisters so definitively inferior to order around. So he is their "go-fer," and when a game is done, with dirty, sweaty smiles of exhilaration, they walk off hand in hand with admiring cheerleaders while the manager is left to pick up their jocks. (Said the *Orbit* of Frank that year: "You can usually find him following Mr. Lavelle picking up the pieces [arms etc.]".)

He liked the responsibility of being manager. Before every game, he had to get permission slips to the players to give to their last teacher of the day. He had to take care of the equipment, make sure it was clean and in good repair. He had a problem with the coach of the junior team. The coach had asked to borrow some of the senior team's sweaters and didn't return them. "I harped on him and harped on him. Every time I saw him, I'd say, 'Mr. Wensley, where're our sweaters?' Finally when he did give them back, he praised me for keeping at him.

"The players were also supposed to take their sweaters home to get cleaned, but they weren't doing it. I said to Mr. Lavelle, if you give me the money I'll get one of the guys with a car to drive me down to the laundromat and do them there. That was sort of my idea. So once a week the lady expected us. She made sure there were empty machines and I helped her clean them up afterwards."

According to the *Orbit* that year:

> This year's senior football team was called everything from the 'miracle kids' to . . . the 'Boston Red Sox of football.' Although these 'miracle kids' might have been 'underdogs' in all their play-off games, they did more than the Boston Red Sox. They won the big one when it counted . . . humiliat[ing] Northview 25-7.

The day of the school's athletic banquet, he saw Mr. Lavelle in the hall. " 'You got your ticket for the dinner tonight?' he asked. I said no. He said, 'Why not?' 'It's the athletic awards,' I said, 'It's for the players.' Well, he got angry, 'No, no, you were a part of the team. I want you there.' I asked if Ron was going." Ron Clarkson was his assistant trainer. "He said, 'Yes,' so I went home, got all dressed up in my blue blazer and grey slacks, and went. The players went up on stage and got their awards, the vice-principal gave a talk, and so did Mr. Lavelle. Then he said, 'I'd like now to present a couple of special awards to people who helped make the team what it was.' I didn't know who he was talking about. Then he says Ron and me. Well, I was shocked. I never expected anything. I just wanted to get out of class and see all the games.

"It was just a little cup, about three inches high. I put it on my dresser and when I got married I took it with me and put it on our bookcase. It's still there." He laughs. "I tell the kids about it every so often." The cup reads,

Manager of the Year

Frank Bloye

D.M.C.I.

67–68

He had begun dating by this time, but had found watching and fantasizing more fulfilling, certainly much safer. His first date had been in Whitby, he had just turned sixteen. He asked a "pretty brunette" named Beth Atkinson to a dance. (That year, Class 10A's poem in the Henry Street High yearbook read: We have a blond cheerleader, her name is Nancy,/Bethy, our bouncy one, is quite fancy . . .)

"I half-expected her to say 'no,' but she said 'yes' without hesitation. Oh God, what am I going to do now, I thought? I'd never been to a dance. I didn't know how to dance. I'd never held a girl before.

"She was beautiful. She had her hair done up and wore a pale-coloured full dress. I handed her the corsage. I was really nervous. She and I mingled a while, then the music started. I confessed to her I didn't know how to dance. She told me that was OK, she'd show me how. I was awful. I stumbled around and stepped on her toes. I was sure everyone was watching. I wanted to get out of there and die. I just wouldn't let myself relax and have a good time. I'm sure I ruined the whole evening for her."

After he had walked her to her front door, he swore he wouldn't go through that again.

The story repeated itself every few months for the next years, whenever his hormones had enough time to rage and overcome good judgment. The next incident was the following summer. He was seventeen. He worked only weekends at Dominion and passed as many of his summer days as he could down at the lake. It was here he saw Nancy, the blue-eyed blonde cheerleader from Class 10A at school. He had been watching her many days before he dared get close, and for many more days before he spoke. Then one day they talked and swam. The next day they were both back, and the next day, and when finally he was sure this was more than mere accident, he asked her to a movie. With no need to talk, dance or hold, a movie seemed the perfect date.

They saw Joan Crawford in *Strait Jacket*. "Nancy was too scared to watch. She asked if we could leave and I took her home. I kept going down to the beach but I never saw her there again."

Always the hopes and expectations, the plans, the build up, the things that were supposed to be a certain way that weren't. This was not fun. This hurt. Who needed it? Why put myself in these situations? I can't talk the way they want me to talk, I can't dance, I don't have a car, why would anyone want to go out with me anyway? Besides, I enjoy working on my models. I like my job. I'm happy. I'm fine.

"So I decided to give up girls. I decided I would remain a bachelor the rest of my life." More months passed, they moved to Don Mills, he kept his word. Then he met Reet Mae. She was tall and blonde with long, folk-singer-straight hair. He had been careful to ask out shy, awkward female versions of himself. This time, "I forgot everything my experience had taught me." He asked her to a *dance.* Two years later, the Don Mills yearbook described Reet Mae this way:

> This swinger's likes range anywhere from sand-casting to square-toed shoes. Next year, she'll probably be making the scene at U. of T. or Simon Fraser. Someday she'd like to live in Sweden. No doubt she'll revolutionize the fashion world if she carries out her plans to design clothes! Her colourful and avant-garde creations (that includes dance routines) will be sorely missed at D.M.C.I.

That night, he swore off girls completely.

Nearly two years passed. Two nights before the annual "Sadie Hawkins Dance," where the girls ask the guys, his phone rang. It was Jan Pauling, a "shy, petite girl" in his class. ("A member of the up-and-coming [and enlarging] Verner-Pauling 'Boys not Allowed' clique," the yearbook said.) He was almost twenty. "She asked hesitantly if I'd consider going to the dance with her. I said I'd be glad to go." It was the voice of reflex, desire, good manners. "Then I started kicking myself." The voice of logic triggered too late. "I told her up front I couldn't dance and usually stayed home for that reason. She said that was OK, she couldn't dance either, we'd learn together.

"I picked her up at her apartment and gave her a corsage. I think she was pleased. We walked over to the school. I felt more relaxed with her than I had with anyone before, but I still dreaded dancing. She showed me what her girlfriends had taught her, but I was still like an elephant walking on eggs.

"I took her home about eleven, stayed for a coffee with her folks, then went home." A better night than most, yet whenever he was on a date, it seemed his only purpose was to get through the evening, to turn present into past as fast as he could, *to have dated.* After leaving Jan Pauling in her apartment, "that was absolutely the last date I ever went on. The last until I met Carolyn, two years later."

He had failed grade 11 the first time, then passed it the next. His sister Sue, two years younger, had now caught up to him and was in the same grade, though thankfully in a different class. In grade 12, things would get easier for him. He could drop French and he no longer needed to pass all his subjects to move to the next grade. He got credit for any course he did pass, so with the passage of time, if not much else, he was closing in on his grade 13 goal. It was this extra time he had needed all his life. Always his world had been pitched too fast for him. All his stories seem so strangely out of time: learning to read *in grade 3*, his first date *at sixteen*, his licence *at seventeen*, building model cars *at eighteen*. Normal, routine things made abnormal by age and time. Everything just took him longer.

And what's wrong with that? If life is for all eternity, what's the hurry? What's wrong with slow and steady, with failing twice and picking up credits like wind-blown apples in slow, extended grade-less years? His grade 13 diploma would look no different. But it's not that simple.

The getting there had changed his life. If someone's ten years old and looks ten years old, he's supposed to do what ten-year-olds do, as fast and well as they do them. If he doesn't, he's a failure. And treated like one, he feels, talks, thinks, walks and acts like one. He sees life through a failure's eyes, expects and does what a failure does. His standards are a failure's standards, it's their ceiling which crowds his head, their walls which blinker his way. It's the story others write for him, the one he writes for himself.

His high-school transcripts tell an interesting tale. They show consistent and slightly below average results in normal years, failure on the heels of change, an aptitude in math and none in languages. They show the results of IQ tests: the first, given to him in June, 1962, a month before his fifteenth birthday, when he was still in grade 9 in Ajax. His IQ was measured at 108, about an average score. Four years later, he took an academic aptitude test with other grade 12 and 13 students, many of whom having advanced this far would go on to university. His verbal score put him in the 43rd percentile, his math the 42nd, much better than his regular class standing. A third test, taken the same year, measured his IQ at 116. A "gifted" high school student might score 125 to 130, a Harvard freshman 140, a freshman in the University of Toronto, three-year general program, 115 to 120.

There is on his transcript only one written comment:

> Poor working habits. No effort is visible. Seems to be the 'baby' at home. Could not always accept correction — would not always see the reason for it. I am sure that with a bit of drive he could succeed.

There is no indication who made the comment or in what year.

Learning in a classroom and demonstrating that learning has also to do with other kids, with teachers, personal relationships, expectations, clues, jokes, ironies, surprises, information that comes from everywhere, status, confidence, pace; comfort. On an IQ test, these are not issues. He had the ability to do better, but who knew?

We learn in school, or so it seems. We find out if we're good learners or bad learners and take that knowledge with us wherever we go, often forever. Because he didn't learn when and where he was supposed to, he was a bad learner, and grew up and into adulthood believing he *couldn't* learn. That he could build a patio and earn "excellent" ratings as a collector at Imperial Oil to him seemed unrelated and beside the point. That was *doing*. Real learning was classrooms, books and tests, and faced with them, he'd freeze, run away and avoid them. In a more competitive, technologically evolving workplace, in a changing future, that matters.

He thinks good thoughts when he thinks of his childhood. "If a kid is too much in the spotlight too early," he thinks, "and doesn't continue there, it'll ruin his adult life. If he becomes just an average guy, he probably can't handle it. I was probably on the down side of average, but I wasn't unhappy at all."

He passed most of his grade 12 courses one year, the rest and some of his grade 13 the next. It was June, 1968, a month before his 21st birthday; he decided to leave school as a full-time student to find a job. When the school year began again, working days he returned to school at night. He was so close to doing what John and Jim had never done, what his mother had wanted for them all. In June, 1969, he finally made it. He passed grade 13. School for him was over; just as those of his generation were moving on to university.

Part Three

"You can go as far
As your heart can see
Be on any road
That you want to be
It's your day
You're on your way
With Esso
Now is the time for celebration . . ."

YOU'RE ON YOUR WAY WITH ESSO

7

It's been four months since that Saturday morning early in June when he opened his pool. And it was a good four months, all in all. July was beautiful, sunny and hot nearly every day, a little rain on the weekends, of course, but that was no surprise. August was cooler and damper, especially late in the month, not what the weatherman had promised, which was annoying. So some days he uncovered the pool and it rained, and some days he didn't and rain threatened long enough that when the skies finally did clear, there didn't seem enough time to make uncovering the pool seem worthwhile, and a day was lost.

He took two weeks' vacation the second half of July and didn't do a lot. It was his birthday the last day of his holidays (what a birthday present!). He is forty-three. He and Stephanie went to mass, Carolyn prepared a nice scrambled-egg breakfast, then he opened his gifts — two T-shirts, socks, handkerchiefs, shaving lotion, plastic storage trays for his workbench in the basement, French brandy and sun-glasses. The kids kept asking him how it felt to be forty-three. He tried pleasantly to ignore them until they wouldn't be ignored, then tried to answer until it was clear it wasn't an answer they were seeking. That night, he realized for the first time he was older than his father had been when he was born.

Carolyn took the summer off to give herself a break and be around so the kids could use the pool during the week. She was working full-time now. She had cared for some of the neighbourhood kids when her own kids were small. When Stephanie was old enough to be in school all day, she started working part-time. Two nights a week and all day Saturday, then occasional weekdays, then more, seeing how much she could handle and not penalize the family. She took a job as a sales clerk at Lizanne's, a fabric store, in charge of notions (threads, zippers, etc.); sometimes she made up the model garments on display on the floor. She was now working as many as four days a week, Fridays until nine. Pay was low; on her feet most of the day she would arrive home tired; the nights at work were hard for the family. But the kids were getting older, they could do more for themselves and for her, Stephanie could go to a neighbour's for the hour after school until she got home. And the extra money was nice. But she thought, if she was going to be working full-time, why not at full-time pay?

So almost a year ago, she started at Imperial, also in the credit-card section. She was "casual," paid by the hour, no benefits, easily terminated, but her wage was much higher and in time she might become permanent staff. She did address changes at first, then return mail. A credit-card holder moved with no forwarding address; using purchase locations and licence plate numbers, she had to find him. She worked at 90 Wynford Drive on the same floor as he did, her cubicle about ten metres away.

Being casual, it was easier for her to take time off, so July and August she was home. The family had never really *needed* her extra pay-cheque. They had always lived on *his* salary, anything she earned they treated as a bonus. He had seen it too many times before, couples living off two salaries, their hopes, their thinking, their image of themselves all based on two salaries, then *bang*, the wife gets pregnant, and they have no idea any more how to live on one. Unable to wipe their memories clean, they can see only what they were and aren't, and now they're miserable. A wife is supposed to stay home until the kids are old enough to fend for themselves. The rest is greed, and trouble.

He had a busy summer, just how he likes it, but nothing was rushed, nothing *had* to get done except when it did.

He had no big projects until September when he painted the outside of the house, but even that took only a few days. He never did get around to moving the front walkway; the patio stones have settled and sunk even deeper. He moved a few bushes, not the red maple, however, that will need to wait for next summer, and the apple tree gave forth its usual bounty of wormy apples. Next year, he's definitely going to spray it himself.

Carolyn got her tomatoes in first, and they came up first, which brought about much neighbourly celebration and abuse. They certainly were plentiful. Next door, John's tomatoes came out eventually and, though not as numerous, began growing fast, and got quite big, bigger even than Carolyn's. Just about then they began to wonder what they hadn't dare wonder before, and John grew more sure of himself. Whenever they would go shopping, they returned to a bag of big, juicy red tomatoes on their doorstep. No note, no name, just John rubbing it in. Carolyn had planted cherry tomatoes.

Lee had her barbecue late in June, all the brothers and sisters were there, but only Clara, Leo's sister, attended from her generation. They were the ones who had always enjoyed this day the most, but so many of them are now dead, or too old and infirm. Jack, Leo's youngest brother, didn't make it either. He usually plans his annual trip east from Saskatoon just for the occasion but, like Leo, has emphysema and the plane ride has become too much. Janine had no such excuse but decided she wasn't going to the barbecue either, until her own pool party seemed suddenly in jeopardy, and she got the message. Then she and Stephanie rediscovered some of their girl cousins and had a great time. Matt hadn't wanted to go either, until the wind shifted and he decided it would be fun to see two of his cousins again who, it turned out, were canoeing with their school class that day, and didn't come. Late in the summer, they all went over to Sue's to try out her pool. For one reason or another, no one made it into theirs.

It was an expensive summer. They knew Matt would need braces, and finally the time came, the top ones in August, the bottom in September, $3,800 worth. What they hadn't counted on was Carolyn: $1,200 for two caps, a bridge and new glasses as well. A few years ago this would have sent them scrambling. Matt's braces would certainly have needed to wait, he might have had to do without them entirely. His teeth and jaw would then have moved imperceptibly into the shape God intended, and not much would be different for awhile, maybe ever. But with Carolyn working full-time, they can manage many of these new expectations, and most of their worst surprises; they can step out of the perpetual present, choose to see more of what is around them, and intervene.

They were even able to begin redoing the living room. It certainly needed it. Their chairs were a mismatch of colours, patterns, textures and styles: two of them had been inherited, one from his mother, the other from Carolyn's dad's cousin; another was a gift from Carolyn's mom, two more were bought from a friend. Now the choice was theirs. They could have any colour, lots of patterns and textures, a few different styles at least. Bound by circumstances so long, however, they were not finding this new freedom easy. And mistakes they still couldn't afford. Whatever they decided they would have to live with a long time. So she wants to go slowly and he wants to get things done, yet if anything isn't right, she knows he will be the one who won't not notice.

If money is much less a source of tension between them, however, it is still a problem with the kids. He and Carolyn know how easily expectations rise, turning wants into life-transforming needs. The kids have never had to learn. They don't know or care about incomes, budgets and debts. To them, needs and wants are the same, and what they need is what their TV screens and the kids at school tell them they need. There is only one world and to them everything in it is real, "Beverly Hills 90210," "Roseanne,"

"Lifestyles of the Rich and Famous" included. How TV kids dress and live is how all kids dress and live. Or should. It's not status. They want to fit in, feel comfortable, be noticed, feel a little bit important to those who matter to them, nothing more than what anyone any age wants.

To him, a shirt is a shirt. If it's clean, covers his back and can be buttoned over his belly, if it was bought on sale, it's a good shirt. A fancy label has no function, so isn't important.

One Saturday late in August, he took Matt shopping for blue jeans. He noticed Zellers was having a sale on GWGs; Matt wanted Levis. After some discussion, he talked Matt into going into the store and comparing the two. He held up a pair of GWGs, Matt a pair of Levis. He looked at them, then turned to Matt, "OK, show me the difference." "These aren't the Levis I like," Matt said. They bought the GWGs.

When they got home, Matt announced he wouldn't wear the jeans.

Except for a week in June that he spent with his grandmother and uncle in Owen Sound, this summer Matt was just "around," doing who knows what, not working, that was what, which was all that seemed to matter. He had worked two nights a week during the school year, usually Wednesday and Thursday, four hours each time, and all day Saturday. It was for a carpet cleaning company, telemarketing, making (numbingly) cold calls into homes, trespassing on people just when inside their doors they finally had time for themselves. Nearly every phone was slammed down in his ear. He made up little games to see himself through the hours. He decided he would yell back at abusive customers every bit as loud as they yelled at him, *after* they'd hung up. Sometimes he even called them back, and when they answered, *he'd* hang up. He always found a way to get even.

Then the job ended and he has been in no hurry to get a job since. And while some can look busy when they're not, not Matt. All summer, he was underfoot. It was such a waste. They are a family. They don't have a lot of money and every one of them has to know and accept that. They have to know there are certain things the family can't afford, so not to ask for them or expect them or make life miserable for everyone if they don't get them. Yet they can't make him not want Air Jordans or Levis; yet so far as they are concerned, their obligation extends to the adequate and wearable; anything more is up to him. But for anything more, he has to get a job to pay the difference, or not ask, neither of which he will do. (Which even if by some miracle he does do, isn't the end of it for them. Janine and Stephanie, too young for part-time jobs, want one-hundred-dollar shoes too. When they tell them "no" . . . "but you bought them for Matt!")

He and Carolyn noticed "Help Wanted" signs in the malls, wrote down the phone numbers; Matt wouldn't call. They asked him pleasantly, suggested in passing, encouraged, cajoled, advised, demanded, threatened; when pretending not to hear wasn't enough, he always had a reason not to make the call. In February, he will be sixteen. He will have driving lessons and gas and some of his own insurance to pay for. If he doesn't have the money, he will lose out. Frank remembers so vividly how he had lost out. And there's a part of him now that wants Matt to do everything right so he won't have to go through what he went through, and a part of him he can't get rid of and can't control that says if this guy won't listen, why should he get off any easier? He's going to have to learn for himself, and if it's the hard way, so be it.

And he still hasn't cut the back hill either.

As for Janine, not much was different this summer. She still spent too much time in the house. Whenever she disappeared from view they always knew where to find her, down in the basement, watching TV. She had gone to an art camp the year before. The kids were chosen by their art teachers at school. It cost three hundred dollars, but after showing her portfolio, she had been awarded three separate prizes of one hundred dollars each! She was so excited. But at camp, some of the kids made fun of the way she talks. It's nothing very different, a little slowly, just enough that when kids need other kids to pick on, they picked on her. So this year she wouldn't go back.

They know she needs to get out more, and they know why consciously and unconsciously she finds herself in front of the TV. She needs to be with friends, and they know why she likes it better alone. So they understand, and push, and understand, and don't know what to do.

Then in August, she said she wanted to learn the piano. Lots of kids say things like that, then a few thousand dollars and a new piano later, they want something else. But she hadn't been like that. Except for The New Kids on the Block and her art, she had never really seemed interested in anything. He and Carolyn let a few days pass, still testing, but when she brought up the subject again, they took her shopping. They looked at a small keyboard first, more toy than musical instrument, yet right away she talked of saving her money to buy one. She even had a spot in her room picked out where it would go.

A few days later, he and Carolyn wandered into the piano store again. They looked around, and saw what they weren't quite looking for, on sale, $120 off the regular price! It was a *very popular* brand, they were told, in the *mid-price* range, *last year's* floor model, but *fully warranted*, and though with fewer keys than a piano keyboard, the keys were *full-sized*, which would make a *switch* to piano easier. There was also a *music school* in the back of the store. The keyboard cost a little more than they intended to spend, but it could be for the *three* of them, for *Christmas*, though they would need to buy it now because the warranty was *ticking away*. But they wouldn't wait for Christmas to use it; that would just *waste* time.

They brought it home, wrapped it loosely in Christmas paper, waited until Matt returned from work, then showed it to the kids. They loved it. Immediately, Janine asked to take lessons. She and Matt sat down and experimented with it until almost eleven o'clock. For the first time unable to out-energize her sister and brother, Stephanie was more subdued.

A month has passed, Janine's lessons continue and though she must practise and face one more hated teacher with one more set of expectations every week, she seems no less interested. As for Stephanie, she wants lessons too.

It was their anniversary August 13th. Nineteen years! They had planned to go out to dinner the night before, but Carolyn's sister called and invited them there. They then planned to go out the next night, but Carolyn had to go to the hospital for blood tests the next morning and thought she'd be too tired, so they ate at home. He ordered a silk flower arrangement and by the time he arrived from work it was there. Everyone was all dressed up, Matt included. Carolyn greeted him at the door with a Manhattan, and he could smell the roast beef in the oven. After his second cocktail, they sat down to a "lovely dinner." The flower arrangement, set in the middle of the table, looked "nice."

They are together so much, yet are together alone so rarely except to do things that have to be done. They almost never go out to dinner or the movies. They don't think about going until they're already on the way home from work, then with so many things to arrange so fast, it doesn't seem worth doing. It's only food and entertainment, they tell themselves, the money could go for things so much more useful. Why not throw something in the microwave — there's a good movie on the tube even if they've seen it before — and stay home? So they do.

Even more often now, it seems, since she began working full-time. The rest of the family hasn't found it easy with her gone so much. Yet the past year she has reminded herself just how much she enjoys being with people. She's more confident now. She never thought of herself as smart and still doesn't, there were always so many things others seemed to know that she didn't and wouldn't and could never learn. She's a good sewer, she made most of the kids' clothes when they were little — dresses, blouses, shirts, even slacks and sport jackets — she still makes most of her own, though not as much for the kids now that designer labels have made her things seem unwearable. She cuts all their hair; he hasn't been to a barber since a week before they were married. And this year she has learned she is good on the phones too. She talks with a human voice, and listens with a human ear. Her supervisor says she is doing well, she is paid what seems to her a lot of money, she is making a tangible contribution to the family; all this makes her feel good.

Combining this job with her job at home, however, has been hard. More tired more often than before, she knows that sometimes she takes out her problems on him and the kids. She can even feel it happening as it's happening, yet can't quite stop herself. They knew they would have much less time to do everything. He and the kids knew they would need to do more, and she do less; they all understood, and accepted.

But their way isn't her way. They don't take the look and running of the house as seriously, haven't had the same lifetime of conditioning, role models and conventional wisdom to set their minds in stone. So when she comes home and the house doesn't look as it should, she redoes it or yells at them to do what seems to them they've already done. Or they forget, and she has to remind them, which she doesn't like doing or think she should have to do, which puts her at the centre of every conflict in the house, making her sound like a shrew, when still she is doing more than her share, and they are doing less. So, mad at them and mad at herself, she turns on them more and can't stop because, in part, she doesn't want to.

They did manage a few family outings this summer, though not as many as they intended. They went to Canada's Wonderland, the big amusement park. Matt and Stephanie went on all the rides, Janine got a headache and

watched, he and Carolyn took pictures. They talked of
going to the "Ex," the Canadian National Exhibition. He
used to go with Trish and Sue, his mother would take them;
John and Jim, older and as boys more independent, went
by themselves. They got the ten o'clock bus at Bryant's
Garage and were there before noon. They would go on a
few rides, spend the afternoon at the grandstand show so
Margaret could rest her feet, then meet Leo for a picnic
supper. It was one of his favourite days of the year. When
he was old enough to go by himself, he liked to go on
Labour Day for the air show.

He wanted to go for the air show this Labour Day too,
but Janine didn't want to waste her money, Matt was broke,
Carolyn was tired, and finally he didn't care much either.
Only Stephanie wanted to go. So he trimmed some bushes
and fixed the downpipes of his eavestrough, and waited for
summer to end. When the kids went back to school, he
spent the last week of his holidays painting the house. He
didn't need all that time, but one day it rained and another
it threatened and, one thing leading to another, the week
passed. But now the job was done; one more thing he
wouldn't have to worry about for awhile. And if a few brush
strokes strayed onto the bricks, "I'll be back in five years,"
he shrugged.

The provincial election was also that week. He voted Liberal because his father voted Liberal and because the Lib-
erals were in power and as the devil he knew, offered fewer
surprises. But they lost, not to the Progressive Conserva-
tives, Ontario's traditional governing party, but the NDP,
the New Democratic Party. For the first time, Ontario had
a social democratic government. He hadn't paid much
attention to the campaign, just enough to say something at
work if he had to. There was nothing much about it that
had anything to do with him. So why be interested? Long
ago, he had learned never to imagine he had in his hands
what he doesn't. That was the perfect recipe for unhappi-
ness. So political parties go their way, and he goes his. And

now he knows he can live without them, even if it isn't in them to imagine he can.

The morning after the election, the whole family was at the breakfast table. "In case anybody says something," he announced, "the NDP won. Just so you don't embarrass yourselves."

The routineness of their fall ended last weekend, however. It was the Friday of Thanksgiving, a sunny, crisp, beautiful day and they were going north to Owen Sound to visit Carolyn's brother, Paul, and his girlfriend. It was about four in the afternoon, he and Carolyn were still at work, Matt was the first to arrive home. Coming up the driveway, he saw the side door open, and in it a big hole where the door had been kicked in. He leaned in the doorway, "You'd better get out of this house! I'm calling the police!" Nothing moved. He yelled again. Taking no chances, he ran to a friend's house to use the phone, meeting Stephanie on the way. She wouldn't believe him, of course, until he showed her the door, then the two of them peered in at a house turned upside down. Janine was baby-sitting across the street; she had gone straight there from school. They ran to tell her, and Janine called Carolyn at work.

Two cameras, binoculars, the TV and a bracelet of Carolyn's were gone from their bedroom. Stephanie's room was a mess. Her drawers were open, her chair on its side, a portable stereo she had bought with her own money was gone and both her New Kids on the Block tapes which were in it. Janine was missing some rings and twenty dollars. The living room, dining room and kitchen were untouched. The stereo, silver and china they got as wedding gifts nineteen years ago, their few antiques, the new keyboard, none of that was taken. Downstairs, Matt's portable stereo was gone, and some of his speakers. His room always a mess, it was hard to tell what else was missing. Their computer wasn't taken, their Beta VCR was (that was the good news). Also gone was assorted costume jewellery, a watch and forty-six student bus tickets. For the TV, stereos, cameras, speakers and Beta machine, he had model numbers, serial numbers, dates of purchase and purchase prices for the police and insurance agent. The total loss: $3,705.00.

In two weeks, all the electronic equipment would be replaced and most of their other things; only the door wasn't fixed to their satisfaction. But the effect of the break-in lingered. It confirmed everything he had ever thought about Scarborough. More than that, it was one more piece of evidence of an outside world he didn't understand. Why would anyone do this, he wanted to know? *Why?* And now, he had come to realize, there was nothing he could do about it. No matter how small and walled off he made his world, he couldn't escape.

On their way back from Owen Sound, they heard news reports on the radio. Imperial Oil will announce layoffs this week, the radio said. Two thousand five hundred will go.

8

The first noise is the swoosh of air conditioning, and inside that, nearly lost, the hum of fluorescent lights which track up and down the room. At 7:00 a.m., the music comes on. Muffled by the other sounds, it reaches into the conscious minds of the few who have straggled in only as it rises to its choruses, setting heads humming, soothing, easing them into their morning mood. By 7:30, the swoosh is buried under layers of new sound, and so too the music. Voices take over. People with next-door faces in clean, ironed, Saturday-night-at-the-movies clothes lean over their metal dividers and talk about last night, and not yet today. In a few minutes, the voices nearly stop, traces of air and music reappear until both are covered again by the hollow peck and cluck of keyboard keys, *grind grind* of printers, stamp of staplers, the collective coughs, sighs, cleared throats and grunts of the eighty or so busy in their workdays. That and the high-pitched burble of phones, always the phones. The layer of sound thickens, thins as midday comes, then thickens again until the hours of the day whittle it away and the music and the air, then the air and the lights, then only the air can be heard.

He works here. It is a big room, bright and institutional like a suburban high-school cafeteria. For those already seated and at work, it shrinks to cubicle-size, six feet by six feet, cluttered, compact, convenience-store-efficient, filled with computer terminal, keyboard, calculator, in-basket, out-basket, phone, note pad, pens, pencils, desk top, drawers, filing cabinet, waste basket, reference books, coat hanger, photos, cartoons, drawings or sayings, everything an arm's length away, no posts, walls, hanging plants or heads visible above, only a big ceiling and a roomful of noise.

Two or three coffee stations are scattered about. "If you take the last cup and make a new pot your coffee is free," their signs read. On personal spaces are personal messages, facing into the office or out and stuck into the cushioned beige burlap which covers each divider. "I've got one nerve left," warns a hand-drawn frazzle-haired man, "and you're getting on it." "I suffer from PMS," says another, with the same sweet mix of whine and threat, "Putting up with Men's Shit."

His cubicle has its own touches. Taped to the back of his chair is a scrap of yellow paper on which has been written, "Bloye," and to his waste-basket another reading, "Bloye 90-1st R6." A few months ago, Imperial's credit-card section was moved a few hundred metres up the road into Texaco's credit-card space. The stickers told the movers to take the waste-basket and chair to 90 Wynford Drive, first floor, location R6 on the floor plan. He hasn't bothered to remove them. On a small filing cabinet he has two framed family photos, one with Carolyn and the kids taken several years ago, beside it more recent pictures of each of the kids. He has taped on the front of the filing cabinet three home-made birthday cards, each decorated with cartoon drawings, done for his forty-third birthday two months ago. One card reads:

> Dad, Happy Birthday
> Do you feel old yet?
> Love Janine

Another:

> To Dad: Good luck on the second hill
> Love Matt

The third:

> To Dad: Happy 43rd Birthday
> Holy cow; Get real; Wow; Get outta here, that old?!
> Signed: Guess who

There is one more drawing on the inside of his work space. It shows a vice in horizontal position, and in it a human figure whose head and feet have been scrunched together. The caption reads:

Go ahead, you son of a bitch. Give it a turn.

I work better under pressure.

On the outside of his cubicle where everyone can see it is a drawing of Janine's. She did it before visiting him at work last spring. On it, she has printed "Job Shadowing." The drawing shows a desk piled high with paper, a phone, its receiver bouncing off the hook, "RING RING RING," and a begoggled, slightly balding man with a moustache, his head flat on the desk, asleep, "ZZZZZZZZZ."

It is 7:55. His work day doesn't begin until 8:30, but already he's at his desk. He can't be sure of traffic on the expressways so he takes Sheppard Avenue and Don Mills Road, and not sure of them, he leaves early and ninety-nine days and more out of a hundred, arrives early. And after a few smiling hellos and comments about the weather, with nothing else to do, he begins early. Around him, co-workers still sip their coffee and chat, about the Leafs who have just begun another NHL season, about the baseball playoffs, but mostly about the "rumours." Two thousand of them are going to be laid off, four thousand some have heard. One woman who knows the secretary to one of the big bosses at "One Eleven," 111 St. Clair Avenue West, the company's head office, says her friend told her that her boss told her that the company was moving to Calgary. On and on. Excited, energized, they seem to be talking about someone else.

He enters his ID and secret password code; his screen hums and flashes to life. The system is up. He sits before his computer terminal in his bright golfer's green slacks, like the bright blue ones he wore yesterday and the bright red ones the day before. He has on a white shirt with thin black and green stripes and military loops on the shoulders, similar to the blue one he wore yesterday. His sleeves are folded, not rolled, neatly up his arms nearly to his elbows. His top button is undone, he wears no tie. Faint undershirt lines run in an arc from his shoulders to under his arms. He is wearing white socks with a single green stripe around their tops, and running shoes. His Timex Quartz watch is two minutes fast.

He types "WPA" onto his blank screen, hits "ENTER" and the day's work-list flashes in front of him. He does his work-list now because he is fresher, because of all the decisions it requires, because the phone isn't ringing. He calls up "on-request" review, accounts which some days or weeks ago he asked the system to see again today. A customer has defaulted, the company has sent a series of sharp-toned letters; the customer has called and agreed to pay. He has sent post-dated cheques, but until full payment has been received his card can't be used. So today the system throws up his unique screenful of numbers and he scans them looking for the payment, to release his card or punch another set of keys and send his numbers permanently out of his life and on to pre-collection.

He has four or five to do, a normal day. He whips through them fast to build up a head of steam, a frame of mind and the bubble of time he will need later. The payments are in; he releases the cards.

Next, "maintenance accounts." A customer hadn't paid after many letters and promises, so he punched more keys and a few days ago telegrams were sent to Esso dealers in the customer's area telling them to pick up his card if he tried to use it. But before they could pick it up, he paid his bill. So yesterday, he cancelled the notice, except the system isn't sure he should have been so hasty. In the customer it sees a pattern of behaviour it may no longer want to tolerate. It sees too much risk that the next time items are charged, it won't see its money. So it gives him a day to reconsider, to look at several years of screen behaviour, and again to make his decision. Punch one key, the notification is affirmed, the card will be picked up and his screen will move on to a senior collector's. Punch another and everything is fine, except a screen never forgets.

Large credit balances come up, he lets them scroll by. Here he can make up more time. Either the customer intended the extra payment, or will request a refund, or the company made a keying error, which is the most likely. A cheque was received for $290.00, "$390.00" was punched in, the credit appeared. Triggered by its size, the system sent its query onto his screen. Before he can issue a cheque, he has to be sure he isn't giving back what was never sent, which requires time to check, which he doesn't have or need to spend, so rarely does.

Next, replacement cards and sub-card requests. A card is lost or stolen, a customer wants another for a spouse or child, so he must look at his credit history, and decide. No, and he punches a few keys, the system prints a letter and declines the request; yes, it issues a card which in ten days is in the customer's hands and into the marketplace, a few months or years from now perhaps, back on his screen as a problem account. He assists a collector who is responsible for more than 100,000 accounts. About 6 per cent go bad. These are his lifeblood.

He is the override to the system, the human eyes that connect the numbers on the screen, and create from them a person. Who is this guy? What's going on? Is he sloppy or young or worse? Is he from the north, has the mine or the mill shut down? Is she from the Prairies, from Toronto, Red Deer or Halifax? Is it tough times all over? Will tough times pass, will they pass soon enough? Is he a good customer having a bad time, someone to stay with, help, bully and nurse so the company gets its money and he keeps buying his gas, tires and candy bars month after month at the Esso sign until the day he dies? Or is he a bad customer, not necessarily dishonest, but out of control, with more needs and wants than he can pay for, about to crash, taking the company's money with him? If he does nothing, the system carries on, it knows what to do. A credit-card application triggers a card triggers a statement a month later, another a month after that and another and so on and so on. And if the system is fed its proper due at the proper time, nothing else happens. If it isn't, it gags and triggers again, interest penalties, letters, nastier as each unsatisfied date passes, offering no shred of human understanding, no recognition that in human lives one month is not the same as the next, allowing no possibility that explanation exists or even matters.

Only he can stop it, something he sees on his screen or hears in the voice in his earpiece, but only if he wants to. Only if he believes that interrupting the system's relentless justice will achieve the company's goals better than allowing it to grind on. It's his job to get the company its money, *and* keep it its customer. To get its money now *and* in the future, and that's not easy. A customer fills up his tank, bills go out in twenty-eight day cycles, on average it's fourteen days before the charge shows up on his bill. He has thirty days to pay it without penalty, forty-four days of free credit in all. After that, an interest rate about 2 to 3 per cent higher than Visa or Mastercard.

So there is another balancing act, but this one isn't his. Is it better to get that money now, or *eventually*, after the interest meter has run awhile? Many other companies let out more line, but with better technologies, they keep closer contact with customers, easing, jerking, always reminding, the bill going up, the customer going nowhere. But he is told only to collect. His job isn't to make the company money, only to see that it gets what it's owed. So he and the system work together. He is its human face.

He goes to NDC. He has registered a problem account with the National Data Centre, an outside agency. The card holder tries to buy tires, the charge is more than seventy-five dollars, the dealer needs authorization and finds it denied. So every morning, the system asks him: is the problem sufficiently resolved to cancel NDC, to save the company payment of its fee, to reinstate the account and get business moving again? He wants his customer back and to save the company its money, so he scans his screen for a reason. His pace slows.

Still ahead are defaults. A customer had been several months late in paying, he called him, they negotiated an "arrangement," his card was cut off, and for a few months his cheques came in on schedule. Then he missed a payment, the system gagged, and his numbers flashed back on his screen. What should he do? Which was the anomaly, the hits or the miss? Does he go easy, extend the time, or punch up a letter demanding full payment at once? Does he lower the hammer, step out from the transaction entirely, isolating the customer from the possibility of further human contact and leave him to the uninterruptable mercy of the system? Trigger . . . response; trigger . . . response.

There is no wrong answer. That's what they told him when he was training, and though that's not how he wants it to be, they were right. He has only to justify his action. To his supervisor, provide a trail of logic; to himself, out of all the numbers, circumstances and story, out of all the stories from all the screens he has seen, a "gut feeling." "I'm flying by the seat of my pants," he says, but he isn't.

"Woooo, this guy's in trouble," he mutters. As he reads his screen, the logic of its story begins to coalesce. "Fairly new account, the seven-hundred-dollar payment didn't bounce though; but they've been bouncing ever since. Think I'd better pull his post-dated cheques and put him in collection." He has his gut feeling and a point on which to pivot his logic. "He lied," he says, his passion gone. "He said no more NSF cheques, and the first was NSF."

"Specials" are next. Statements are run every night, printed, sorted and prepared for mailing. But there are some that he told the system he wants to see again before they're sent out. "Ooh, look at this," he says, his numbers and symbols not looking quite right. "A new account, $1,700 the first month, gas purchases every day. Looks like gas and cigarettes." He spots an entry for $220.83. "Ooh, that's not gas and cigarettes," his eyes jump up the screen, "and from a truck stop. And here's another for $135 at the same truck stop the next day." His story is finding shape. "Then $101 the next day." His voice is rising. "Then another five days later." He looks back up the screen. "That's no personal account. That's gotta be a business." Personal accounts are allowed minimum monthly payments except on gas; businesses must pay the full amount. "I gotta cut off his revolving credit."

His phone is about to ring and he knows it. It was worse a year ago when he was new to the job and knew he couldn't do it as he always knows such things. Everything moved too fast. He couldn't read his screens, sort them out, understand, formulate, make good decisions and know they were good. The pages kept turning before he was done. Every decision seemed reflex, knee-jerk, random, off-the-top-of-his-head, wrong, or non-justifiably, unsatisfyingly, mysteriously right. Either way, he didn't know what he was doing or why.

He felt like a machine himself, punching this, punching that, but worse than any machine, slow and inconsistent. Everyone else knew what they were doing. He'd ask them advice; they could explain. Sometimes he got so wrapped up in their words he forgot to listen to their answers. Why did the company bother? Why did they insist on putting him into things like this? He told his supervisor right from the start he couldn't do it, he was only hurting the company. His supervisor said he was doing fine, to try a little longer, give it a good shot, and if still he didn't like it, Imperial being Imperial, he could go back to his old job; to customer relations, problem solving, research, letter-writing, where he had more time. It was that round-trip promise that kept him going.

Now, he speeds through his work-lists, cuts corners, knows more, gets better, yet every morning his race ends before the finish line is in sight. This afternoon he'll have to go back to these lists, he promises himself, but that won't happen. Still, he is now almost used to things. Not many months ago he just waited for the sound, and when it came, he could feel his body scream. Now, there's just a tiny scream.

The phone rings.

"Good morning, Esso Petroleum."

"I want to cancel my wife's card." It's the voice of an older man.

"Can I have your account number, please?"

"See, my wife left me and —"

"Your account number, please."

"Oh yes," and he gives him his number.

Before he can say anything else, Frank stops him, "Just a sec, please." A maze of numbers, acronyms and words flashes onto his screen. His eyes zero in on the top left corner. "Mr. _____?" and he reads off his name.

"That's right."

"What can I do for you?"

"Well you see, as I was saying, my wife left me and she's got a card that's in my name, and my son has one too. Anyway I asked her to return it, but I haven't got it yet." He sounds anxious and not at all sure of himself, as if he's been putting off this call for days, rehearsing his story and nerve. And because he hadn't thought about his card number, now he's out of synch, off balance, and a little flustered.

"Well, you know you're responsible till you get that card back."

"Oh, yes sir, I understand that."

"I can have it picked up if you like," Frank offers. "Do you want us to pick up your son's, too?"

"Oh, no, that's OK. He's in jail. He won't be out until March anyway."

Just one more detail in his story. Frank doesn't blink. "OK, I'll clean this up for you today."

"I mean, I've got a good credit rating eh, and I want to keep it." Frank is silent. The man wants to talk; he's out of things to say. "I'll make sure I won't use the card till after the divorce." His voice trails off. Frank has stopped listening.

"Yes sir, I can do that for you."

He has already punched the keys that have added more letters to the screen and sent a message to the dealers in the caller's area to pick up the card the next time the man's wife tries to use it. When he hangs up, the job is done; his phone burbles to life again.

"Good-morning, Esso Petroleum."

He sits with his left elbow propped on his desk, his left thumb pushing into his cheek, his left index finger resting against and running across his forehead. Hunched between his left shoulder and ear is the cradle of his phone on a small shoulder-piece, both his hands are free to work at his keyboard. He is a two-finger typist, using only the middle finger of each hand, mostly the right one. In his right hand is a yellow Bic pen, a small note pad is on the desk in front of him. He sits looking into the screen, as if looking back at him amongst its numbers is the face of the voice he hears. He looks puzzled when it puzzles him, angry when he is angered.

He doesn't wear a headset because it puts too much pressure on his ears; because "it looks silly." His voice is high-pitched and pleasant, but carefully unfamiliar. It's a voice that doesn't have all the answers, but is willing to listen; one that will try to work things out, but is not your buddy and you are not its. It is loud, but not aggressive-and-insistent loud, as if straining over the top of everyone and everything to be heard. It is unnecessarily-inappropriately-annoyingly loud, loud when it doesn't have to be, as if he is partly deaf though he isn't. When every office noise seems to blend with every other, his doesn't.

He works to his left, his body angled that way, his phone, calendar of billing cycles, reminder notes, out-basket and appointment calendar all there, his calendar entirely blank except for "Wynford Challenge" printed on the 17th and "Do Wendy's work-list" a few months before. On his right is his calculator, next to it his in-basket and further to the right a filing cabinet he rarely uses.

He reads the screen from top left to top right, to bottom right, bottom left, to middle left, then across, down, across, up, in increasingly smaller rectangles. It was the way his first trainer taught him, and now it's as instinctive to him as reading a page of type. On the top left is the card holder's number, name, and date the account was opened ("DO"); on the top right, its current status ("ST"), type ("CT"), use ("CU") (personal, business, etc.) and a behavioural score ("BS") estimating the probability the account will go bad (the lower the number rating, the higher the probability). Finally at the bottom right is a cluster of letters and digits, which, like a paint-by-numbers portrait, gives him his best card holder's profile.

Across the top of this jumble are thirteen letters, the first letter of each month with the first month repeated, in reverse chronological order so current behaviour is first ("SAJJMAMFJDNOS"), a pattern of personal history revealing itself behind it. Beside and beneath these letters are six horizontal columns measuring different behaviours. On top, "PH," pay habits, less than 30 days, 30 days, 60, 90, over 90, when a card holder pays his bill, "0," "1," "2," "3" or "4" in the code of the screen. Next down, "DH," dunning habit, for Joe Dun, the fifteenth-century bailiff of the Town of Lincoln, the number of collection letters sent and, read against the column above, how they affect behaviour. Next, "PS," pay schedule, "F," "M," "P," "U," or "C," how much of the bill a card holder pays, full, minimum, partial, "under" minimum, or credit; "NP," the number of purchases he has made, scaled from 1 (low) to 9, "PV," the purchase value of those items, and lastly, "NS," the number of NSF cheques he has sent.

He has been an Imperial credit-card holder himself ("DO") since "8802," February, 1988. He has never defaulted ("DD"), his account status ("ST") is "A1." His highest ever balance ("HIB") was $346.74; on his credit card last year he purchased ("PU LSTYR") $1,266.04 worth of Imperial Oil products. In his important bottom right corner, beside "PH" and "DH" are thirteen "0"s, beside "PS" four "C"s and nine "F"s, four credits and nine fulls, beside "NP" one "2" and twelve "1"s, beside "PV" a mixture of "2"s and "3"s. Along his bottom line, "NS," are thirteen more "0"s.

Another burble.

"Good-morning, Esso Petroleum."

"Hey, none of you guys know what the other's doin'?!" The voice is angry.

"Excuse me, sir?"

"I said, none of you guys know what you're doin'?! I got this bill that says I didn't pay and I paid last week. What goes on here?!"

"Can I have your account number, please?"

"I don't have it," he snaps.

"Sir, if you just check the top left corner of your bill —"

"Huh?" and he snarls off his number. "Look, I paid —"

"Just a sec please."

"I got this bill —"

"You are Mr. _____?"

"Uh huh."

"I see your balance here but I see nothing about a cheque. When did you send it?"

"I don't know, last week, four, five days ago." More information, not even certain about it this time, he's beginning to lose his fight and beginning to know it.

"Well, we wouldn't have received it yet, sir. It takes five days just to get across the city, so from Saint John —" Frank has won. Then graciously he backs off. "There's nothing I can do about the post office." Nothing *either* of us can do, no sir.

The man is reduced to a murmur. He had been feeling fine this morning, then he received his bill and everything was suddenly wrong. Everything he hadn't let bother him in his life, that he had put away, locked up, put under control — injustice, arrogance, ineptitude, powerlessness — came rushing out. He was furious; yet he was happy,

gleeful. Alive. *He was right and they were wrong.* He had them.
He could give them back everything that all his life they
had given him. On his bill was only a phone number and
a name, "F. Bloye," and "F. Bloye," he knew, would just spew
out stupid, corporately correct excuses which would only
make him madder, *and* more right. He had them. It was
their stupidity, *their* ineptitude, he had every right to feel as
he did and say as he'd say.

Then it got confused. There was another story. Maybe it
was more his fault than theirs. But then Frank had let him
off the hook. The post office, that was it. They were victims
in common.

"No, nothing any of us can do," the man grumbles,
everything under lock and key again.

Whenever he wants to separate himself from his callers,
when he thinks their problems are their fault and wants
them to deal with them, he invokes "the system." "There's
nothing I can do now," he might say. "It's out of my hands.
If you don't pay, *the system* will automatically send your
account to collection," though he knows he can stop it if
he wants. But when he thinks that what has happened is
just the way things are, he introduces the other system, the
post office, and shares their troubles with them.

Another call comes in, another bill, another cheque has
crossed in the mail. Another Imperial-Texaco mix-up.
Within the first few seconds of nearly every story he knows
the rest, but they don't know he knows and it wouldn't matter if they did. He can't interrupt. People call for all sorts
of reasons, not just to resolve their credit-card problems.
Some want to talk, to anyone, taking any human voice for
human contact. Some need to get angry, some to win and
some to lose, some need the relief of working down personal checklists, to feel the achievement of getting things
done. But whatever the reason, it is theirs. *They* made the
phone call, it's *their* problem, *their* complaint, *their* story to
tell. Don't interrupt.

Knowing how their stories will end, their words come at

him in super-slow motion. His impatience is palpable, his need to finish everyone's story nearly irresistible. Yet he resists. Then he takes his callers back through their stories, what happened and why, what has been done, what needs to be done yet.

These are real-life histories coming into his earpiece. These voices owe money. They are in some kind of trouble. Most have gone through calls like this many times before, they know how the system works, they are aggressive, take the offensive, try to control the conversation. They admit nothing, offer nothing. Pushed into a final corner, they promise easily; it's more water off their backs. They feel nothing because the system feels nothing for them. They say yes because that's how the game is played and when they hang up, it's no.

For some, this is new, humiliating, terrifying. They don't know the system. For them, it's the first step on the way to jail. For them, it *is* personal. Fundamental. A matter of blood and bone and character. They are truly, deeply sorry, it has never happened before and won't happen again. Not because the same thing can't arise, because they can't live with the way they feel right now. They may learn.

It's difficult not to get hardened, not to turn cynical and cold. "Time to talk to the animals," radio phone-in hosts come to say when they've done their jobs too long. His are the bad-news people, the "dirtbags" or "scuzzballs," his co-workers call them, the 6,000 out of 100,000 who are trouble. The good ones get billed and pay. They are left to go on with their lives, their reward is the system's indifference. His are the bad apples or people with bad-apple problems. They lie, play him for a fool, abuse him and hold him in contempt, yet he is to treat their calls as if he's two people. One, filled with the experience of having heard all their stories before, the other, deaf to the inevitable patterns of those stories which turn every next person into a category, a box, a bloodless voice.

Like radio phone-in hosts, collectors get the audiences they deserve.

Another burble. "Give me a break," he mutters. It's the first sign of impatience of the day.

"I'm looking for Mr. Boyle," the voice says. Brittle and frail, it belongs to an elderly woman.

"I'm Mr. *Bloye*. How can I help you?"

"Mr. Boyle," she repeats. She is trying very hard to keep her composure. "I have just received your letter —" As background is about to turn to detail, her voice begins to quaver. Before she loses it entirely, he stops her, "Can I have your account number, please?" He punches in the numbers, "Just a sec, please." His screen fills. "Miss _____?" "Yes," she answers. He scans her coded story: *A single woman, had her account a long time, good customer, small volumes, small amounts, must be a spinster, no problems, everything paid up, a little late last month, a letter sent out, no big deal, her cheque just in.* He knows what he's about to hear.

"Do you know how upsetting it is to get a letter like this?" she can no longer stop herself. "I've never had a problem like this before. Never." In her voice is anger and fear. Her age, her gender, her circumstances, a letter like this, it strikes *dead centre* at all her vulnerabilities. Suddenly she's too old, she can't cope, what's to become of her now?

"I always pay my bills on time. You can call any of my credit cards. You have to when you live alone like I do. Now this won't go on my record, will it? It's very important to me. I always pay my bills on time."

Anger turns to confusion and hurt. "Can't you just send out a letter saying you didn't receive my payment, and wonder why? You can see I always pay my bills on time. Then I get a letter like this. You tell me I might lose my card. Do you know how upsetting that is?!" The system assumes wilfulness, not mistake, inadvertence or circumstance. Not honesty. If a bill isn't paid, it's a bill being avoided. It's stalling, juggling, gamesmanship. You're trying to get away with it and I know it, I'm trying to get you and you know it.

Nothing personal. You win a little, I win a lot and always in the end. For games players, it's an exhilarating chase. The rest get hurt.

"Well, m'am, it was a very mild letter, actually the mildest we send. It's just a reminder, really." He seems taken aback. Years ago when he was on the other side of this game, in debt, he got letters like this and almost got used to them. Now, he just punches them up, nothing personal. He can't remember the last time he actually read one, although he has heard complaints. Even the Texaco people were surprised how "stern" they were. We should really rewrite them, he thinks, except the "we" who would get that done is way out there somewhere, deaf and blind to what's going on, motionless unless someone like him gets him moving. Sometimes he goes to his supervisor, but he can't go very often; and though he's feeling slightly guilty now, it isn't enough to stop him in his tracks, interrupt the burble-to-burble rhythm of his day, the evenness of his mood, to break down *his* defences. Like this old woman from Kingston, he has to cope too.

He tries to soothe her as best and as quickly as he can, and moves to another call.

In the next hour, he gets another call for "Mr. Boyle," one for "Mr. Bloyle," and two for "Mr. Lloyd." One caller swore continuously, but not *at* him, so he didn't mind. He brought up the post office only once, with the same useful result. Two of his callers said they had been out of town: "Like I've been in northern Quebec eh," said one, so he hadn't gotten his bill and hadn't paid but would have a cheque in the mail before the day was out. The other was less concerned. He gave Frank his account number before he could even ask for it; not a good sign. "I've been away, you know," the man said. "I'm just trying to put myself together. Like when you come back, you gotta put things back together, you know." He knew. "So next week you'll pay the full amount," Frank said, interrupting his story. "Well no, like you can't do everything at once, you know.

Half next week, half when my next bill comes."

Among his other callers was a judge. It began as a "Look here, I'm a judge, I make it a point of keeping a perfect credit record" kind of call, until Frank pointed out his account was sixty days overdue and his record had been anything but perfect the last thirteen months. He did so respectfully, of course. Back on track, they worked out an easy resolution. When they were done, more as statement than question, the judge said, "When my bill is paid, you will erase all this."

"No sir, I can't do that," he said, and the line turned chilly again. A screen like this may be the most penetrating history a person has. When a mistake is made and the system makes it, Frank can change it. Whole lines of a person's life can be wiped away, rewritten, *just like that*, a whole new story can take its place. But not if it's the customer's mistake. "Sorry, buddy," he is saying to himself. "The past is done. You can't change that no matter who you are. History is history."

He doesn't always keep his composure. Yesterday he lost a customer, all over thirty-eight dollars and he knows he will hear about it. The call started simply enough, then the man got belligerent and he got stubborn and the rest followed too easily. He had been ninety days overdue on his account and made payment at his bank, the man said, but there was nothing on the screen to indicate that. This made no sense to him because, like everyone else, he assumed bank payments were credited instantly, which they're not. Frank tried to explain, but by this time everything he said sounded to the man like an ass-covering lie. Things would get worse.

Frank couldn't reinstate the card even if he wanted to, because it had just expired. The man needed a new one. But for a new one, his account had to be paid up (which to the man it was). Frank said he'd issue a new card when his payment arrived; in ten days he'd have it. The man wanted it now. Frank said he couldn't do that. The man said he could, that he was only "playing by the book." He was. But he was going to keep playing by the book because he didn't feel like getting him a card any faster. He had been so obnoxious. He knows his supervisor will tell him to cut the card, but there's no way. If he wants him to have it, he can cut it himself.

If there is one criticism that keeps coming up on his evaluations, it's that he plays too much by the book. He is a "black and white" kind of guy, his supervisors say, he likes the security of rules, sometimes he just doesn't know when they should be bent or broken. And if some of that has to do with insecurities which probably will never change much, some has to do with his own sense of propriety. His own values, which are the real book he plays by.

Late in the morning, two calls come in back to back. The first is from an old woman, a retiree, who owes more than six hundred dollars on her account. She isn't very well, it seems, though she doesn't say so directly, and her husband, who had always done the family's finances, isn't able to do them any more. So she does her best, and at times he does forget they don't have as much money as they used to but, she says with affection, he is her husband and what can she say. She is trying to find a way to pay off the debt and Frank is trying to help her. She wonders if sixty dollars a month for ten months would be OK? He seems troubled, yet is reluctant to push too hard.

"You don't think you could do better than that?"

As cheerful as before, she replies, "No well, I don't want to promise anything I can't do, you know. If I promise one hundred dollars and can't send it —" her voice trails off.

"OK, then," he says in a proper tone, "so you'll send me ten post-dated cheques. Now you realize with interest charges you won't be able to clean everything up in ten months."

She says she understands. She will write out the cheques and mail them today. "Oh no, I can't mail them today," she scolds herself. "I need some stamps and can't get out. I need somebody to do it for me, you know."

He says the end of the week will be fine. The next call doesn't come in right away, he has several seconds for his mood to cloud over. This call is from a much younger woman, a single mother with a young family. A quick look at the screen and he can see she's in trouble.

"Your outstanding balance is more than thirteen hundred dollars," he says, his voice pitching higher and louder. "You paid only fifty dollars last month. Your service charges alone were twenty-six dollars. Your bill only went down twenty-four dollars. Can't you do a little better?" He seems to be asking more for her sake than his.

"My husband has left me," she says, her voice anxious and hurried. "He's the one who ran up my Esso card. I'm just doing what I can."

He nods. Into his screen and through his ear-piece, he can see a thirty-five-year-old woman who looks ten years older. He will agree to the fifty dollars a month for a few months, he tells her, but will keep an eye on her account. He punches the information into the system, in fifteen days its numbers will flash back onto his screen. As he hangs up, he mutters, "She's not goin' anywhere. Fifty bucks a month. She'll never get it paid off." And shakes his head.

It takes so little. One misstep which leads to another, and another, and he feels for them, and gets angry at them. It's the anger of a fellow-traveller who saw the light and cured himself. Can't they see what they are doing? Don't they realize they can't get away with it, that everything will come crashing down, the harder and more unforgivingly the longer they wait? And there's a part of him that believes they *should* be punished, they did wrong, that punishment is necessary for learning and healing; and a part of him that gets angry when they don't seem to feel the pain or the immensity of their wrong, when *maybe*, they think, *maybe* they might just get away with it, and *not* be punished. That would be so unfair. He had to go through it. He had to live its hobbled life, carry its wisdom and stand judged against it. "Live within thy means"; "Neither a borrower, nor a lender be." They need the wooden spoon.

Forty-five days in arrears, he sends them a note telling them to contact him, and they don't, and the numbers on his screen go higher. "They just live by the card," he mutters and shakes his head. And his screen, he knows, is only one of many, his card one in a whole deck, Eaton's, Sears, The Bay, Canadian Tire, Shell, Petro-Canada, Sunoco, Visa, MasterCard, whoever will give them one. Each month, juggling minimum payments, robbing Peter to pay Paul, the squeakiest wheel getting the grease, the total going higher. The house of cards about to collapse.

The numbers, which were climbing in slow, steady increments, suddenly leap upwards. They've been cut off somewhere else. Now everything is going on their Imperial card. They get a consolidation loan from the bank, everything looks clearer, feels cleaner and better, they keep buying; it's one more charge to pay. He talks to them: just having a bad stretch, had a job interview today, everything looks good, wife's been sick, should be at work soon, trying to turn the corner, almost there, everything'll be fine. Next month.

"I used to think I was the poorest guy in the world," he says. "Now I see these people . . ." So sometimes he is too inflexible. There *is* a price to pay. There must be.

It is almost noon; he needs a break. Another call comes in, he thinks about redirecting it, then picks it up. It is the voice of a younger man. He is uncomfortable, anxious, afraid, and trying to sound older, calmer and too much in control, he tries too hard. Every explanation begins a story and every story gets him in deeper. He keeps wanting to start again.

"Anyway, what really happened," he says for the third or fourth time, "ahh ahh you know, is that I'm not workin'." With a new beginning point, his next words tumble out easily. "I'm very sorry, you know. You know, but I'm not going back to my old job. It was —"

Finally Frank interrupts, "Have you applied for UIC?"

"I'm not — oh oh, UIC! Sure, I've applied. But I, you know, I'm not sure how it all works. You know. But we're gonna get this bill all cleared up. You know, soon as possible."

"I'm going to have to restrict your card until then," he tells him.

"Hey, I understand that. I understand." Feeling he has survived the worst, he becomes less willing to please. "I mean, until I get Christmas done I may only pay small amounts, you know. But then we'll get this done, eh? You know."

He's had it. "I hate people who say, 'you know,'" he mutters as he hangs up the phone. "All it was with this guy, 'you know. You know.' He just doesn't want to get the story out."

It's time for lunch.

He likes it out there, on that floor. The people he works with, their noise and energy, their bitchy, whiny, funny spirit. They make him laugh. He is far from being at their emotional centre, co-workers don't find themselves drifting over, hanging around, leaning over top his work station. When someone is bursting with gossip, he isn't the first one they look for. But that's OK for him and them. They know each other and have learned not to expect more than the other can give. To some, he may seem a "loner." He eats lunch by himself when he eats, and reads by himself when he doesn't. In company, he laughs, smiles, conveys a gentle, genial, easy-goingness, still the happy-go-lucky roly-poly kid of long ago. He uses the techniques of closeness as his way of blending in, getting along, hiding, keeping his distance. If you don't look happy everyone wants to know why; smile and the world leaves you alone. But that's allowed. Here, he can be what he wants to be: around the action, a fly on the wall of whatever goes on.

Most around him here are women; nearly all the men are several years younger. Most are married and have kids; a few are divorced. The women are better dressed than the men. Most of their spouses work, many at Imperial, and

when their incomes are added together most earn about
the average Canadian household wage. Most have their
own houses and years of mortgage payments ahead, the
older ones, like him, live on the outer edges of Toronto's
central and eastern suburbs, in Scarborough and North
York, the younger ones, raised with the same expectations,
have been pushed by housing prices beyond suburban
boundaries to Ajax, Pickering, Whitby and east, fifty kilometres and more, to the once sleepy, rural towns of his
youth. The company's rising stars are not here.

He had always been careful to keep separate his work and
home lives. He wouldn't bring home work or talk about it at
dinner the way his father did. He made it a point never to
socialize with people from the office. When Carolyn started
at Imperial, they made a deal. It was his idea. At work, they
wouldn't be husband and wife, but co-workers. They
wouldn't talk to each other unless as co-workers they
needed to, they wouldn't eat lunch together. He had seen it
too many times before. "Husbands and wives drive in together, take coffee together, eat lunch together, go for a
smoke together, drive home together. It's just not healthy."

One day last June, however, he had an idea. He talked to
Carolyn about it. She was reluctant at first, but slowly
agreed. They were both working with the same people now,
maybe together they should get to know them better. The
next day at work, he sent around a note asking anyone
interested in a pool party to sign up. He was careful to
make the note look like a party "feeler," not an invitation,
so if the whole idea came to seem foolish, he had a way out.
Fifteen people signed the note. He was disappointed. But
after sifting through dark thoughts, he decided that, vacation time and all, fifteen wasn't bad, and went ahead.

He asked them not to bring anything, instead he and
Carolyn collected five dollars from each of them to pay for
food. He made about fifty invitations with directions to
their house and passed them out, giving those who hadn't
yet signed up another chance. By July 9th, three days

before the party, he had collected eighty dollars and sixteen responses, only three from former Texaco employees. He and Carolyn went out that night and bought hamburger meat, buns, vegetables, everything they needed. While he was at work, she, Janine and Stephanie spent the next few days preparing salads and vegetable platters, repairing lawn chairs, doing what needed to be done. Everything was ready. At work on the 12th, everyone was talking it up. It looked good. He could picture the whole scene: people milling about his backyard, lazing in the pool. There was lots to drink and eat, lots of talk and laughter.

Only nine showed up. The weather didn't cooperate; it was cold, but it wasn't bad enough to imagine that that was the only reason. They sat around one table, nobody went swimming, the vegetable plate "wasn't a success," they had too many hamburgers and too much salad. This was what he had been afraid of.

Two weeks later, back at work after his holidays, he couldn't help but bring up the subject. In case anyone had any ill-feelings, which they hadn't, for a bad party, which it wasn't, he'd turn on himself first. Make himself the proper brunt for something others hadn't noticed or had certainly forgotten. When he was finished, he decided never to have a company party again.

He finds his spot on a park bench behind 90 Wynford. It is a bright, early fall day. He doesn't eat lunch now. Stephanie has noticed his thickening middle, another problem of a pool, so he reads. Thirty minutes later, he reaches the end of a chapter, reinserts his bookmark, and looks at his watch. His timing is perfect. One block of time ending, the next about to begin. He looks around, a smile on his face, some of his co-workers hang about the back door dragging the last drags on their cigarettes. His smile fades. His body resettles on the bench, he opens his book again. Just a few more pages, he thinks.

9

In the year and a half since the merger, change has been everywhere. Nothing has felt settled, everything feels on the way to *somewhere*, none of them knows where. There have been rumours, and because the merger was so massive, so far beyond their own experience, because decisions are being taken on things they know nothing about in places distant from them, everything is believable. They were just getting used to new Texaco and Imperial faces when still newer faces began appearing on their floor, wearing the kind of identical, earnest expressions they didn't recognize and suits they never wore. Something was happening. All the company handouts, so many more than before, their tone so different, more soothing, more inspirational, *why?* And now they're being told to read those handouts because they're important, even read them *on the job* if they need the time, which makes them laugh, "Excuse me while my phone is ringing off my desk. I'd like an hour to look at this stuff."

They don't read them, of course, now or later, for what do they have to do with them? Things are changing, things are going to change, there's nothing *they* can do about it. They aren't bitter, that's just the way things are and for them have always been and always will be. It's the rest that bothers them, the task forces, committees, meetings, even more than before, the company's overwrought solicitude. Who does it think it's fooling? *I'm* supposed to know about these changes so *I* can decide whether *I* want to work with this new Imperial Oil? I am an empowered worker, I own my own job, I am a true stakeholder in all I do; I am the good, productive worker which the future demands, on which the future depends? Maybe. But don't tell me about empowerment now. I do what I'm told and do what I have to do, it's the way I've been trained. Here, everywhere, all my life. Twenty years ago, I felt empowered about a lot of things. Now I know. And now I'm so out of practice I wouldn't know where to start. And you don't either. Every word you speak says "empowerment," every action, every instinct in your corporate body says "control."

So the men put their handouts in a drawer and the women put theirs in their purses. And without reading them they know what's in them, and about that they're neither soothed nor inspired.

To those on the floor like him and Carolyn, things are a mess. To those who write these handouts, everything is "on course." They might both be right, but they can't both be right for long. It may be that big mergers are so complicated, disrupt so many things for so many people for so long that merger experts have developed a completely *other* sense of time. They've learned to stand so far ahead of the present that out of the dust of its collisions they can detect increments of movement, a tiny vector arrow straining forward. In the long run we may all be dead, they seem to say, but we all succeed.

So they have done their jobs and the merger is a success. And in their caps another proud feather to parade before any future client hungry to merge. To anyone else, that's not good enough. They have a business to run. Every collision and cloud of dust is an ulcerating glitch in the way of getting out a product, increasing market share, turning a bigger profit. But eighteen months into the merger, though their patience has been tested, still they trust the process they have set in motion. They must.

Others don't. Their perspective can be no more distant than the voices in their ears, and they can't stop remembering how it was. Until the merger, until Texaco. Everything was fine then. They were Imperial, and that was all that needed to be said. What kind of company do you work for? How is it doing? Why would you want to work there? Ever think of going someplace else? Ever regret? To neighbours, families, to themselves, they never had to explain. Imperial did things right. *Everyone knew.*

They needed just to do their jobs because Imperial would do its job. Hire the right people, make the right decisions, find oil when oil needed to be found. Imperial had discovered Leduc. Imperial was first into the oil sands. It was the one affiliate *not* wholly owned by Exxon. And wasn't it Imperial's Chairman, Jack Armstrong, certainly not the all-American boy, who had told a doubtful Exxon about the oil sands, "Thank you for your advice, but I think we're going to invest anyway." That's the way Imperial did things.

The first, the best and always. As kids, the men who now rule Imperial from its head offices at One Eleven spent wintertime Saturday nights in front of their televisions, with their fathers and mothers, often sisters and certainly brothers, watching "Hockey Night in Canada." They remember as vividly as any of the players the smiling, good-neighbour face of Murray Westgate, in his crisp Esso uniform and angled Esso hat, his snappy salute of confidence, and his words to them each week, "Always look to Imperial [slight pause] for the best." Just as they insisted that their mothers buy the cereal or corn syrup their heroes used, they wanted only hockey's gasoline for their families' cars. It was the beginning of a lifetime habit.

Other companies would struggle, disappear, be taken over, Imperial would go on and they would go on with it. As long as there was oil in the ground, so long as the sun shone from the sky. Imperial paid more and offered better benefits, listened to their problems, treated them as if they, and what they did, mattered. Why would they go anywhere else? Many had fathers who had worked with the company, some had mothers and spouses, many, as kids, had had summer jobs, some had gone to university on company scholarships. It was Uncle Gen who had gotten him in, just as he got his own son into the company, just as Frank had gotten in Carolyn. Uncle Gen had been at Imperial forty-three years. At ninety-one years of age, twenty-eight years after his retirement and years after his death, his wife, Frank's Aunt Clara, still gets *The Reporter*, because Imperial still sends it to her, and she still reads it.

The Imperial family and the families of Imperial. It recruited the best from the best schools, the top 10 per cent, *Imperial material*, and from them, and from the thousands across the country hired to support them, who weren't stars, it wanted something more. Good people, decent people, people with *values*. People who cared about family, community, country, who like them would care about their company. Because this was no short walk in the woods ahead. At stake was a full-time, lifetime job, from school-leaving until retirement. If they stuck with the company and worked hard, Imperial would stick with them.

To work side by side for so many years, they would need to get along, feel comfortable, be compatible. In style and culture, Imperial would need to be collegial, genial, methodical, patient, as frictionless as Teflon or so it had to seem. There could be no big winners or big losers, no face lost, no bridges burned, everyone had to look good. They would have to tip-toe around each other's feelings, their messages subtle, beneath the surface, behind the back, gracious, agile, seemly. In time, they would come to think alike, be alike, be each other's best friends not because they had to, because they liked each other. They were each other's "kind of people." Through countless, timeless meetings, they would need to listen to and respect each other's opinions. Differences would be met like an airplane meets a runway, slowly, moving in the same direction, easing together, gently touching down. Decisions would be group decisions, everyone to be heard out, everyone to be "on board." If that took time, it was a necessary price easily paid. The company was profitable, there was oil in the ground. Those frustrated and suffocated by this would weed themselves out and go.

These were values from another time. As if the product of years of living on the land, knowing its hardships and plenty, knowing its defiant uncertainties. Every Imperial chairman since he joined the company had been from an agricultural region, all but one from a small town. Bill Twaits, born in Galt, Ontario, raised in Sarnia; Jack Armstrong from Dauphin, Manitoba; Don McIvor, Winnipeg; Arden Haynes, Esk, Saskatchewan. Armstrong, McIvor and Haynes, all graduates of the University of Manitoba. They understood about the fruits of the land, those above and those below, and knew if there were any certainties in life on that land, they had to do with family, community, loyalty, hard work. In them was a sense, more than history, of continuity and destiny, of the connectedness of things. Today owes itself to yesterday is responsible to tomorrow. What you reap, you will have surely sowed.

Even down on the floor where he is, away from the teeth-baring action of One Eleven, where work can be tedious and routine, where privilege is neither an experience had nor a concept understood, where a job is not a career, that same belief persists. For all these lifetime employees, there develops an attachment, a loyalty, something deeper than habit, a true identification. They will work longer at Imperial than their kids live at home, than they live in one house, in one neighbourhood, one city, longer than most friendships and many marriages survive. They will work at tasks more time-consuming, reward-giving and mood-determining than nearly everything else they do. "It's the best thing I ever did," they will say, as Frank says, of his decision to join the company, as his wife and children listen on and no one interrupts. Father, mother, spouse, family man, Imperial becomes part of identity itself.

Yet since the merger, things haven't felt the same. All the new people around and the different ways they do things, ways they brought with them from Texaco that they think are right and better too. The little incidents — two weeks ago Irene's coat disappeared, last week Angie lost one hundred dollars from her purse. Things like that never happened before. For old Imperial people, it's been like bringing strangers into their home for a visit, opening the front door, and finding the living room left a mess by their kids. They don't need to impress these outsiders, but they want to, and now they can't show them any more what made them proud, nor make them understand. We're really not this way. You should have been here last year and every other year, *before* the merger. The outsiders are inside and have seen for themselves.

And they are shocked. That richly greener pasture down Wynford Drive, the "Cadillac" of the industry; and they can't and they won't hide their feelings. It's not how they thought they would react, nor what the company needs of them in this confused post-merger time. Yet with a deeper, longer stake in the past, they eke out revenge on what was *them* and now is *us*, to win yesterday's battles, to be prouder of what they surely were than what they are not yet and may never be. They need their jobs, yet this perverse little part of them wants only satisfaction.

At Texaco, it had been one long boot camp, and like boot camp survivors, they resent anyone who has never had to survive it. They want to test them, see what they are really like. You never had to live in that big competitive world, they say, because you were *it*. You always looked down your nose at me, the way I did things, my ethics. You never approved. Nice, tolerant, generous Imperial, but now *your* world has gotten bigger. Just how long are you going to listen and respect now? Just how nice and tolerant and generous are you going to be? I want to see how *you* do.

It was a merger that wouldn't fail because Imperial would see to it. As many as three-quarters of U.S. mergers had failed, but Imperial Oil and Texaco were too good a match.

Imperial needed low-cost oil reserves to balance its expensive Cold Lake reserves, Texaco had them. It had a modern refinery and long-life gas reserves. It was stronger in the east, Imperial stronger in the west. The merger made too much sense. It would be made to work. Even the companies' work "cultures" which might seem so antagonistic, black and white, Jekyll and Hyde, with a slight twist of a receptive eye might seem "complementary."

Each was what the other wasn't and needed to be. Together they would be it all. Texaco, hard-driving, "lean and mean," an American company in Canada to do business. *Period.* To make money. *Period.* To make the most at the least cost and return the most to head office in White Plains, New York. Industry spokesman, community leader, corporate model and good citizen, *why?* Those are just smoke screens to hide the soft, insecure mind, to smudge the bottom line. To win the perception game. To make everyone think you are doing a great job with none of the pain of doing it. Profits are the test. Texaco was a "shareholders' company." And inside, bosses bossed and employees, overworked and underpaid, did what they were told. And if they got it wrong, they did it again and again until they got it right. Ready, fire . . . aim.

Ready, aim, aim, aim . . . That was Imperial. Don't fire until it doesn't matter any more. A people company, an employees' company. But together with Texaco . . . that would be something.

It would be a "model" merger, a "breakthrough" merger, Imperial said. And to do it right, it brought in the best merger minds to help. They imagined five possible "merger outcomes." A simple "sum of parts," Imperial + Texaco = Imperial + Texaco. For all its money and time, not what the company wanted. On either side of this median, an outcome slightly worse, "lowest common denominator," or slightly better, "best of both"; and on the outside, the extremes, both possible, "disaster" or "breakthrough synergy." To Imperial, why not the best?

And this was a "merger," Imperial insisted. It was the far bigger company, it had put up the money and bought all the stock. But its insistence was more than a generous gesture of welcome to Texaco employees. It was symbolic. Texaco Canada might cease to exist but what it stood for must not. Imperial needed a dose of Texaco, some bottom-line toughness, an edge, a splash of cold water from the outside real world. If Imperial couldn't quite generate that from the inside, it would buy it, to infect itself if possible, to stand side by side if necessary. More than the sum of two greater parts, they would create a bubbling, boiling synergy, some new *third* way uniquely their own, and greater still.

It would not be easy. With its consultant experts Imperial put together a merger plan of near-unbelievable dimension and complexity. Bob Peterson, then Imperial's president and chief operating officer, headed the Merger Steering Committee, a senior person from each of the old companies were his committee co-chairs. Certain basics were agreed upon, the new company's name, "Imperial Oil Limited," its primary brand name, "Esso," its corporate values, Imperial's, etc. Beyond that, everything was on the table.

Reporting to this Steering Committee were four "Leadership Teams," one for each segment of the business: upstream (exploration), downstream (refining and marketing) and corporate; the fourth was communications. Reporting to these teams were several "Functional Teams" (human resources, tax, etc.) and "Business Line Teams" (retail fuel oil, etc.), which in turn created "Synergy Teams," *five hundred* of them, to define "Issues" raised by the merger and how each might be resolved, not to *status quo ante* of either company, but to achieve a "breakthrough opportunity." Each Issue was assigned a priority: immediate, high, medium, low. Related Issues were grouped as "Projects," defined and given to appropriate Synergy Teams to investigate, analyze and offer their recommendations. These recommendations then passed to the appropriate Functional/Business Line Teams for approval, or to a Leadership Team or several Leadership Teams, to the Steering Committee or some other higher authority, which in turn developed an Implementation Plan, again with definitions, responsibilities, timing and relative priorities.

Where Issues overlapped affecting more than one Team, a separate category was created, "Joint Issues," and another, "Referral Issues," where one Team was affected predominantly. For each such issue, a separate Synergy Team was created. All Issues were compiled on a master list, numbered and entered into a computer database, the "Issues System," managed and operated by Issues Coordinators. Project System Coordinators and Data Analysts did the same for the Projects System. More than five thousand Issues and six hundred Projects were dealt with in all.

But any process is only as good as the people in it, and what did Team members know about mergers? Conditioned to things as they were, to change in tiny increments along broad, well-trodden paths, what did they know of contorting their minds, leaping ahead in all directions to who knows where for "breakthrough results"? So Imperial hired "change management" consultants to conduct "Capability Development" seminars. It hired "systems people" to monitor the merger process. Experts in understanding and evaluating systems, they proved experts in *creating* them too.

Communications were critical. The challenge: how to make informed the 90 per cent of workers not directly involved in a process which was determining their futures, or which they feared was. If no one gave answers to the questions in their heads, they would provide their own. Information *would* flow, employees *would* talk, they would speculate, worry, imagine and create the truth out of all manner of things that seemed plausible enough to enough of them. They would distract and upset each other until their work was affected. The question for the company was which information and whose information would prevail? Rumour and misunderstanding; or some consistent, constructive, official version?

The day of the merger, a "Day One" information kit was distributed to all employees. In it was a letter from Imperial Chairman Arden Haynes, welcoming Texaco employees into the Imperial "family," an outline of merger plans and a button with three stylized faces, a red one for Texaco, blue for Imperial, a grey one (grey?!) to symbolize the newly merged company. On it were the words, "Joining Forces." There would be "Joining Forces" bulletins, about two a week, offering merger updates, posted on bulletin boards and distributed to each employee. There was a "Questions-and-Answers Hotline," a video for managers to help them answer employee questions. Employees could punch up information from the computer on all Issues and Projects. There were Open-House Sessions, ten in all, held on company time, where employees could speak face to face with merger leaders. There were thirty-nine Employee Focus Groups measuring attitudes to the merger and the effectiveness of merger strategies.

Everything had to be done 'according to an urgent timetable. Phase I of the "Four Phase Merger Approach," "conceptual planning," one month: merger guidelines set, top-level organization created, etc. Phase II, "detailed planning," one to two months: merger teams created, Issues defined and prioritized, Projects coordinated, master plan developed. Phase III, "short-term implementation," five to six months: high-priority Issues set on fast track. Phase IV, "long-term implementation," one to three years: a single merged organization.

As Teams did their work, upper management created the organization. Business would be conducted with an eye to two scenarios. In the immediate ten months post-merger, consideration had to be given to the practicalities of transition and the realities of merger promises made, most importantly the commitment to no employee layoffs.

Second, three or so years into the future, after all the struc-
tures and functions had been integrated, synergies gained,
after regular and extraordinary merger-generated attrition had cut the workforce, the "vision" organization.

Who would do what in this new company wasn't yet clear,
but soon would be. The Workforce Integration Synergy
Team designed a process to match "employee skills and
preferences with the work required to achieve the business
goals of the organization." Each job would go to the can-
didate best qualified. Each employee would set down
career and personal choices which were entered into the
Workforce Integration Information System and matched
against job openings. Within a year, all employees would
know their roles.

It wouldn't happen, just as most things in this process
didn't happen when timetables said they would. As some
deadlines slipped, many more slipped, and many more
because of them until finally new deadlines were imposed
which had nothing to do with the work to be done and
everything to do with the time that was backing up, frustration that was building, and the simple, urgent need to
get things done. There were other setbacks. The merger
had to be reviewed by the federal government. Investment
Canada offered its approval the following day. The Bureau
of Competition Policy took longer. The new Imperial
would have a heavy concentration of service stations in
Atlantic Canada, and control nearly half the refining
capacity in Ontario. The Bureau allowed upstream integration to proceed (exploration, etc.), but required the
downstream business (refining and marketing) to be held
separately until a final ruling, which took almost a year.

One more straw for the camel's creaking back. "Minor
issues," the consultants called them, scores of them, office
moves, parking locations, things that create "anxiety, stress
and dysfunctional fears." Determined to do the right thing,
Imperial expanded an Employee Assistance Program to
provide special counselling on merger matters. Everyone

was supportive, sympathetic. "I am very aware of how hard people are working on the merger," Arden Haynes said in a special merger issue of *The Reporter*. "I can assure you that all your efforts are appreciated and valued." But as the months passed, the straw piled higher and the phones kept ringing.

Everything Imperial had done made sense, except human beings make their own sense. They were being counselled now when they weren't before, but before, they didn't need counselling. They were being advised from inside and out, trained to turn their minds inside out to think different thoughts, were taught how to change. They were sympathized with, their feelings were understood, they were supposed to feel grateful. Wasn't the merger great? Weren't they now so much better off with their new mix of low-cost oil reserves and high-cost Cold Lake reserves? Wasn't that Nanticoke refinery a blessing? Their joy was not apparent. And perhaps it would have been wonderful to be informed of merger happenings if they had read what was there to inform them, which they might have if they believed that reading them would have made the slightest difference to them. But why spend time reading what seemed to them only explanations for why they had so much less time to do their work in the first place?

Did ten new Synergy Teams mean the merger was going ten new teams better? They *knew* how the merger was going. Their customers told them. And those customers didn't care about any merger, they wanted service. They wanted to *tell* Frank and everyone else that their precious system that was always right, that had just told them what every other system had always told them, that they had screwed up *again*, hadn't paid on time *again*, and should be treated like criminals, is wrong, that *it* screwed up, and you, the ears of that system, are stupid and wrong . . .

They knew. They weren't Team leaders whose only job was the merger, who had no accounts receivable, no concrete measures that let everyone know if they were doing their jobs, who spent their time defining Issues and

Projects, drawing up recommendations and timetables;
whose real job was to tell those above them that everything
was fine so that those above *them* could tell those above
them that everything was fine, and so on and so on. Everything had to be fine for them, that was their job. And if it
wasn't fine, that meant trouble for everyone above them
who had trusted them and who would oversee their
futures, which would mean extra time and money spent to
set things right, which time and money no one had nor
wanted to hear or think about. But if everything was fine,
the merger would be a success, Team leaders would be
happy, reputations would be made, futures would continue on track and, no excuses, day-to-day work would be
done profitably and well, and if it wasn't, it wasn't their
fault. *They* did *their* job.

Imperial's experts also advised there would be considerable attrition. People would be unwilling to put up with
new systems and jobs, and leave. So while the merger pro-
duced massive overlap in operations and people, Imperial
could promise no staff layoffs, satisfy its external (and
internal) audiences, the government and public, and still
be safe. Attrition would do the job for it.

But almost no one left. The economy was strong when
the merger was announced, when final government
approval came it was falling into recession. The Canada-
U.S. Free Trade Agreement was generating its first fallout,
layoffs had become the copycat pattern of the day. New
jobs would be hard to come by, so people hesitated. They
had heard stories of other companies, their mergers and
broken promises. They knew there were too many of them.
for the work to be done, that sooner or later commitment
or not, Imperial would cut back. So they stayed and waited.
If they had to go, it would be with a big severance package
in their pockets.

This was a watershed time for Imperial. The merger and
Free Trade Agreement had caused within it a fundamental self-examination now beginning to pick up steam.

Where was it going? What would it need to be? How would it need to change? Its corporate body already exposed and open from the merger, it brought in more consultants to poke around. McKinsey & Company was hired. This new process at times dovetailed with and complemented the ongoing merger process, at times ran parallel to it, more often it confused it, overwhelmed and overburdened it and rode it into the ground. Too many straws. From this work, however, had come a new focus for Imperial, a new goal and theme, "The Premier Challenge," and a new campaign to get it there.

Beginning early in the summer, a series of "Premier Challenge" handouts were distributed to employees. The first offered a "Vision Statement for the Imperial Oil Family of Companies."

"Our vision sees Imperial Oil as the premier corporation in Canada."

From these opening words, the booklet continues for fifteen pages under such headings as "Canada and the World," "Stakeholder Expectations," "Beliefs" and "Corporate Core Values," a methodical blend of inspiration and bureaucratic apple pie. More interesting was its follow-up, an open letter to employees from Bill Innes, President of Esso Petroleum. The letter arrived a few weeks ago, shortly after Labour Day. Imperial's self-examination had been moving ahead quickly, Innes was preparing the final ground. He began:

"I·am writing to you, in this unusual format, because at Esso Petroleum Canada we are now at a *critical point* in our history — a *turning point* beyond which we will see wide-ranging and fundamental changes in our company." [my emphasis]

He tells his employees that everyone will be affected by these changes but for the vast majority, the changes will be positive. "They will lead to secure employment and more fulfilling and rewarding work in a more dynamic, successful and forward-looking organization." Then as if to grab his readers' flagging attention, he changes his tone. "I must tell you, however, that the Esso Petroleum of the future may not be for everyone." No matter what came before or what comes after, to everyone on the floor at Wynford Drive, in red neon letters, this is Innes's message.

To be "premier" means "being in a class of our own," he tells them. It is "a liberating vision," challenging and exciting, something to be proud of, one which puts "no limits on our potential as individuals or as an enterprise." More specifically, a premier company has to be strong financially for that is its "essential foundation." It must meet shareholders' expectations of a "quality return" on investment, and give back an amount "equal to what the investor could earn elsewhere." This hasn't happened.

"Our profitability has been below the cost of capital, and below the average for the Canadian manufacturing industry as a whole." In every year of the 1980s, Texaco's rate of return was greater than 10 per cent, in every year but one, Imperial's less than 10 per cent. This is "not acceptable," Innes writes. But the story is worse. Its Canadian competitors, Petro-Canada and Shell, are in the midst of drastic changes which will make them more efficient and competitive; worse still, Imperial's traditional standard for comparison has changed. "Elsewhere" is now a much bigger place. "Since the advent of free trade with the United States, we have been operating in a North American rather than merely a Canadian marketplace." So while the company's "premier" vision is Canadian, to achieve it "our goals are expressed squarely in a North American context: we intend to be North America's most profitable marketer/refiner." As a result, "we must double our current earnings."

This is where McKinsey comes in. Imperial must find ways to generate new revenues, but mostly it must lower its costs "substantially." It has been living in a fool's world, a cozy, content, hermetically sealed Canadian world, beneficiary of its power relative to the Canadian marketplace, of size and its easy efficiencies, of cheap oil it could raise from the ground from easy-to-access Alberta fields, in the 1970s and since of stunning OPEC price rises which turned everything it owned to gold. For years, it had been able to pass on its high-cost way of doing things, losing market share to low-cost independents, yet still remain profitable. "In a very real sense, we have been operating on borrowed time, mortgaging our long-term future simply because we have been unable, or unwilling, to change."

Now things are different. "We do not have the option of standing still. There is no safe ground somewhere between success and failure. Our choice is between changing and prospering, or refusing to change and withering on the vine." And this time, that means real change. "We must undertake a deep, serious and clear-eyed re-examination of everything we do in our company, to determine whether we really should be doing it, whether it creates or adds value to our business."

So to Imperial's Merger Steering Committee, Leadership Teams, Functional and Business Line Teams, to its five hundred Synergy Teams, merger consultants, change management and counselling consultants, McKinsey & Company was added. "Effective immediately," Innes writes, "change leaders" have been designated from within Esso to work with McKinsey, "using proven technologies such as activity value analysis (AVA), operations performance improvement (OPI) [and] pivotal job design (PJD)," to identify where costs can be cut and efficiencies generated so that "premier company" status can be achieved.

"I want to assure you that the objective of the process is not to make people redundant," Innes writes, anticipating his readers' reaction. "The focus is on identifying valuable work and new opportunities, not on the individuals who do the work. I want to emphasize that this is a *building* process, not a *tearing-down* process." [his emphasis] "At the same time," he continues, about to drop the other shoe, "it has been clear for some time that there are job duplications as a result of the merger, and that we currently have more people than we have valuable work for them to do. Through this process we will better understand the real dimensions of this situation and . . . take steps to correct it, where appropriate, *in a manner which will preserve the dignity of the people affected.*" [my emphasis] For anyone who has read this far, the red neon lights have just flashed again.

About to close, he writes, "I'll turn now to the most important question of all: What will these changes mean, in the final analysis, to us as employees — what's in it for us?" He asks his employees to leap ahead in time to a moment when the big disruptions are over and their company *is* the premier petroleum products company in Canada.

"Imagine what it will be like to be part of a truly dynamic and successful company — one that sets the standards for excellence in its industry, and whose future is secured on its financial strength and the support of its stakeholders.

"Imagine," he writes again, "what it will be like to be able to test and extend the limits of your own capabilities — to *know* [his emphasis] that everything you do has value, and is valued by the company, and that you have the authority to do it in a caring and collaborative work environment."

And one more time, "Imagine what it will be like to be relieved of the bureaucratic and process-driven tasks that now take up so much of our valuable time and energy, and to be free, too, of the pressures of continual rounds of incremental cost-cutting we've experienced in the past, able to pursue our business and personal goals with confidence." Without a doubt, he says, the company of the future, "challenging and demanding," will be a "more exciting and rewarding place to work."

He takes a deep breath, and returns to the present. "Our train is now starting its journey," he writes quietly, "and each of us has a choice to make . . . Each of us can choose to get on the train and take the journey . . . some of us may choose to get off the train, and that's fine. Not everyone welcomes change, or can cope with it when it happens. But we mustn't hold the train back."

To those on the credit-card floor, however, they can't *imagine*. And what they *know* is that even if all Innes's imaginings come true, things will not be much different for them somehow. *What's in it for us*, indeed? Except layoffs, to make the company strong enough to protect many more jobs in the future, except that's not the way it feels. Challenging, demanding, exciting, rewarding? It's a job, a good job, the best they've ever had and that's why they want nothing to change. What does the rest have to do with them? They are *already* on this train. Long ago, they made their choice and they're not getting off. They can't get off. What other train could they take, and where would it take them? No, if Imperial wants them off it will have to kick them off. The packages are coming soon, to them that's what the Innes letter is saying, and for the rare people who have read this far, they have a red neon message for him. They won't even think about getting off this train until then.

"Our journey leads on to fortune for all of us," Innes concludes. "I hope it's a journey you'll want to take."

These were handouts written *by* those who always managed change, *for* those who always managed change. To control the largely uncontrollable by reducing it to what they can control and understand and tame. Substituting paper and structure for the real thing in order to make themselves feel better. If this is done, that will follow; everything at, everything emanating from their own fingertips. It is their training, their life's expectations and view. It is what they know and feel, and what they need to be. Having to live the way the other guy lives and feel as he feels, they don't know how.

About two weeks ago, three more handouts arrived. Using the change technologies, AVA, PJD and OPI, all work would be re-examined, the handouts said. Was it profitable? Did it offer a "quality return"? Could it ever provide a "quality return"? Should we do it at all? Every non-essential step or task was to be reduced or eliminated, so when the dust cleared, left would be fewer employees working faster, doing more meaningful, productive, rewarding work. Simple "change" had become cliché; "step change" was the new order of the day.

Already seventy-two AVA units had been created, each with its own unit manager, each reporting to the twelve-member Advisory Task Force which reported to a Steering Committee of senior management. Shaping and driving "the overall change agenda" were "change leaders" who, together with Task Force members, constituted the "action team" and reported to the "change centre," a senior management group responsible for "the overall change process" and not just AVA. More streamlined than the merger process, more urgent, it was geared to building the kind of excitement and momentum that could slingshot the company towards its target.

As usual, communications would play an important role. Handouts, progress reports, electronic mail, hotlines. As usual, few paid any attention.

But a layoff was coming, that they knew. And minutes ago at lunch while Frank was reading those extra few pages in his book, a memo was dropped on their desks.

To: Credit Card Services Personnel
Re: Workforce Realignment Programs
A presentation to you of Esso Petroleum's Workforce Realignment Programs is scheduled for Wednesday, October 10th, in the cafeteria. Two sessions are planned, 8:00 a.m. – 9:30 a.m. and 9:45 – 11:15 a.m.
Please confirm with your Supervisor as to which session you should attend.

Attached was a copy of a hand-printed note from each supervisor setting out the appropriate session. His is second.

It had finally happened. Mike Gamble, one of his supervisors, glances at the sheets. He is in his early forties, dark haired, broad and tough looking, for twenty-one years he had worked for Texaco and until the merger had never worked anywhere else. "It's been tough these last forty-five days or so," he says. "It's the rumours." He gets halfway out of his chair and looks at the people on the floor. "I mean, you can hear 'em. *Buzz buzz buzz*. You just want to say, 'Forget it. They're just rumours.' But there's nothing you can do. People come and see me, they're gonna lose their jobs. They got families, mortgages to pay off, a recession's coming, they're scared. 'Don't worry,' I tell them. 'If anything, we're understaffed here. You'll be OK.'" He stops, "I mean, I don't know that for sure."

He has seen other effects. "Morale's a way down. Productivity's down, our receivables are up 20 per cent, September to September. I figure about 5 per cent is the recession, 15 per cent the rumours. People just aren't doin' the job. This isn't a happy place." He brightens, "But you'll see some smiles this afternoon." In a few minutes, he will start bringing people into his office to tell them their new roles under the re-organizational plan. "A lot of people are gonna get promotions. Then tomorrow, we'll see.

"If I was fifty-five sure, I'd be worried. You got a mortgage, your kids are in university, how're you gonna afford to leave? You got plenty of years ahead of you, but what're you going do? Who's gonna hire you, especially with a recession on? But we can all see the writing on the wall. You know who's going to get it. You gotta look out for yourself. The company's not gonna. Not any more. Loyalty's dead. People who stay with one company all their lives, they're dinosaurs.

"The real problem with packages like this is you lose the wrong people. It's the weak ones who stay. They know how tough it'd be somewhere else. The good ones know they've got a chance."

He goes quiet a moment. "Loyalty's a funny thing, you know. The guys who are loyal to themselves, they're the best workers. They're the ones who give 110 per cent. They've got ambition. It's the ones who say they're loyal to the company who don't put out. They hide behind the company. They're just looking to pick up a cheque until they retire."

He admires Imperial Oil, and in these last many months he has tried hard to feel for it what he thinks he should, and can't. "You know, at Texaco," he says, "there was a pride. There wasn't any great loyalty to the company, it was to ourselves. To each other. We were small, we didn't know what any other company was doing and didn't care. We just knew we were working hard for not much pay and *doin' a job*." It is his ultimate compliment. "Here, we don't have that pride." Hearing himself, he backtracks. "Not yet, I mean."

Mary Chiswell sits next to one of the coffee stations not far from Frank. She looks worn out. She was at Texaco for thirty-three years and for the last fourteen years, she has worked in this same building, 90 Wynford Drive, on this same floor, in exactly the same physical space. The merger which brought him and Imperial's credit-card section from 825 Don Mills Road took place around her. It is her job to take credit-card applications and key their information onto her screen. She has just received her memo too.

"I don't like change very much," she says quietly. "I never have. I don't know why." She thinks on that a moment, "Maybe because any real changes have been bad ones." She is plain-speaking more than blunt; and her answer now clear to her, she feels no need to explain. But she is thinking about change now. She is not yet fifty-five so tomorrow's packages may not be for her, or may not be rich enough. Still, she is hoping.

"Everything's paid for. I own my own home. I've got no debts, no habits I can't afford. I'd like to just stay home, do some antiquing, maybe something in real estate." She stops herself and stares at the truth. "Really, I just want out," she says. "I've never had a break since I finished high school at seventeen. I've been doing the same job for thirty-three years. It's so boring. At the end of the day, my shoulders, my neck and back, they just ache. My fingers are OK, but my eyes, looking at that screen. At the end of a busy day, you're no good for nothin'. You just want to sit in front of the boob tube like a zombie."

She angles her head to one side, a smile crosses her face. She is years younger. "You know, I like keying." Her voice is an excited whisper. "I really like keying. It feels good moving my fingers." She smiles again, "And I like it when I get an application and can hardly read the writing. Everyone else starts swearing, but you're like a detective. You figure it out bit by bit and when you've got it, you feel such achievement." She breaks out laughing. Her laugh is such a surprise.

The weight of her day returns. "But it's a nothing job. Everybody's job is a nothing job, on this floor, I mean. Upstairs, they gotta use their brains a bit. That's probably more interesting. But down here when anybody pretends it's not a nothing job, I laugh. They think they're doing something special and something great's going to come along. They're kidding themselves. Anybody can do what we do. Not necessarily well. I mean, not everybody has the patience to sit in front of this screen or talk to angry people all day."

She looks at her memo. "A lot of people will go," she says evenly. "If people think there's room for two presidents, two comptrollers, two anything, they've got to be stupid. If you've got a merger, it's got to happen. That's the way business works. I laugh when people pretend nothing's gonna change. They're kidding themselves. They don't need all these people. Everyone's busy now because they screwed up the credit cards. But that'll get straightened out, then all this can be done with fewer people."

She thinks back on her time that may be about to end:

"I started here. I had some plans to do other things. You know, *a year from now*, always a year from now. Then a year passed, I'd have other plans and suddenly it's thirty-three years. But I've made good money, everything's paid for. I just need a change."

He reads his memo and lays it back on his desk. Tomorrow is tomorrow. This afternoon he gets his new assignment, and that is what worries him. He had been part of a task force this summer whose job was to come up with a plan to integrate customer service and collections. People should work in "teams," it was decided, each with at least one senior collector, one senior customer service person, one assistant collector and one support staff. The senior people would be level 17s, the assistant, a 15. The structure and job descriptions presented them little difficulty. Fitting people into this structure did. There were too many 17s, not enough 15s and some 16s which didn't fit at all. Would the 16s move up or down? Responsibility, prestige, money were at stake. He was a 16.

Too self-interested, the discussions became snarled, then heated. He spoke up in his loud, blurting way when he had something to say or felt he should. At one meeting, Mike Gamble joked about him speaking his mind, hinting he might be one of those demoted. Frank didn't realize he was teasing. He vowed in front of the whole group not to speak that entire meeting. The others thought *he* was joking, but for half an hour he kept his promise. Then, unable to hold himself back, he blurted, "No!" about something, louder than he intended, threw his hand over his mouth and tried to turn the incident into a joke. The moment passed, but the source of his future problems had already taken root.

He now had in his mind that they were being "led down the garden path" to a result management had already decided. Their work was a charade, an *exercise* in empowerment, a game for everyone but them. You are our greatest resource. Nothing is more important than you, our employees. Give us your time, your energy and dedication, and we will let you redefine your jobs, remake your future workplace. The company was "managing perception" one more time. Task forces, merger and "premier" processes, they were just techniques, bottom-up managing from the top down.

Well, he had had enough, and so had everyone else, he could tell. Just tell me what to do. I don't care if you consult me. You'll just do what you want anyway. So do it now. And still they met in their task forces.

It happened a week later. Task force members were examining the functions and responsibilities of each job within the teams. Texaco had reorganized its credit-card section before the merger, making customer service equal to collection. After the merger, Imperial had done the same. The collectors didn't like it. The pecking order had been violated. With a chance to set things straight, two Texaco people, Mike Gamble and Ernie Anslow, Frank's supervisor, had decided to save face. He had it all figured out.

He thought he heard Ernie say senior collectors and senior CS people would be at the same level. That was the trigger. Before his thoughts were clear, he accused Ernie of "cheating," management of trying to protect themselves. They were being railroaded, and from the faces around the table he could tell everyone felt the same. Except they didn't. "Oh Frank," said one of his co-workers, "let's just get it over with." He threw down his pencil, "Fine," he snapped, and stormed from the room. It was a graceless performance. A lifetime of feelings swarmed back. He was immature, had been too big for his britches, had gone onto that task force and had no right to be there. God had shot him down again. Properly.

At a meeting the next day, he didn't show up. One of the managers went downstairs and found him still in his cubicle. Only when he told him he wouldn't leave without him did Frank go with him. As he shuffled into the meeting room, he felt a need to tell everyone how he had misunderstood their feelings. It was his way of apologizing. After the meeting, Ernie came by his desk and thanked him for coming. He hoped the little incident wouldn't keep him from speaking his mind, he said. Good ideas often come when someone speaks before he thinks of the consequences. It wasn't the Imperial way, but Ernie was Texaco.

Last week the task force's recommendations were finally approved. Each team will have six levels, not four: a senior

collector and senior customer service rep (both level 17),
a customer service rep (16), an assistant collector (15), and
two support people (levels 12 to 14). For him, this is a problem. He is an assistant collector but also a 16, and he is the
only one. It is moments before Ernie brings him into his
office to tell him his new role, and he is worried. "If they
keep me at 16, I'd make the same pay, but lose all my
accounts. They'd all be handled by 17s." He thinks on that
a moment. "I'd be pissed off if that happens."

Every few minutes he looks in the direction of Ernie's
office; his door remains closed. Each time it opens, heads
pop up and someone else is motioned forward. About an
hour later, the door opens again, Frank looks up and Ernie
looks back at him.

The door opens a few minutes later and Ernie appears.
No Frank. Ernie leaves, then returns and closes the door
again; more minutes pass. Finally the door opens and this
time Frank walks out, a smile on his face, both his thumbs
are up. "I'm a 17." There are now two levels of 17, one customer service, one collection. He is customer service. "I
don't have quite the experience the others do, but enough
to back up. I got a raise too, retroactive to September 1. I
guess all my worries are over."

He can't worry about much in his life. That's not being
immature, it's not denial. Without the money or power or
skills to immunize himself against the future, most things
simply have to go fine, turn out, be all right. He has to
depend on time, nature, wellness, goodness, on the light
side of human nature and whatever other forces there may
be, to cure him and see him through. His roof won't collapse, the sky won't fall, no motorist will run him down. It
is the way it has to be, the way he must live his life. He is in
God's hands, and while most around him at some point in
their lives believe the same, his is no last resort belief. He
gives over control earlier because he must. If things can't
be in his own hands, in whose hands would he prefer,
Arden Haynes's, Brian Mulroney's or God's? What he can't

control is or will be. All his worries really may be over.

He spots Carolyn. "When you're done come back over, huh?" He's so nonchalant she misses the point of what he's saying and several minutes pass before she returns. He goes back to the phones, but now a little chirpier. One of his co-workers stops by and he tells her the news. Word spreads.

"I'm calling from a station in Vancouver," a voice shouts in his ear. "The last few days some people have been chargin' up all kinds of miscellaneous things, cigarettes and stuff. We're lookin' at heavy-duty amounts." He checks his screen: customer reports new card not received; $2,700 in charges since the beginning of the week. "It's definitely suspicious," the voice says. "The Capilano station alone got burned for over $300. I've got a description and a licence plate number. A black BMW, looks like a runaway."

He confirms some details, then hangs up. "I hate frauds," he mutters.

Another burble.

"Aw, shit."

The calls keep coming, the day gets shorter. He is tired, the sing-songy lilt has gone from his voice. He can feel himself losing interest in the stories of woe more and more sounding to him like lies. When a story turns complicated, he can't seem to cut through the dreck to the point that will save both of them time and whatever energy he has left. Yet only rarely does he escape to the safety and comfort of automatism, close his mind, turn on his computer voice and system sensitivities. To out-machine the machine. Years ago, someone had told him he was the voice of the company. Not Arden Haynes or Bob Peterson whose voices are internal, within central offices and board rooms, within the tight symbiosis of business leaders, politicians and media followers. "We represent the company," Frank says, and he means it. "We are the voice they hear. If we don't deal with them in a friendly, courteous manner, they'll go somewhere else." And as with other gospel truths in his life, he holds this one without question. He is not instinctively outgoing, isn't easy with people, so much about them he doesn't understand, so much has hurt him, so many of the easy human, personal skills he has never learned. But whatever else comes across in his voice, there is one thing which forgives the rest. He cares.

When he and Carolyn decided to have a family, he made himself a promise. He would work hard, be on the job every day and on time, he would provide for his family the way his family had provided for him. But he wouldn't be like his father. He *would* be a nine-to-fiver. He would leave work behind, take nothing home, no briefcase, no laptop computer, he wouldn't think about work, he would *do* no work, until tomorrow, until Monday, until after his holidays. Until it was time. Physically and emotionally, he would be there for his family.

One Friday night some months ago, his phone rang at home.

"Hello, is this Mr. Bloye?" a voice asked.

"Yes."

"Mr. F. Bloye who works at Esso?"

"Yes."

"Oh, am I glad I reached you. I'm calling from Calgary. You see, last week I got a letter saying I was behind on my payments and my card had been cut off. I tried to use it today and the dealer picked it up. I sent you my cheque a few days ago and really need [the card] this weekend."

He had been following the man's words until they began suggesting a meaning which made no sense to him. Assuming he was lost, he began retracing his memory steps. "What?!" he finally cried.

"I really need my card. I was wondering if you could go down to your office and reverse all this so I could use it."

"You're calling me at home!"

"Yes, sir, I know." The man still didn't get it. "I need my card and was wondering —"

"*This is my home,*" he repeats.

"Yes, sir."

"How did you get my number?"

"Well, I just called the operator and there aren't many Bloyes. Actually you're the first one I called, and —"

Fully caught up, he explodes, "How dare you call me at home! You have no right to call me at home!" And all weekend he rehearsed how on Monday he would refuse him a card and close his account when he called. He never called.

For more than nineteen years, he has kept his promise. But since the merger, as surely as in briefcases and laptops, he has begun bringing the office home in energy, patience, will and mood lost or ill. His promise will now be harder to keep.

He looks at his watch again. "Five o'clock," he smiles. "Time to quit." It is 4:56. He never did get back to his worklists, he'll just have to do what he can tomorrow. Lots of faraway voices now feel better than they did this morning which makes him feel useful, but tomorrow, he knows, the same voices will be back. No matter how good a job he does, he is never finished, never ahead. He wishes only he could plan out his day a little more, feel the routine of it, get to things in order and get them done, feel himself at the *end* of something at least some of the time. Instead, he is always at some infinite middle with no beginning or end in sight, with no signposts to know where he is or how he is doing. Today is always another day.

The clucking of keyboards continues but not as before. Printers and photocopiers have gone silent, the voices are fewer, the layers of sound fall slowly away and slowly the music and swoosh of the air return. Some still sit at their screens, more than just finishing what would be forgotten and lost in the overnight, and will be here for some time yet. He arranges a few things on his desk then starts to shut down his system. Carolyn walks by and sees him still at his screen.

"You working overtime?" she asks.

"No," he smiles, a trace of triumph in his voice. "I'm goin' home."

10

It is only 8:00 a.m. but the sounds of air conditioning and music have been long covered over. There are no clucks, no stamps, no grinds, no work is being done. Half the floor is empty, the first session is meeting downstairs. Session Two waits, and talks.

Tables filled with donuts, muffins and fruit, juice and coffee have been set up downstairs outside the cafeteria. Glenn Kirby mounts the stairs two at a time and bursts into the room near Frank's cubicle. He spots Wendy Peace, a big friendly woman about fifty, talking with Frank.

"Ooh," Glenn says, a smirk on his face, "you know it's big when they bring out the food."

Wendy laughs. "Looks like 'The Last Supper,' doesn't it."

"You know what you're goin' to do, Wendo?"

"Oh, I don't think I'm interested in a package," she says. "I mean, I'm too young. I can see if you're married and have a mortgage to pay off. Take the lump sum then work part-time or something. Or if you're going back to school. But me, I'd just have to get another job so I might as well stay right here."

The same conversation is taking place all over the floor, all over all the floors of all the Imperial offices across the country. You ask the other guy if he doesn't ask you first because you have to talk about it. And you ask not to know, because no one is listening much except to their own internal clamour, but for the chance to spill out your own words, take your own centre stage, make *your* life and *your* future seem as important as everyone else's. Still everyone knows.

To all their practised certainties, however, they hedge, qualify and leave doors ajar because they must. This isn't a time for closed doors. Their deck of cards is being reshuffled. Big changes are happening that can redirect and remake lives, and maybe make them better. So maybe I won't take the package, surely I won't, but maybe I will. This is my chance. I *have* to be interested. How often does the momentum of life's inertia get interrupted? *This is my chance.* And at 8:15 a.m., Wednesday, October 10, there is no better time than this. Not knowing, not able to know or having to know, nothing can be better than *right now*. For those downstairs just beginning to know, that moment is over; passed. But here, now, nothing is not possible. Mortgages, families, kids, college educations are tomorrow's cold shower. My future is in my hands. Now is the time to dream.

In the cafeteria, portable chairs have been rearranged in rows; in front of them a podium, microphone and large TV set. Session Two takes its seats, spreading out, filling in, as if in church the first few rows left empty. First to speak is Gord Beddome, manager of the credit-card section. In his mid-thirties, short and trim, he darts about in nervous, nervous-making bursts even as he waits. He has on a dark blue pin-stripe suit, white shirt and dark Paisley tie, a white handkerchief sticks from his pocket. His suit jacket is unbuttoned, beneath it a shirt-tail half out peeks at his audience.

Since the merger, he says, the company has faced three main challenges. Getting people settled into their jobs, which by and large has been done, he says. Integrating and solidifying the business, which again has mostly been done. Repositioning the company to give it the strength it needs for the future, he says, which is what he and those who follow him will talk about today. His audience begins to squirm. *Just give me the packages.*

He relates the story serialized in the summer handouts, beginning with "Vision of the Enterprise," then Innes's letter. Our employees, our community, our shareholders and customers, are "all number one," he says. But how are we really doing? For our employees and community, "very well." For shareholders and customers, "not very well at all. We can't deliver the goods and services [at a price] that customers will pay," and market share has been eroding. As for the shareholders, are we really satisfying them, he asks, when they could put their money in a bank and get a greater return, with less risk? We're not even meeting the cost of capital, he says, and they are edgy.

He moves to "The Premier Challenge Change Process." Imperial wants to be the premier company and "to be seen as 'premier' by all its stakeholders." It's a goal it must achieve. But for that to happen, the pace of change must pick up. "Step change" is required.

He speaks with practised intimacy, calling his audience, "you folks," but he holds himself apart, treats every speck of information as if a secret, and he is its keeper. After fifteen minutes, he introduces the video presentations.

The room goes quiet. "A Message from the Chairman," flashes onto the screen, then Arden Haynes himself. He too is dressed in a dark blue suit, white shirt and handkerchief. In his lapel is an Order of Canada pin. He is in his office, dark wood panelling surrounds him, an oil painting and computer terminal are partly in view behind. He is in close-up. He is serious and solemn.

"I have attempted to restrict these appearances," he says, "to times of significant importance to you and the company because I realize it takes up your time and mine, and interferes with our busy work schedules.

"However, the time is again upon us when we face another major challenge."

The company has had three main tasks this past year, he says, paying down a debt pushed up by the merger, completing the merger "efficiently," and improving productivity. "I can report today that we have made significant progress on the first two of these initiatives." As for the third, the company has fallen short, so "voluntary staff-reduction programs" must be introduced. "I said [they] will be voluntary, and I mean that. But it is important in reaching your decision that you have available to you as much [data] about your prospects in the company as possible and that these are weighed objectively against other opportunities." It is your decision, he is telling them, but first now, and last later, it is his. At the moment the momentum of his words and generosity of the scene make him want to say, and them want to hear, that if they do decide to stay "we'll be glad to have you," he doesn't say that. He wants three thousand of them to go. Only then will he be glad to have the rest.

If his audience has somehow missed his point, he crosses the final "t." "In the end, if you decide you wish to stay with the company in some capacity, that will be your choice. This is of course no guarantee for the future. I simply could never promise that to any employee. If we are still overstaffed at the end of this program it may be necessary to introduce selective *in*voluntary programs later."

Frank has sat attentive and impassive all these minutes. Only twice has something escaped his mouth. When Haynes told them the company had reduced its debt by $2.5 billion, he said, "Mmm." When he mentioned the possibility of *involuntary* programs, he said, "Oh, geez."

Haynes begins explaining the rationale behind the programs. In the minute or two it takes him, it's unlikely anyone is listening.

"And now the programs," he says, and with that Frank begins to write. There are three: Pension Enhancement Program, or "PEP," for those fifty-five years old and over with at least ten years' service; Pre-retirement Enhancement Program, "PREP," for those over fifty with ten years' service; and, Career Change Assistance Program, "CCAP," for the others, him included. Haynes gives only a few program details; they will be explained by the next speakers, he says. But "before I turn this discussion over, I want you to realize that I feel a great deal of empathy for you." Your decision will not be easy. At the time Texaco Canada was purchased, "I said that no one would be laid off as a result of the merger," most overstaffing would be taken care of by normal attrition and "anything left over would be dealt with in a way that preserved the dignity of employees. While the current rate of attrition has been a surprise," he admits, "I feel the commitment I made has been fully met." These programs have been introduced, he says, only "*to speed up the normal attrition process.*"

". . . I searched for reasons not to introduce these programs," he says, "and found none worthy of consideration." The programs are necessary to stay competitive and "to achieve the status of the premier company we all seek."

"You are without question our most valued resource. In the weeks ahead, as we go through what will be a trying time for some, in our actions we will adhere rigorously to our fundamental belief that people, that you, are in fact 'the company,' and that you will be treated with fairness, respect and dignity, without compromise.

"I want to close by wishing each one of you the very best in whatever decision you choose and to thank you for your loyalty and contribution to the company."

The TV screen goes blank. Sympathetic and sincere, this was no pitch but a father's sober message. When the session finally ends and they slowly climb the stairs to their cubicles, he says only one thing, "It's the first time they ever said anything about *in*voluntary."

"It's a pretty sweet deal," someone says.

"We'll never get another like it, that's for sure," not with any other company, not with this company any other time. They had seen it coming. It had to happen. There is little or no bitterness.

Glenn Kirby is beside himself. "I haven't been so excited about this company for years, and now I'm leaving," he laughs. "You're not gonna take it are ya, Audrey?"

"I don't know. I could pay off my mortgage. I'll think about it. I'm keeping my options open."

"But Audrey, this place wouldn't be the same without you." They both laugh.

Glenn Kirby is still bouncing. He is twenty-eight years old and lives in Newcastle, past Whitby and Oshawa, about ninety kilometres away. "Oh, I'm takin' it. I've got ten years, so I get ten months' salary. I can go back to school. My wife's working, I won't have to pay three hundred dollars a month for gas." Several years of thoughts and feelings come out. "So far as this company is concerned, I've gone about as far as I can go," he says. *This is my chance.* I just know if I don't take it, I'll regret it."

Mortgage paid off, ten months of holiday, back to school, something new, different, better: for most, this is a time to dream. A chance to do what you always wanted and knew you could; to be what you knew you were. Fundamental dreams, risky dreams. Can I get another job? Will it be as good? Should I take the chance? Can I afford the chance? With the car I drive, food I eat, house I live in, shoes my kids wear, with a lifetime of needs, habits, expectations and obligations, can I do it? *Do I dare?*

It is a difficult time. Not because the right step is so unclear because for most it is totally clear. Because you must face your own dreams. And dreams pursued can be dreams unmet. What then? Yours may not be the best of all lives, but it *is* yours. You've become good at it. You know how to live it. No surprises or worries, you can live it the rest of your life. But if you dream and fail, what do you dream then? Worse than dreams unpursued is a dreamless future. On the brink, most back away. The risk is too great. What is is good enough.

For them it's a time for dreams deferred.

Since the merger, since the rumours and handouts, the news stories and yesterday's memo, he has said little. He hasn't asked others what they intend to do, and no one's asked him. He hasn't schemed and bargained with himself about his future. He hasn't dreamed. He has listened and gone about his work.

More than eighteen years he has been at Imperial. And five days a week, forty-eight weeks a year, in sickness and health, he has been, in Mike Gamble's phrase, "doin' a job." But now at this very moment he could get up from his desk, walk into Ernie's office and tell him he's leaving, enough is enough, and for eighteen months do whatever *he* wants, sleep in, go where he wants, come back when he wants, and still his cheques would keep coming in. But he won't take that package, he won't even look at it and wonder because if he does, he might be tempted; because in his life he can't afford to be tempted. God would shoot him down as God always does. The untempted life is tough enough.

With every reason to leave his door ajar, a few days, a few weeks, to dream with the rest of them, instead he shrugs his "who am I kidding?" shrug and reaches for his burbling phone.

"I'm not going anywhere," he says.

Part Four

"The past isn't dead. It's not even past."

WILLIAM FAULKNER

11

Carolyn Norma Thomson was nearly twenty-two when she and Frank first met. She was still living at home with her mother, Muriel, and younger sister, Lois, sixteen, in an old brick house in Scarborough. Her older brother, Paul, a teacher, was married and had recently moved with his wife and infant son two hundred kilometres north to Owen Sound. Their father, Leonard Thomson, had died three years before, suddenly, two months before Paul's wedding day. The pains he had felt in his chest all that last week of his life, which had always been indigestion, eating too many fatty foods too fast, the product of a salesman's life on the road, had really been a series of small heart attacks. He was fifty-one. Carolyn was nineteen.

She had been born the day after Christmas, 1946. They were going to name her "Holly" at first; she became their Christmas "Carolyn" instead. Life was just beginning to go Len Thomson's way at about the time his daughter was born. Through the Depression and war, he had managed to make ends meet and not much more. Muriel had worked as a proofreader for a printing company, then quit as married women did, and was home with Paul. She had wanted more children but having suffered a miscarriage after her son was born, she had almost given up hope. Then Carolyn arrived, truly a Christmas gift. When six years later another girl, Lois Janine, was born, she came as very much a surprise.

Len Thomson joined Chocolate Products after the war, and just as Leo Bloye was discovering fifty kilometres away in Oshawa, it was a good time to sell. Windows and other glass products might have been necessities for the postwar building boom, but chocolate ice cream, chocolate milk, chocolate *anything* was just right for families finally able to treat themselves a little. He sold mostly to dairies and vending companies as far away as North Bay. He'd leave home on Monday and not be back until Thursday night; Friday he spent in the office doing his paper work. When big events in their lives were about to happen, he could sometimes rearrange his schedule and be there. But when the bigger events came — a first tooth coming in or lost, a first word, a trip to the hospital — he was away.

It was Muriel who ran the household which, given their personalities, was just as well. A smile on his lips, a spring in his every step, Len Thomson was a good-news guy. You can't sell chocolate with doom and gloom. So Muriel worried for both of them. She angered and resented and fought and feared when each was required, because he wasn't there. She was the family disciplinarian, so he was their favourite. A dad coming home was a lot more fun than a mom always there.

Carolyn was a happy little girl, shy and pretty and neat. Whenever she went to play in the backyard, not an hour would pass and she was back in the house, up in the bathroom, washing her hands. Then she'd go back to play. There was no kindergarten in her local school, so like the other kids she started in grade 1. She liked school and dreaded it; nothing seemed amiss. Then she began to stumble. It was her reading; but reading is hard and lots of kids have trouble, they thought. So her teachers waited, pushed a little, worried a little, and finally got angry. What's wrong with her? She looks normal. She doesn't need glasses, doesn't look retarded, she's no DP just off the boat. She comes from a good family, her mother is home. Everyone else is doing his and her part, *what's wrong with her?*

At home, her mother sat her on the floor beside her and had her read out loud. Every time she got the words wrong, *whap*, Muriel's right hand would shoot out against the back of her head, and she would stop and try again. Her mother doesn't remember that, but she remembers. And no matter how many times she got hit, "was" was "saw" and "saw" was "was." "Eventually, I did figure them out," she laughs. "If I saw 'was' and got a whack, I knew it was 'saw.'"

She failed grade 1 and again grade 5. Paul was smart, the big older brother who could do everything. Lois was so little that anything she did seemed a miracle. Years later, Carolyn said something to her mother about how she had had two smart kids and a dumb one in the middle, saying it sort of off-hand, as if the words just came out, but they didn't and it wasn't. It was, in part, her apology, in part said in bitterness, part incomprehending, part looking for the response she hoped she would get, but her mother got angry. That's not how it was, she told her. That's just how it was, she remembers.

Whenever there was a problem, it was always her fault. "Stop teasing your brother." *But Mom.* "She's just a little girl." *But Mom.* The curse of the middle child. It was never Lois. She wouldn't take it. Tiny and overmatched, she would stand up to her mother as she stands up to her now. She had this sense of herself, of her own value, a selfishness and self-possession that said, Look, my thoughts, my feelings and time are as important as yours. *I'm* as important, and I'm not going to listen to you and do what you want me to do if I don't want to do it. And you can't make me. Somehow she knew that as much as bread and water, fighting back was survival too.

Carolyn always took it. She didn't demand of her mother and teachers more time and attention. She had caused them enough problems. She had no right. The least she could do was go quietly. If her mother noticed something was wrong and went to her teachers, what could she really say? Carolyn was letting *them* down.

In class, she didn't raise her hand because she knew her answer was wrong, and if it wasn't, she didn't raise it the next time because the next time, it *would* be wrong. She belonged to no teams, no Brownie troop, no church or other group. She liked it better alone. If someone tried to explain something to her, "yeah, uh huh, sure," she'd say, even though she didn't understand a thing, just so they'd go away, so no one else would know. There might be lots of things she'd never know and lots more she'd never learn because she didn't, but that was much less painful than knowing she didn't know, and having others know that too.

Her second year in grade 5 was her best. She seemed finally to have turned the corner, but she hadn't and wouldn't. Every new grade presented another new corner she could only manage with much struggle and hard work. After her first year of high school, she transferred to vocational school. She was fifteen. Her mother had told her a story about her own father. As a teacher, he had seen so many kids who knew so much, who in school seemed to know so little. They needed so badly to know how much they knew, to feel they could learn *in* school and find pleasure doing it. "If you can't learn with *this*," he used to say, pointing to his head, "learn with *this*," he said, holding out his hands. She never heard her grandfather's words, but her mother knew them by heart. Muriel taught her to knit and sew and make her own clothes. At her new school, Bendale Vocational Institute, in a secretarial course, she would learn once more with her hands. At seventeen, she graduated and went to work.

It was 1964. Frank was still living in Whitby, having just struggled through his first year in grade 10; his father had recently given up the Oshawa store and was beginning to commute to Toronto.

These were good years and not so good years for her. She liked being out of school, learning by doing, staying in a job until she could do it well. Then not having to move up to something she couldn't do and have the same old feelings return; instead, doing the job, do it better than anyone expected, not because someone was pushing her, but because of her. Because *she was good.* Moving into an adult world certainly more complicated, surely beyond her, she was discovering just how much she could do.

At home, it was harder. Her dad had quit his job at Chocolate Products. Forced out. Taken off the road by a president who didn't like him, stripped of his commissions, his lifestyle, most of all his identity. If one door slams shut, look for a window. A little charm, just the right words and no window can hold out for long. Except this time, he had met the person he couldn't sell.

Now in his late forties, he had to find something else. He got a job at People's Credit Jewellers as a collector, this time the bad-news guy, and he hated it. He worked at Becker's, as manager of one of its convenience stores, until he discovered an employee, a moonlighting policeman, was ripping him off. He quit there too. The kids were told nothing. They ate the same food, wore the same clothes; he and Muriel got one more year out of everything; busy and happy, the kids didn't notice. They had had hard times, then for all the years at Chocolate Products, the years of Carolyn's life, good times. The country was moving, there was no reason to believe anything would ever be different. Then the bad times returned. Too tired to struggle, they had it all to do again.

Then he got a job at a Liquor Control Board store, dealing with people happy to buy his product, people he could have fun with, and he loved it. His income was steady, the pieces were coming together again. Then he died.

The last night of his life, Carolyn had come in from a date. She always kissed him good-night, but it was late, he was in bed, she decided not to. In the morning, he was gone. It is her one big regret.

She had grown up without many dreams. For awhile she was going to be a nurse, then her mother had a friend who made gowns for CBC's "Juliette," so some day she would do the same. But what she really wanted was to be married and have a family, to live in a house not much different from hers in an area like Scarborough. And now she was ready to begin that life. Her brother was married, the people at work were married, everyone around her was talking about kids. She had lived at home long enough, yet knew she would remain there as long as she was single.

Late June, 1968. She was sitting at her receptionist's desk inside Superior Propane's offices. It was early in the morning, the first day of a new week. Up the stairs and through the door came a skinny young man in a black suit, white shirt and black tie. They must have glanced at each other, neither of them remembers. He was the new office boy. Shy, firm in his convictions that a date meant a date gone wrong and a friendship ruined, she would have a while to wait yet.

It might have been early July, at his desk or hers, at her initiative or his, their memories differ. Somehow they found themselves sitting in the same place eating lunch together. According to him, he had been reading, had never given her any hint he was interested, when one day she walked over and asked if she could join him. According to her, there was an empty chair in the reception area, and one day he joined her. (Ah yes, they remember it well.)

They talked about their families, about movies and music, sometimes they played cards. Outside work they didn't see each other. She was dating other boys. For him, eating lunch together was a pleasant habit, he liked her, that's all. Nothing had to lead anywhere, everything was fine as it was. Try to turn things into something they might never be and lose what you've got.

No first impressions survive, just a few lasting ones. He was awkward and shy, she recalls, yet had this sudden loud voice which leaped over volumes others used only for anger or excitement. Yet he seemed not to notice. She remembers the nasal spray he had on his desk. He had broken his nose playing high-school football, he told her, it was the first and last game he ever played, his mother had seen to that. His sinuses had been messed up. So several times a day, *snort snort*, she would swirl around and see him, his head and chair tilted back, glassy-eyed. His father had emphysema; in his house nasal spray was as common as facial tissue, snorting as blowing. To him, the sight, sound and act were routine. To her, one more curiosity.

She has one other early impresssion. Before they knew each other well enough and he had the right, he brought out a book of poetry and read to her. The poem, by Ogden Nash, was called, "Oh Shucks, Ma'am, I Mean Excuse Me."

> The greatest error ever erred
> Is a nice girl with a naughty word.
> For naughty words I hold no brief,
> They fill my modest heart with grief . . .
> At least let's send them back again
> To where they come from: namely men.

He opened doors for her and helped her with her chair, he did lots of little things like that. No flourish, no show, he just did them. It wasn't manners or chauvinism or old-time thinking, it was respect. She could do every one of those things herself and he never pretended otherwise. He liked her, that's all. He wanted to do things for her, in his own often awkward way he wanted to treat her nicely. It was loving, or liking, by doing just as it had been in his house. And because he respected her, she should respect herself. Be a little special, talk properly, don't swear, just because you can doesn't mean you should.

In the fall, he signed up for night school to complete his grade 13. He was living at home, paying room and board. With money in the bank and more to come, he decided to buy a car, a bright red 1969 Volkswagen. He was twenty-one. A few days later, he and Carolyn were again having lunch. They began talking about movies. She mentioned *Dr. Zhivago*, which she hadn't seen in its first run but which she noticed was back in town. His breeziness disappeared. Hearing what he thought was hint in her voice, his defences retaliated:

Look, I've always said I'm not going to get married and I'm not going to get married. I'm not interested in getting married. I don't enjoy myself on dates. I like girls, I love to watch girls, but face to face I get weak-kneed. Besides, she gave her hint, I didn't pick up on it, so it's done.

A few days later, another voice peeked through:

Ask her.

Helpless, he got up from his desk and walked to the front. "How about you and I going to see *Dr. Zhivago?*" "Fine," she said. Walking back to his desk, his voices returned:

What are you doing?! You'll just ruin a perfectly good friendship. You'll probably end up having to leave your job because she'll be all angry and you'll be embarrassed and . . .

He drove over in his new red "Bug," met her mother and Lois, and the two of them went to the theatre. The show was sold out. Before *that* part of him could scream, they noticed *West Side Story* was playing down the street. Everything was fine. They liked the movie, he had fun, she was good company. He had known that already, of course, but she was good company even *on a date.* Most of his previous disasters had been at dances where there was no way to hide from himself that he was on a date, when he had to do so many things he had never done before. But he was good at movies, he was used to sitting beside people, this time it was her that's all.

He was so comfortable with her. No bumps or rough edges, she just blended into his life. Work turned to lunch, they ate and talked, lunch turned to work, they went home, Friday or Saturday night they shared a movie, the weekend turned to Monday again. Going where his feet had always taken him, except now she was there too. It wasn't that she was *his girl* or anything. He wouldn't even think about that. They were friends. That's all.

The pattern continued for months. She stopped seeing her other boyfriends; they went out once a week. And so long as they went to movies and plays and did things friends do, he was OK. But she was ready for more. A few times, she invited him to Thomson family functions, and he hated that. Things were moving too fast, towards something he knew nothing about and didn't want to know. Why change anything?

She was pushing him, he told her, and he hated being pushed. He was living at home, not making much money, still in a struggle to finish grade 13. He had found a nice, easy rhythm for his life. Everything was finally under control and could stay that way for ever and ever. The challenge of life wasn't finding new challenge, but turning life into a habit he could repeat over and over until he could live it in his sleep. That way *he* was in charge. That was freedom.

This wasn't. New commitments, new responsibilities, and worst of all, new expectations. Having to live up to something he might not be able to live up to. Don't ruin it. She wanted to do things that could only lead to other things. Stop pushing. Back off. He could feel it happening. Three times he stormed out of her house, avoided her at work; each time he apologized and asked her out again. He loved her, she loved him. She was ready, he had to be ready or would lose his chance, maybe forever.

Two years passed. It was a day like every other day except they were stuck in traffic. They had gone to the Sportsman's Show at the Exhibition Grounds. Leaving the parking lot they were surrounded by cars with no movie screen in front and little to do but feel uncomfortable in silence, or talk. He had in his head none of his usual voices of warning. He was just sitting there. All of a sudden, that tiny voice peeked through again.

It was as if it wasn't him, he'd say later, as if the real him had jumped into the back seat and some stranger had taken over. The same one who had talked back to his mother, made smart-assed comments to his teachers, who later would stand up in meetings at work and ask questions which congenial, collegial members of the Imperial Oil family would never ask. Then disappear, leaving his poor stunned hulk to live in the mess.

"I love you," he said. "Would you like to get married?" He was as stunned as she was.

The rest was a blur. His impish other self quickly skipped off; his real self and voices returned. "But not right away," he blurted, inside his head or outside, he isn't quite sure. "We should wait a year or so."

"Yes," Carolyn said, "I thought you'd never ask," and burst into tears.

There were obstacles to come. He would be married in St. Bonaventure Catholic Church which he had attended since moving from Whitby. Unfortunately, she would be married in Washington United Church. Catholics had to be married in Catholic churches, everyone knew that. Catholics might marry non-Catholics, his brother Jim had married one, but that had been contortion enough for the church and especially the Bloyes. Similarly unthinkable was for a bride to be married anywhere but in her own church. So obvious was all this to both of them that neither thought to bring up the subject, for awhile.

After the initial confusion, amusement (was he being teased again?) and shock, it seemed not so important after all. It was still a long time before the wedding, he/she loves me, he/she will realize just how important it is to me/my mom (and dad), how unimportant it really is to him/her and her/his mom (and dad), how it just has to be this way. He/she will understand. Then time began to pass and what had seemed a little important became *important*. Central, basic, not a subject for negotiation, even civil talk. If we can't agree on this, maybe we should forget the whole thing, etc., etc. He hoped the subject would go away, but one night at dinner with his mom and dad, it didn't.

Well, you see, actually I was meaning to talk to you about that, he said or something like it. I'm having a little problem with Carolyn. You see, she wants to get married in the United Church [pause; room darkens]; her mom wants that too. I know, I know, I know (I'm on your side), but she's insisting (oops, wrong word). I know, I know (I'm on your side, remember), she just doesn't understand. I keep telling her but . . .

"Well, you *have* to get married in the Catholic Church," Margaret said finally. "Otherwise," Leo stormed, "we're not coming."

Margaret suggested he see Father Bryant for his advice.

This was genius, he thought. Father Bryant will tell him what he already told Carolyn, he'll tell Carolyn, better yet he'll have Father Bryant tell her himself. That will be the end of it. So he went to see Father Bryant. He told him how he had just become engaged, that his fiancée wasn't Catholic and wanted to get married in her own church.

Father Bryant looked surprised. "Well, what's stopping you?"

More surprised, Frank stared at him. "Thanks a lot, Father," he finally blurted, inside his head or outside, he isn't quite sure.

"No, really," Father went on, "if it's that important to her, why don't we try to get you a dispensation?"

That was *not* the answer to his problem.

"Why would *you* get special dispensation?!" his mother thundered. "Who do you think you are?"

"I know, I know, I know . . . "

He'd have Father Bryant talk to his parents, that was the only way. Slowly, they began to soften. When more weeks passed, however, and no dispensation had been received, he grew panicky and angry. At least three times he had gone to see Father Bryant at his office. Now it was night-time, but this couldn't wait. He and Carolyn drove to Father's rectory, knocked on the door and insisted the housekeeper let them in.

"You said you'd help us work things out, and you haven't." It was a real tongue-lashing, he remembers.

Father Bryant looked at Carolyn, "Is it really important for you to be married in your church?"

"Yes," she said.

"Fine," he smiled. "I've been delaying this just to see how much it mattered to you."

Within a week, he had his dispensation.

He can't quite remember if it arrived before his father died. Leo Bloye had been getting worse for some time; two years before he had had to retire even from the lesser stresses of head office. But moving out of a life he could no longer handle, he had moved into one which offered him little meaning. Since fifteen he had worked, for forty-nine years with the same company, and sometime during those years he had lost the habit for anything but work. That young man who in the mid-1920s filled his nights with bowling, skating, dancing, playing cards to the early morning hours, the still youthful dad his kids watched through the upstairs bannister, jacket and tie off, doing the Charleston; his Friday-night poker games, the annual Knights of Columbus bash followed by his annual morning-after, when Margaret would tell the kids, Dad has the flu. Responsibility first, then health, then age and health together had remade him.

In all those years, what time had he to step back and see where he was going? To see how he fit into his own life's picture? To plan, invest money and time for his different futures ahead? Eight kids, a store to run and air sacs so swollen he could hardly breathe would turn anyone into Pavlov's dog. The light of day goes on, he moves. No whys or what ifs or what abouts in the long run.

Now his kids were grown and he had no job. He'd never had the time for hobbies, never had gotten to know his kids well enough to get involved in their lives, especially at this late date. There were still Christmases and family occasions to preside over, but at home were only Frank and Sue. And Margaret.

For nearly forty years, he had run the office; she had run the home. Now he was home too, and this was her domain. They had most of their lives invested in each other. To get along the way they needed to get along, he now had to accept meekly more things than he had ever accepted meekly in his whole life. Every so often he would chafe a bit, less often he would fight back, insisting on doing certain things his way because his manager's mind and lifetime of experience told him that his way made more sense, that what she had been doing for forty years actually was all wrong. Under one roof instead of two, nothing seemed so perfect any more.

Carolyn remembers the first time she met him. She had been going out with Frank only a short time. She and Frank, Margaret and Leo were sitting in the living room watching TV, when suddenly Leo started coughing. "This man was turning blue," she shouts in recollection. "I thought he was dying right there in front of me. And they're just sitting there!! Nobody's doing anything! They're watching TV!" She kept looking around, no one else even noticed. Was she crazy? Was this "Candid Camera"? Finally, she nudged Frank. "Huh? Oh, he has to do that," he said, and went back to watching.

Sue remembers as a little girl sitting on her dad's lap, her ear to his chest, listening to him breathe. Ann still remembers his prescription number from Courtice Pharmacy in Whitby, "2155," for the Prednisone that would perk him up and little by little eat at his lungs and kill him. Trish remembers calling 911, her mother screaming into the phone, "My husband can't breathe," and minutes later the firemen running in with their axes and rubber coats, Trish with her dad on the bed, holding him, the crisis over; Trish suddenly embarrassed, still in her housecoat. The two or three times he had cancerous cysts removed from his bladder, able to have only a local anaesthetic because he needed his whole body, conscious and working, to breathe.

Frank was home from work that day, he remembers; he had a temperature of 101. Leo's duodenal ulcer had ruptured, he would need the operation he couldn't survive. Frank drove his mom to the hospital, the whole family was there. When he died, Margaret cried in Jim's arms. She may not have shown it, she sobbed, but she really loved him.

He didn't cry then, nor when he saw his dad in the casket. In memory's quirky way, he remembers instead how the funeral home had been so careless. There was his dad, laid out, dressed up to greet eternity, and his tie was wrong. He would never have stood for it. He always wore a big Windsor knot in a perfect triangle. This knot was lopsided and small. Someone told him it didn't matter any more. "That's not Dad's knot," he said.

It wasn't until his dad was finally in his grave that he cried. It would be another four years before his own son, Matt, was born and he began thinking about fathers and sons and how families should be, another eight years before his mother died and he was able to make some sense of what on March 3, 1971, at age twenty-three, was already inside him. "I only cried once when my dad died," he recalls. "With Mom, I cried for days."

He and Carolyn began attending marriage courses, first through the Catholic Church, then through hers. Each course was given one night a week for two hours, each lasted six weeks. The Catholic course was for those about to enter mixed marriages, to explain the Catholic religion and practices to non-Catholics, to help them understand the life their Catholic partner was expected to live. She had been pressing him for months for answers about his religion. If it's so important in your life, she told him, it will be important in mine. So why do you do this, and that? And stumbling around, eventually he'd say, "It's just the way it is," and she would say, "That's not good enough."

Offered in an informational, non-evangelical way, the course proved useful to both of them. Ever since he had proposed, she had felt a relentless, low-grade pressure to convert, a sense from him and his mother that one day, inevitably, they would turn her Catholic. "OK, we're not here to recruit you," Father Bader had said in his opening words of welcome. "We've got enough bad Catholics." A year later, Father Bader would himself be married.

The Catholic course had been compulsory; they took the United Church course "in retaliation," as he puts it, Carolyn's tit for his tat. Its approach was more practical: marriage is more than romantic love. It means living together, getting along, avoiding as many of its destructive stresses as possible, learning how to deal with the rest. Accountants advised them on budgeting, buying houses, planning their financial futures. Other speakers talked of marriage routines, husbands and wives coming home from work, the tasks that needed to be done and, traditional roles or not, who would do them. On weekends, the laundry, cleaning, and grocery shopping, the nuts and bolts of living together. There was little in the course that surprised them, little with which they didn't agree. But here in one complete package they found a marriage blueprint, something to live by. It was here, he thinks, he first heard the advice that has guided him all his married life: whether both spouses work or not, live off one salary. And it was here too that she found the words to express what she has grown more and more to believe: no matter who you marry, any marriage will work if you work at it.

Time was almost up. He couldn't quite believe things had gone this far. Inside, he was beginning to feel something which only years later would reveal itself. Nothing that would have made him want to change anything, just a feeling. He had dreamed like every teenager of the time when school would finally end, when he'd move out of his mother's house to a place of his own, when he could live by his own rules. He'd had longer to wait, needing to pass his grade 13, but there came a moment, in June, 1968, when he was no longer in school, had a job and was making his own money, when things might have changed. But he was too young (he was nearly twenty-one), it was too soon, he wasn't earning enough, it would be irresponsible, a waste of what money he had to pay it to a stranger. A few months later when it wasn't too soon, there was a car to buy, there were dates with Carolyn, then more dates, the pressure of the future, the need to save, the web of adult life closing in. Then he proposed and his moment was gone.

"I went from my mother's house to my wife's house," he has said. "I had no time on my own."

How did it happen? Why did he finally marry? And Carolyn, why did she choose him? They were different in so many ways, they liked to say: she loved dancing, he hated it; she liked her coffee cold, he liked his piping hot. But in most essential ways, they were alike. "I never thought much of myself," he tries to explain. "Carolyn is a bright woman and has lots of common sense, but she didn't go far in school either. The girls I knew in high school were smarter than me. Carolyn was more on my level. That's not very nice to say, but that's how I felt. She didn't talk over my head and I didn't talk over hers. We were comfortable. We worked good together."

For her, it was in the way he opened doors for her, helped her when she needed help or when help would make her life a little easier and nicer. He was so aware, so tuned in to her, so little absorbed in himself. With him, there was a you and an us, and so little me. Not flashy or smooth, he could seem stingy about almost everything, especially his emotions, but what he had, what his teachings and ways allowed him to give, he gave, and always more to her than he kept for himself. He had shied away from commitments, not to keep for himself a catalogue of personal needs, but because he was sure he'd always fall short and let others down. Now he was making a commitment to spend the rest of his life with her. To do what he could to live up to her needs and expectations and those of their children, to make them happy. He was willing to set loose his carefully controlled little world and face a rarely kind unknown. She knew how hard this was for him, how seriously he took his commitment. And once he had made it, she knew he

would see it through, of that she couldn't be more certain.
He would be good to her. In good times and bad, for better and worse, he would do his best.

Lois was maid of honour, Carolyn's cousin Dale, the
bridesmaid. Unable to choose between them, John and
Jim were ushers, his cousin Michael Northcott, the best
man. When the reception ended, Carolyn decided not to
throw her bridal bouquet, and the two of them drove off
in his bright red Volkswagen to spend the night in their
new apartment. In the morning, they left by car for their
honeymoon in Cape Cod. On their way out of the city, they
drove to the cemetery where she placed her flowers on her
father's grave.

They were gone nine days and came home two days
early. They had work ahead of them on Monday, had wedding gifts to move to their apartment and didn't want to be
too rushed. She was working as a clerk at the Scarborough
Tax Office, he had left Superior Propane and for the last
nine months had been at Montreal Trust. His title was
"Multiple Funds Pension Administrator." Several hundred
small companies had pooled their pension monies and
were sharing the profits of a fund run by Montreal Trust.
Each company specified the type of investments it wished,
bonds, equities, etc., and each month a report of the fund's
performance was sent from head office in Montreal to his
desk in Toronto. He supervised a staff of ten. It was their
job to calculate the results for each company in each investment category, prepare reporting letters, and issue pension cheques to retired workers. He was inexperienced,
had no training in accounting and was younger than most
of those he supervised. Being Frank, he also assumed he
knew much less than he did. Still, it had been too good an
opportunity to avoid.

The first month or so everything was fine. The man he
was replacing stayed to train him and to prepare the yearend report. Without having to know every answer, it
seemed he knew most of them. Then the man left.

Suddenly he could see only what he didn't know. He had never been able to do accounting, had gone bankrupt on two of the three paper routes he had. The numbers were too big, the responsibility too great, he was too young. He had reached beyond his grasp *again* and everyone knew.

They were depending on him. Each month the books had to balance, letters and cheques go out. If his books didn't balance, neither would theirs. If something wasn't done, he had to stay at the office until it was. There had always been tomorrow, next year. He had failed twice in high school, but had stayed three years longer and made it. At Superior Propane, he had to balance an account that hadn't balanced in two years; what did six more months matter? Here he faced unfinessable, inescapable, unpostponable failure every month. He was a man who couldn't swim, in water lapping over his nostrils eight hours a day, every new morning having to walk into that water again. He hated it. Every month falling behind, sprinting, catching up at month's end to fall further behind again. But it was his first year-end that finished him.

Many of his numbers weren't right, so he did them again. He stayed nights, came in Saturdays, his deadline coming at him faster than the light at the end of his work. It was like school all over again. Everyone he looked at was looking at him. "They think I'm stupid. They think I shouldn't be here." In the middle of his push to deadline, he told his boss he couldn't handle the job. His boss told him to stick with it, give it a few more weeks until the reports were done, then they would see. When they were done, his boss agreed.

He did so in the nicest way, told him he could stay a few weeks taking time off whenever he wanted to look for another job. In time, without hiding the details, he would learn to say he quit. The effect was devastating. Carolyn met him at the subway, they were several months married by now. On the ride home, he tried to say enough so as not to have to say more, but when they got back to their apartment she followed him into the bedroom. What's the matter, she asked. "I got fired," he said, tears in his eyes. It had been the worst year and a half of his life.

For more than twenty years, every step forward had been followed by most of a step back. Then his life seemed to change. He graduated from high school, met a girl he loved and who loved him, got married, moved to an apartment of their own, was hired for a job that seemed beyond him. He was taking chances. And with each chance he took, he was more likely to take more. But again he had learned. Work was no different than anything else. Why would he ever have thought otherwise? Foolishness. Craziness. Did he like pain? Put your finger on a stove, you learn. Why didn't he?

He didn't need a million dollars, big desk, fancy title, people to push around. As a supervisor, earning more than he ever had, he was miserable. There was a message here. He needed only to know himself, learn where the pain in his life was lurking, and live somewhere else. Then he'd be fine.

He would never be ambitious again.

On Monday, April 10, 1972, at 7:30 a.m., he started at Imperial Oil.

They were living in a one-bedroom apartment in a low-rise building on Biggin Court, between his mother's house on Talwood and her mother's house on Cedarbrae, a little closer to his. They had a clear image of what a home should be, how as married people they should live, what as a husband he should provide. It was the image of the television family, of their own families, of parents many years older, more settled and established, of older sisters and brothers they saw only on dress-up occasions, who had their own houses and everything else they seemed to need. He and Carolyn had put away her salary in the credit union at work when they were first engaged. Now they had enough money for down payments on that image, and like everyone else they made them. The smaller pieces, their coffee,

TV and end tables, not so vivid or central in their matrimonial minds' eyes, he made himself.

They had a difficult time "merging families," as he puts it. They had no real problems at all, she recalls. But if both brought with them a lifetime of habits, he brought more. "I was a pain in the ass in the kitchen," he admits, "because she never cooked meals the way my mom cooked them." Carolyn liked to take the meat out of the oven and let it cool, to make it easier to carve though *she* did none of the carving, he did, and he was perfectly willing *and* able to carve it hot. So he sat down night after night to cold dinners, or so it seemed to him. Why is this so difficult, he wondered with his tongue, his eyes, his being? Just keep the dinner warm! And night after night, she grumbled to herself what she knew he was grumbling even when he wasn't. *That's not the way my mom would do it. Why do I have to eat your way?* And she'd get upset, and he couldn't help himself.

She liked vegetables. If he had to have a vegetable, he wanted corn. Sometimes she served peas or beans; when they went to his mom's, she always served corn. He liked liver, she didn't. She liked the apartment cool, he didn't. He squeezed toothpaste from the bottom, so none got trapped, no time was lost, so the tube didn't split and the paste squish out like a Chia pet. She squeezed wherever her fingers hit the tube.

She liked the apartment clean and tidy, except for her parts, her side of the bedroom, her side of the bed, her side of the closet, which he thought, because he could see them, were his parts too. He liked to hang his shirts with his shirts, the whites with the whites, blues with the blues, his pants he hung together. Her slacks, blouses and dresses were hung up, what did it matter where? They had a double bed. He liked to sleep in coffin-position, flat on his back, hands clasped across his stomach, elbows to his sides, feet sticking up; the covers pulled up to his chest. She liked to turn and toss and burrow her way into whatever position felt comfortable; her covers pulled under her chin. Lying on his back, his feet straight up, when she tugged up the covers she pulled up his toes. *That* drove him crazy.

They took turns making the bed. He did it his mother's way, the hospital way, sheets taut and crisp, every morning rearranged to their original position, every corner tight and sharp. She made the bed as she found it. So every night, just a little, the sheets pulled up from the bottom; being taller, his feet got cold (hers didn't), which also drove him crazy.

The hardest time was at Christmas. They each had their own traditions, their own habits and smells, the "Sputnik" on the tree, without which Christmas wasn't Christmas. Len had died, Paul was in Owen Sound, her mom had only Lois at home. It was Margaret's first Christmas without Leo, the older kids had their own families on Christmas morning. Only Sue was left. What would they do?

It wasn't so much having one's own way as it was not having things his/her way. They were independent people now, living on their own, able to make their own decisions. They were adults. Always they had been told what to do, had lived by someone else's rules, what was the point exchanging a mother for a wife/husband? I may love you and want you to be happy, we may be a couple, an "us," but I'm also still a "me" and always will be, and to me what's good for us seems what's good for me as part of us, and that's the way it is. So *dear*, I think we should do it this way, and *darling*, don't you think that would be better? In their own families, neither had fought back; here, well matched and equal, at the same starting point at the same time, creating something of their own, they did fight back. And the more they did, the more they would.

If Christmas was a symbol, so were their mothers. He liked his coffee piping hot because *she* always had it on the stove, perking and perking until she almost burned the bloody stuff. His way was her way, just as Carolyn's was her mother's, and if his way or her way might someday be *their* way, there was no way her/her way would ever be theirs. So every battle was joined and every simple habit got caught in complicated baggage. I am my own person, independent of my mother, why isn't he/she? It was harder for him because, more set in his ways, every other way seemed a challenge that had to be met, because more under his mother's thumb as a boy, he felt a greater need to parade **his** own authority when finally he had some. Are you *her* daughter or *my* wife?

He wanted to go to his mom's at Christmas, she wanted to go to hers and wherever they ended up didn't feel right. They would learn to take turns, one year dinner at one, a visit at the other, Christmas eve at one, Christmas day at the other, but that was later. Until they had kids of their own and his way and her way had reason and the chance to be *their* way, with no tradition of their own Christmas wouldn't feel the same.

12

Their one year lease was almost up. They had some furniture and appliances now, their habits and routines were slowly becoming their own, yet they would never truly have the feeling of playing house without a house. Their sisters and brothers, the Cleavers, Nelsons, Andersons and Petries all had houses; as a married couple they would be failures until they had one too. Unable to afford Toronto, they began looking beyond the city's commuter hinterland, east, where their jobs were closest and they were most at home. He had lived much of his life in Whitby, his three oldest sisters were still there or in Oshawa. She had an affection for Scarborough, but if a choice had to be made, a house was more important than where it was. Besides, it wasn't for ever. They would be gone three years, five at the most, and they were young.

It was two storeys high, red brick and semi-detached, in a new subdivision cut from farmers' fields on Oshawa's west (Toronto) side. It cost $25,000, $5,000 paid down out of Carolyn's savings, a mortgage for the rest. A new Catholic school had been built behind and beside it, making the house affordable. Once more, God had provided. They moved on November 25, 1972, he was twenty-five, she a month and a day from her twenty-sixth birthday. John and Jim, Trish's husband, Camille, and Sue's fiancé, Bob, helped him pack and load the rented truck, and with Lee's husband, Pat, helped Carolyn unload at the house, which still looked empty after they were done. They bought a refrigerator, a stove and dryer, deciding to make do a little longer with her mom's old wringer washer. No single purchase proved too much of a burden, each month they paid down each bill a little, filled another space and drew closer to fitting the image they needed to fit.

Their jobs were now in distant Toronto. Each morning, they got up at five and by six-thirty were on the road in his suddenly aging red Volkswagen. He started work at seven-thirty but liked to be early, so he dropped her off on his way though she didn't begin until nine. When he was finished at four, he drove to the Tax Office and waited until she was done at five. By this time the middle of rush hour, they wouldn't be home until six.

A few months later, he was put on around-the-clock shift work. They would need two cars. With two incomes and her savings, they could just afford a new silver-blue Chevy Nova, the car he always wanted.

Little by little, they were getting themselves in trouble and didn't know it. Living on the financial margins, every change in their lives made them twist and contort a little more. Marriage meant a house, a house meant furniture, appliances and home-making things to fill it, a long-range commute, long dead-hours, a new car, more gas, more insurance, rides on winter roads alone. She quit her job in Scarborough to look for one nearer home. It took her only a few weeks, but it was a few weeks without income to pay off their growing mound of monthly payments. Then the old wringer washer gave out, then the TV. Tired of her mom's old kitchen table, they bought a dining-room set. Flush with her new job at Whitby's Tax Office, they bought a camper trailer, sleeping bags, a stove, lamp and dishes to go with it.

Now they had something for weekends, holidays and times together that married couples were supposed to have. And one more monthly payment. Her salary had gone into savings, and out into a car, furniture and anything else they needed. His salary had gone for food, clothing, life insurance, the mortgage and minimum payments on their credit cards, for all their daily needs. Living on one salary as they always knew they should; the details didn't matter.

Then just about the time she began her new job, it happened; and just after they had bought the new camper, they found out. She was pregnant.

Husband, breadwinner, homeowner, he had filled all of his adult roles but one; she was a wife. They were ready; it was time.

She loved her days being pregnant, feeling something growing inside, feeling fundamentally, irreplaceably important. Her friends had just wanted their babies to be born; she wanted that time, *their* time, to go on and on. She and Frank planned the nursery, the baby's room would be on the second floor at the front of the house with its nice big window that overlooked the street. They bought furniture and baby clothes, and weeks before they needed to, packed her bag and put the old Volkswagen in place at the bottom of the driveway, just in case.

It was a little after midnight, he had just come home from the afternoon shift, she was waiting up. She wanted to go for a walk. It was a beautiful, cold February night, inches of snow had fallen in the hours before, the sidewalks were covered, they shuffled down the empty streets through the trench-like tire tracks. In the morning, she had to pick up new licence stickers for their cars, so he showed her the route. About an hour later, they were back home and in bed. About an hour after that, she awakened. Her water had broken. She screamed to him and ran to the bathroom. He threw on some clothes, grabbed her bag and called the hospital to tell them they were on their way. He brought her some old clothes, then went to the top of the stairs and waited. The bathroom door stayed closed. The leaking wouldn't stop. He yelled for her to hurry. Excited, scared, embarrassed and very uncomfortable, she finally emerged. He bundled her up in her winter things and got her out the door. As he helped her down the outside steps, a thought came to him which has embarrassed him ever since: *Thank goodness the VW [with its leather seats] is last in the driveway. The way she's leaking, how would I ever clean the [cloth] seats in the Nova?*

They reached the hospital at 3:00 a.m. She wasn't yet in labour. At noon, still not in labour, the doctor decided to induce her. More than ten hours later when still nothing had happened, the doctor took him aside. He was afraid of infection, he said. She should have a caesarian; it was up to him to give the approval. He knew nothing about caesarians. A little frightened, he called Ann and talked things through with her. He asked if she would come to the hospital to keep him company. She said she would. He gave the doctor his approval. Just before midnight, Carolyn went into the operating room. A few minutes later, at 12:02 a.m., February 13, 1975, Matthew Leo Bloye was born, 10 lbs., 1 oz. When they were taking him to the nursery, past the waiting room where Frank still stood pacing, he saw him for the first time. Matt filled the incubator from end to end.

Frank rushed for the phone, but he had left his money at home (*If I have money in my pockets, I only spend it,* etc., etc.). Borrowing a dime from Ann, he called the operator:

"I'd like to place a long distance call to Toronto, please, to a Mrs. Bloye, and charge it to my home phone?"

"Certainly. What is your home number, please?"

He couldn't remember. He shouted to Ann but she couldn't remember. He stammered and tried to explain what he couldn't quite believe himself. "Heh, heh, actually my wife just had a baby and I, heh, heh, can't quite remember the number. Could I look it up in the phone book, please?"

Later, he would describe Matt's birth as the most exciting moment of his life.

There was now lots more to do around the house, but for him it was time that was long set aside and waiting. When Matt awakened in the middle of the night, he got up, changed him and brought him in to nurse. She had so much to do during the day, to feed and clean him, dress and undress him, all the wash, the walks, the shopping and errands now so much more complicated, the trips to the doctor, pushing him on swings until she thought her arms would fall off. The planning, the thinking ahead, the need now to see everything through two sets of eyes, could he do it, should they try, learning what was right for him.

It was during this time he began to think about his father. He had accepted so much as a kid. He loved him, he was the best father in the whole world, he guessed, so tall and smart, the stories others told of him, the respect they showed, the way his mother treated him. She didn't treat anyone else like that. He was beyond question, beyond reproach. If he did something, it was right. If he was at the office, it was because the office had to be at.

Or did it? He was wondering about that now. Later wonder would turn to doubt and anger as he came to hear old stories differently. He was making his own life now. He was becoming something. What would he be? How would he live? What would he do? And how would he do it and be it? He would need to accept what he was, knowing, denying, ignoring, doing whatever it took. And whatever he wasn't, he would need to be able to explain away. More and more he thought of his dad, taking in stories of him the way he now needed to hear them. What he would be, he decided, was "not him." Not a businessman, not a "not-a-nine-to-fiver" And he would be there.

He liked being home. It was where he wanted to be. In his life, he had spent more time at home than anywhere else, he was more comfortable there. His mother had trained him. He could cook and clean and when anyone needed him he could be there as well as anyone could. He had an aptitude and instinct for it. At home, no one was older, smarter, tougher or richer. He could get up and go to bed when he wanted, eat what he wanted, drink his coffee, hang his clothes, wash and dry his dishes the way he wanted. He could watch TV shows he wanted to watch. He was good at home; less clear to him was how good he could be everywhere else.

He would do his job at Imperial, but at home he would go any extra mile.

It was also about this time Carolyn began to understand. It had been a bit awkward those first few years of marriage. As a teenager, he had heard so much about sex, how incredible, how so much beyond everything it was. The way the boys talked about it at school, different from hockey or baseball, even cars, as if those initiated into it were members of some secret society of the blessed. Insiders to life's great experience. They knew and no one else did. No one else could.

And certainly they must be right, he thought. Being naked with someone, touching her, being allowed, being touched. It was so much beyond his own experience. His parents had had eight kids, his brothers and sisters lots more, but never in them had he seen anything that connected in the slightest way to what he had heard. What *was* there out in that vast unknown that could turn something so magical? He would soon find out.

As his wedding day neared, he grew excited, and afraid. Dating, dancing, so many other things were supposed to have been great too, and had only confirmed what he already knew, what everyone knew, what he didn't want to think about and go through again. It's just not fun coming face to face with what you can't do. He was good at model cars, at smiling, being pleasant and fading from view, at doing things on his own time, being alone, being there. Anything else was someone else's pleasure, and that was trouble.

If sex was so great, why would it be so great for me, he thought? Why would *I* like it; why would *I* be any good at it? The "not liking" and "not being good at" he could live with. He was used to that. But what about Carolyn? Sex had to do with her as well, her expectations, her needs and feelings. They had managed to work out other things. She liked dancing; he didn't. They didn't go often; he went when he had to. But this wasn't dancing.

It was fine, it was nice. But really, what could live up to the build-up? He wasn't surprised. It wasn't the sort of thing he *would* like. His mom and dad had never shown affection. It was the boys who weren't like him who always talked about it. Besides, he was as he was. His story was already too far along in its writing.

But in her story, sex *was* all it was supposed to be. Before they were married, he had shown his love in so many ways, and she had shown hers. Now they were husband and wife, having singled each other out as the ones in all the world special enough to bestow a unique gesture of love. Marriage. And to symbolize that gesture, the one thing that made every day after August 13, 1971 different from every day before, the act of love.

And he understood how she felt; but love for him wasn't big brass bands. It was all those things in the hours and days between, when no parade was in sight. It was little things. *Doing.* And those he could manage. It was a good woman and a good man, side by side at life's labours. And she understood; but what's wrong with big brass bands? "You don't love me," she'd say. "Of course, I do," he'd say. I take out the garbage, hold doors and pull out chairs for you. I cook and clean and wash. *I love you.* I take care of you when you're sick, I come home every night. I'm there for you. I do all these things as well as anyone. I will do them until the day I die. Please, can't you see them for what they are, see me for what I am?

Sex is just one more act of love. And I like it. But it's so much to live up to; so much can go wrong. And so much can be riding on it. The moment to moment details of life that have to get done, the feelings we have for each other, the things that can't be risked. Life is hard enough. So please, as we lie here together, let the moment pass into sleep, no thoughts, no expectations, no rancour. I love you.

It was probably after Matt was born, when he did so much to make her life easier, that she began to understand.

To live his nine-to-five life, however, he would need to find a way to provide. He earned $11,350.09 in 1975, the year Matt was born. Carolyn earned nothing. (Average family income in Canada that year was $16,993.) Somehow he had to match the practical demands of life and marriage, the images and myths he held, with the money he earned and what it would buy. Until now, it had bought them much more than he earned, but with their credit-card balances approaching their limits, without her income and savings and with a new family need, the slope would get more slippery. He had been told to live on one salary because some day they would have only one salary to live on. Nobody had taken that message more to heart than him. Extra money didn't matter. If you've got it you only spend it, what you buy you come to need, what you need you need more of, and nothing else in life comes to matter. Want rules. Power, control, freedom are lost. Keep wants small, and everything you want you can have. And you are free.

He had been caught in his own fiction. His purchases were the necessities, he told himself, hers they could do without and would do without when they had to. They were living off one salary; yet really, they were living off everything they had, even pushing that to the limit. Two salaries, his, hers, and buying on down payments, a third, their creditors'. Now one salary stopped, another was drying up.

By early 1976, "We were beginning to sink, and were too dumb to know it."

His Nova was a lemon. It got just fourteen miles to a gallon and back and forth to Toronto more than two hundred times a year meant too many gallons at high OPEC prices. In damp weather it wouldn't start, on snow-slick roads was dangerously overpowered, its engine rusted out. His Volkswagen, now seven years old, was in and out of the repair shop so often he decided to sell it, and his Nova too. He bought a new car, borrowing more than half its purchase price from Carolyn's mother. It was the cheapest family car he could find, he told himself, an American Motors Hornet stationwagon, completely stripped, so basic the dealer had to order it specially from the factory, had even to have it pulled from the assembly line just to meet his specifications. A few months later, she was pregnant again.

On February 9, 1977, Janine Lillian Emily, 9 lbs. 5 oz., was born, nearly two years to the day after her brother. Janine was Carolyn's sister's middle name, Lillian her mother's middle name, Emily her mother's mother's name on whose birthdate Janine was born. When it was clear another caesarian would be necessary, the doctor recommended that while she was on the operating table he tie her tubes, that two caesarians were enough for anyone. She had wanted a large family, four kids or more, until just before they were married he took her over to his sister Lee's. In the din of a houseful of kids, she decided two was enough. Still, in the stress of giving birth, she found such a decision too final to make.

They talked about it when she was out of the hospital. Their money situation was not getting better, and by now they knew it would never improve much. Carolyn's income was being missed, and with a boy and girl already they had a "millionaire's family." Two was enough, they decided. Because she had had two operations, she asked him to have a vasectomy. He stalled for more than a year, then made an appointment to see a urologist. He talked to him, the doctor wanted to talk to her, they all talked, several more months passed, she got pregnant again.

His mother had had as many children as God had provided. They weren't wanted or not wanted, put off, spaced out, fitted in; they happened. She had her first child ten months after she was married, her last at age forty-three. With each new baby, their lives changed, so they changed, Leo got a raise, God provided. Frank would never have been born if it had been any other way. He had grown up in the teachings of his church. He had heard many times that the object of marriage was to propagate, yet now as an adult and a practising Catholic, he was deciding forever to have no more children.

He found the decision easier than he thought. He believed in the basic Catholic doctrine, in the infallibility of the Pope in religious matters. But the Pope was a man, and corrupt popes had sold penances and done all manner of ungodly things in the name of God. That was their human side. In worldly matters, they had shown themselves eminently fallible, so in worldly matters he had come to question them.

So many of their pronouncements he saw as abrogations of God's great gift to man, individual free will. God had guided him in his daily life as He did the popes. He had guided him to Carolyn, to Uncle Gen and Imperial Oil, to Oshawa, to have children, even to Montreal Trust, though there, so filled with the blare of money and power he hadn't heard Him, and had to learn His/his lesson the hard way. But where in the midst of all these directives, he wondered, was free will? Where is freedom? choice? Where is real sacrifice in taking a right road when all others are blocked and can't be travelled? Everyone needs sacrifice. Where is goodness if one is taken by the shoulders and shown the way? He had to decide, right or wrong; to experience one to know the other.

So after they were married, they chose not to propagate, made a down payment on a house, furnished it, and gave themselves some time to live on their own. Then they chose to propagate. After Janine was born, they faced another decision. It had nothing to do with religion or convenience. It wasn't to have more TV sets and nicer cars and trips twice a year to top up his tan. It was a matter of personal responsibility, and from what he was feeling, he knew what God wanted of him. Frank wanted only to provide for his kids, for them to have what other kids had. Nothing extravagant, nothing that would spoil them. Maybe they would always need to make do with cheaper things, a three-speed bike instead of a ten, but that was OK. Just so they didn't have to do without. Why should it be them?! Not everybody can have a college education and make lots of money. He wanted a *decent* life for them, that's all; to have enough so they could live their lives and not be so fixated by what they didn't have, to be blind to what life offered and demanded. Wasn't that more important? Didn't they have that right too?

But they couldn't keep having kids and live that life, he knew. Yet if choice was taken from him, what could he do? He couldn't give up sex entirely, that was biological, but more kids meant he would have to work longer and harder, just as his father did. He wouldn't be there, she'd have to work, the kids wouldn't have her when they needed her, they'd all end up tired, frustrated and unhappy. And wasn't that when kids got abandoned, mistreated and trouble began? Surely God didn't want that; He was responsible too.

So when Carolyn got pregnant the third time, certain of His guidance (with the horse already bolted from the barn), he had a vasectomy. (After Stephanie was born, taking no chances, Carolyn had her tubes tied too.)

On July 8, 1980, Stephanie Dale Bloye, 10 lbs., was born, named for Carolyn's cousin and bridesmaid. Carolyn had just turned thirty-three, he was thirty-two, Matt nearly five, Janine almost three. He would earn $16,471.20 that year; home with the kids, she earned nothing. Average family income in Canada in 1980 was $28,533. He had earned 66.8 per cent of the average five years before; now five years more experienced with five years of pay increases behind him, and three more mouths to feed, he was earning just 57.7 per cent.

The vasectomy was the first step on the road back.

In his story, there is nothing tragic. No series of misfortunes hiding in the shadows, rubbing at their palms, waiting to crash down on him. He is no life's victim because he doesn't see himself that way. Some things have gone wrong; things go wrong. No one said everything would be perfect, least of all his mother. Put together the moments of a life and they can add up the wrong way; just as easily they can add up the right. Same moments. It depends on how you add, on how you see yourself.

So which life is yours: older parents, older brothers and sisters, bullies, dyslexia, father never there, school, debts, etc., etc.? Big family, loving family, mother always there, smells from the kitchen, Christmas, a God who loves you, etc., etc.? For him, it was easy. He had reason to be happy, he wants to be happy, he has a stake in being happy, *presto.* He's happy. Besides, what can be so bad?

Every two weeks he brought home his pay-cheque, put some of it aside for groceries, paid the mortgage, the rest went into the bank. That same night, he'd write out his cheques, paying only enough to keep his accounts going; overnight his money was gone. He had no savings; at age thirty-two, he could see no different future. If he didn't do something now, he decided, they would be "dirt poor all the time."

So they gathered up their credit cards and put them in a safety deposit box. She began making their clothes. He paid cash for gas or didn't drive; he began car-pooling to work. For years, he had paid only the minimums on his accounts, robbing Peter to pay Paul as he put it, until finally robbing them both to pay everyone down the line. Now he began attacking one account at a time, making minimum payments on the rest.

To cut his costs, he thought about leaving Imperial Oil. It was for the first and only time. He had been there eight years, the company had been good to him, it had taken him in when he needed it most. He had a lifetime job there, and every two weeks a pay-cheque safe and sure in his hands. Still, working closer to home, he wouldn't have those gas costs, his cars would last longer; he could replace them with smaller, cheaper ones. He went for job interviews in Oshawa, and almost made his move. Then he discovered an Imperial benefits booklet, and realized all he'd be giving up: a medical and dental plan, accident, life insurance, savings and university education plans. He decided to stay.

He also discovered the "credit union." In cutting off his credit cards, he had found a way to force himself not to buy. The credit union got him to save. Willpower, he had learned, was too weak a force to keep him in line. If he had money in his pockets, he'd spend it. If he didn't, he wouldn't, and because he'd survive in either case, he didn't need what money would make him buy, and would escape its temptation. So once he was living more than just hand to creditor's mouth, every pay-cheque he had fifty dollars deducted, untouched, unseen, and put into his credit union account. And every January, one half his annual raise, nearly five hundred dollars a month at one point, also went into the account. He talks today as if the credit union was an instrument of God. It's what saved me, he says, without hint of exaggeration. It gave him simple steps to follow, a new pattern of behaviour he could manage. More importantly, it made him feel strong when he was weak and had to be strong.

By 1982, they were escaping their hole. He was earning $21,751.69 now, up to 63.3 per cent of the national average. They had new habits, new routines they could sustain; there were no big surprises, no new babies, no cars to buy that would again throw everything into a snarl. And the more in control, the more blessed they seemed to be. They bought some insurance, found themselves short of money one month when the bills came due, then a cheque arrived from Allstate. They had been overcharged on their premium. Or the baby bonus would arrive. Something. They had closed their financial gap enough that good things could happen. Someone was watching over them.

These were the hardest years, when their kids were

being born. There wasn't much money, yet he had in his mind what a family should be. He would work, she would stay home; he would provide. Other families might have nicer clothes, their kids might have more things, but only at a price too great for them and everyone, now and later. So he had resisted. They hadn't really lived on one salary all that time as they liked to imagine. They had needed what Carolyn earned and saved, what they borrowed from her mother, what the system allowed them to run up. Yet through all this, he had given his kids a mother at home when a mother needed to be home. That was the point, that was his achievement, and about that he was very proud.

It was during these years that Margaret Bloye died. She had had a minor stroke in 1975; a few months before her death eight years later, the arteries hardening in her brain, she would suffer from confusion and deteriorate rapidly. But it was those years when the kids were leaving home, especially after their move from Whitby, that her life had changed the most.

She had given them birth, raised, nurtured, schooled and churched them, directed and redirected them, taught them right and wrong; she had been the emotional, psychological and functional centre of their lives. Every path outside them, into the world and back, to and into each other, connected through her. But as they got older, more distant and busy, they began building their own connections separate from her. She found that hard to take. At family gatherings, they reverted to their old roles, Mom was still Mom, and they would defer to her force and being, though not without tension. She still needed them to need her, loving was doing, but having raised them to be strong she was reaping what she had sowed, and they needed her less.

Because she always did so much, everything she did had seemed for everyone else, and every failing she had was excused from sight. She was so busy, so tired; with eight kids and a husband who wore a clean white shirt every day, sometimes two, how else could she be? And all the kids nodded to themselves. That was her story, fully, completely written in their minds and souls, and in hers too. Except now so late in their lives, who was this other woman, so cranky and hurtful?

When her kids visited her no one could come often enough, stay long enough, be agreeable enough, have raised their kids well enough. She took out her various angers on anyone around, the better she knew you the angrier she got. Sue stopped taking her friends home, never knowing what her mother might say. It was hardest on her, Frank and Leo, those still home as the 1970s began. Her mother had no less of a need to lead, they were fewer, older and less willing to be led; the collisions grew harsher and more frequent. After Leo died, things got worse.

Was this some new woman emerging from nowhere or, a thought too frightening, the same woman in the light of their more mature eyes? They needed her to be someone new, someone they could excuse by age, illness and the last hard days of her husband's life, her sudden turn an unimportant, forgettable sequel to her story. The alternative meant rewriting her whole life's story and theirs too, but to what? That was too risky. It was all so confusing. Surely she must have felt the same. I am a devoted mother. I gave my life to raising those kids, I did everything for them. Any time, in any situation, I was there. Why do I feel this way? Why am I saying these things? What made me what I was? What makes me how I am? Am I, is she, a lie?

Motherhood was duty, but it was also living at the centre of things. Which did she love best, which drove her more, or could it be both? Motherhood was loving by doing; and being loved by having things done. It was being needed and needing to be needed, selfless and selfish, being there and having others be there for you. It was being an icon, and being a human being in a human role. But what happens when circumstances change, when she can't be there, when she has no further duty, can't do, isn't needed, can't be selfless, when she no longer inhabits that centre? How does motherhood feel then? And how does she act? Her needs no longer softened by her duties, she seems utterly changed and doesn't know why. Nor do her kids, and she doesn't like it and they don't like it, and her story and their stories, all their lifetimes invested in them, seem suddenly false.

After Sue was married and no one was left, she moved to an apartment. It was the happiest she ever saw her, Sue recalls. Alone, she depended only on herself and outsiders, not on her own kids who had always depended on her. There she could be what she was, and not be reminded always of what she wasn't. She had taken back a mortgage on the house and had some monthly income. She had a little yellow Maverick to get her where she wanted to go. She helped care for the church rectory when the housekeeper was away, was a Red Cross volunteer at North York General Hospital. Twice a year for a week at a time, she baby-sat eight rich kids in a sprawling house on one of Toronto's wealthiest streets, The Bridle Path, civilizing them slightly before returning them to their parents.

It ended with her stroke. The kids, worried for her health, insisted she not live alone. She moved in with Trish, but Trish had a baby and two other kids under five. But really Trish found her mother too difficult to live with. Ann was next. Her house was bigger, Margaret had her own bedroom, bathroom and family room, and for ten months she was there. It was awful. Ann's five kids would leave the dinner table *before* dessert just to get away. There seemed no solution. Then one day Margaret decided she would live on her own, and that was that.

Her daughters helped her find an apartment; her spirits picked up. She went to mass every day, Ann took her shopping Thursday mornings, Frank and the others drove to Oshawa to visit her nearly every week. She attended all the birthday parties for all her kids, every summer there was a family get-together with the grandkids, now thirty-nine in all.

Early in December, 1983, she went into the hospital. The day after Christmas, Carolyn's birthday, the kids formed into teams and stayed with her around the clock. Three days later, she died. Frank was with her.

She had been hard on him. She put him down when put down too often he had needed a mother to pick him up. Her way was to turn every little thing into a showdown, and in a mismatch of ages and natures she never blinked. For reasons of her own, she had to win even when those she loved had needed to win more. But he loved her, he nearly worshipped her. Even now in his head when he searches for guidance, it's her voice he hears before he hears God's. For him, the matter was simple. In spite of everything, *she was always there.*

His father never yelled; always he was gentle and calm. But always Frank had the feeling his father disapproved of him. His father liked watching hockey games on TV, he couldn't play; his father was a successful businessman, he went bankrupt on his paper routes. When he told him he and Carolyn were getting married, his father was stunned, "Are you serious? Why don't you get a job first?" He had been working nearly two years. In his father's eyes, he was never good enough and for reasons that were all his own doing. His father made him feel inadequate; his mother never did.

"Mom's death hit me harder than Dad's," he says now. "I miss them both, but I miss Mom more."

"Whenever I'd be sitting in church, and do something I shouldn't, Mom would give me *that look*," Sue recalls. "Her lips would go all thin and straight, her mouth would set like stone." When her mother died and she saw her lying in her coffin, Sue whispered to Trish, "She's still got that look on her face."

They had stayed in Oshawa much longer than they imagined. It would be three years, or five they promised themselves; it was thirteen. Their neighbours were changing, their families were growing up, bigger and older they needed more space, older and earning more money, they could afford it. Newer, younger families were moving in. With three children of their own in two bedrooms, they were more cramped themselves. He was tired of commuting. Their finances were now mostly in order, it would be now or maybe never. For Carolyn, it was time to go home.

13

"Toronto's purr-fect mieuw-sic mix, CHFI, FM 98."

The words sing into his ears as he turns the ignition. She piles in beside him. In the hundred metres between the outside door of 90 Wynford Drive and the parking lot, their energy has returned. He hits the accelerator a little too hard, then the brake, then the accelerator, they lurch and squeal like Bonnie and Clyde at a getaway. They are on their way home.

"Now here's Darryl Dahmer and more CHFI airborne traffic."

He reaches over and turns up the volume to hear what he knows he will hear. The Don Valley Parkway northbound is slow, bumper to bumper in stretches, volume is heavy; in the southbound lanes an accident, the cars are on the shoulder, but northbound traffic is slowing for a look. His energy clouds over, "I don't know why they insist on gawking," he mutters. She looks pleasantly ahead, hearing neither the radio nor him.

"OK, thanks a lot Double D," the DJ's voice sings again. "And now a little music . . ."

He waits his turn then shoves into the line of cars jammed up along Wynford Drive. A white Chevy pulls up to the curb; he watches it. It waits, he slows and motions the driver to move ahead of him. Behind, an old Chrysler powers after it, but he had been watching it too. He hits the gas, jumps into the gap and blocks it off. He whirls around to see the driver's face. "Typical," he mutters. It wasn't his turn; he had no right; it wasn't fair.

He stares into his windscreen. She is bubbling on; he

isn't listening. He turns down the access ramp, crawling ahead a car length at a time. The Chevy, and soon the car behind him, continue along the outside of the access road; he works his way to the inside and sticks his nose against the traffic. The cars roll by as if they don't see him.

"Thanks a lot, sir!" he snarls at one car, then another.

"Thanks a lot, buddy!"

He bounces the car forward hoping the sudden movement will make on-coming drivers blink. Freed from work, their minds are elsewhere. His mouth lengthens into a leering, sneering grin,

"Thank you, sir!" he snarls again. A few more cars go by. All day he had to put up with so much more, but that had to do with the company and not just him. There, he was protected by telephone and distance; here, the outside world is in front of him. Others spend many of their hours drifting in the indistinct light of past or future, hope or fear, as purposeful refuge from the present. He is immersed in the present. What he sees is what is before him, every scene in drenching sunlight, every colour rich, shadow deep, contour etched, contrast clear. Everything unmistakeable, unmissable. Like his mother, he has a need to correct. *Semper vigilate.* And what he sees aren't acts of blindness or inadvertence, but symptoms of a selfish, uncaring world.

The cars keep passing him by. Nothing is personal, and everything is.

"Thanks again, buddy!"

His mouth tightens. He slams his foot on the gas and leaps into an opening only partly there. Once more he has put the world to the test; and once more it has let him down.

"That's 'One Heartbeat,' with Smokey Robinson, here on the station everyone can agree on, CHFI, FM 98."

She is still talking about work. As something they share, it is something to talk about. To him, anything that has to do with work is work, and work is over. When he finally hears her, he changes the subject.

"Have you got anyone else coming in?"

Stopped mid-sentence, she has no idea what he is talking about. "We could do that one night next week."

Now that she knows, she sits back in retreat. Since putting in the new carpet and painting the front rooms last summer, they have wondered what to do about their furniture. It needs reupholstering, but in what colours and materials, and when?

"No, I'm still not sure —" she says, trying not to be defensive and not succeeding.

"We've got to get moving on that. It's the chairs or a rug for the back bedrooms. One or the other."

It is *not* one or the other, her look says. It's the chairs, done slowly and properly, or nothing. "Let's just do one room at a time," she says.

"OK, OK, but how long's it been since we put in that living-room rug, a year and a half?"

"Frank, it's been eight months."

"Anyway, you know what you want."

"Frank, we have *five* chairs to do. We can only do two this year, but I've got to know what to do with the other three before we start." She begins calmly, until more sure of herself her passion begins to show.

He shifts his probe. "What're you doing for curtains?"

"I think just sheers."

"Yeah, but sheers and what?"

"Sheers and sheers," she says, her voice rising again.

"I thought you didn't like people looking in."

"You can't see in with sheers."

"But then it's not dark."

"Night is dark."

With the living room now on her mind, he goes on to something else.

A big black BMW swooshes by on his left. He had been watching it in his rear-view mirror, had speeded up as it approached, but blocked by the car in front, the BMW went by. He checks his side mirror, snaps on his blinker, and pulls into the passing lane. Traffic has broken up and for the moment is moving well. He slams down his right foot. Travelling comfortably at eighty kilometres per hour, his speedometer is now at one hundred and rising. He pulls up alongside the BMW, glances to his right, and eases past.

It isn't as much fun as it was. "I'd see a guy in front of me in some big, fancy car, I'd put my foot down and *zoom.* 'You gotta a $40,000 car, mine's $9,000, and I'm passing the hell out of you. Whatsamatter?'" And he'd laugh. Now he has a fancy car too. Not *that* fancy, and a van actually, a Dodge Caravan. He had been tempted for so long and for so long he resisted. Buy only what you can afford; don't go near what you can't because wants turn to needs and everyone is weak; avoid bells and whistles, any four wheels get you where you need to go.

Anything he didn't have, he needed not to need and for anyone who had it to be foolish. Power windows? My arm works fine. Besides, power windows now means power windows forever, and every few years a few hundred more dollars from the credit union to pay for them. So can I really afford them? Everything is a lifetime decision. The car he had before, his old Dodge Aries, had black-wall tires and bench seats and could go faster than any speed sign and pass any big BMW he was likely to meet. So why buy more?

Then he bought the van. It had 38,000 km on it; it also has on it air-conditioning, tinted glass windows, chrome side-steps and a V6 engine. There is now no going back. "Well, it's only a *mini-*van," he explained, confusing the mind he wanted to confuse. "It's probably not any *longer* than my old car. And periodically I do get a *station wagon,* then go back to a sedan. To me, the van is really more *like a wagon. The next time* I'll probably just go back to a *regular* car." Wind your road around enough, and maybe you *can* go back.

The salesman had told him to go into his office, that he would make him a deal. This was the part he hated. He got too excited. He knew it was only a game, nothing personal, but in this game there would be winner and a loser and he knew he had to lose. If the salesman didn't give him his price, he couldn't back away and go someplace else because the salesman had given that price to everyone else, he was sure. It was his fault, he was a lousy negotiator, a loser if he made no deal, a loser if he paid more than his price. Or if he did get his price, it was because he had set it too high and was the fool for setting it there. Or another dealer around the corner would have sold it to him cheaper. He wanted only for the salesman to give him a price and be done with it. Spending a few hundred dollars more was a lot easier to live with than losing.

The salesman looked him in the eye, "With the trade-in on your car, I can give it to you for *this*," he said. It was exactly his price. So he held out for more, and got the warranty and rustproofing thrown in.

It cost $17,550. He would pay it off $405 a month for five years. He had never spent more than $9,000 on a car before.

The next Sunday morning, he was sitting in the living room reading *The Sun*. He turned to the car ads. A dealer downtown was having a sale, Dodge Caravans, one year newer, with everything but the tinted windows: $16,000.

He couldn't resist.

Traffic is backing up again as he approaches 401. Road conditions have been so good he is ahead of the next traffic report and now he isn't sure whether to take 401 or stay on the Parkway. He takes a chance and goes 401. As he turns onto the access road, he wishes he hadn't.

"Happy going on 401 eastbound near the airport, but east of the Parkway it's extremely busy, so stay away from there." He shakes his head.

"Thanks again, double D. Not too hard, not too soft, the purr-fect mieuw-sic mix, CHFI, FM 98."

He has stopped listening.

He likes being in his own vehicle. When he had to take the bus those early years in Scarborough, he had felt so cut off without a radio. When he got to work he'd hear people say, "Hey, did you hear about this?" and he hadn't. He had to pretend, which he was never good at doing, or shrink back so far into himself that he faded from view. Now he listens every morning. It's a different kind of news on radio. Most is local, car crashes, layoffs, lots of murders and rapes. Everything gets spit out quickly, dispassionately, so stark and spare, day after day so hammering and obsessive. Who is the crazy one here? he sometimes wonders. The people doing all these terrible things or the voice twice each hour which speaks of them, can't get enough of them. Is this really what's important, what I need to know, what makes my life different from yesterday? What an evil place this must be. The editorialists, witty, abrasive, controversial, delivering one minute certainties for every coffee station debate. Everything so awful, so simple to rectify. Everyone else so stupid. "And now back to you Double D . . ."

It's not his world, yet it is one he can imagine, just out of sight, around every corner, over every next hill, lying in wait, for him, his wife, his son and especially his daughters. Incomprehensible, beyond his redemption, a world to be avoided and escaped. It wasn't like that when he was a kid, he's sure. He may now be the parent who knows too much, still he knows what he feels. The world is getting worse.

It's why he likes to drive. Behind metal and glass, he can witness it and not be touched. Buses and subways may get him where he needs to go in not much more time, at much less cost, but that isn't the point. Like hundreds of thousands of others who jam up the roads, he wants to get away. His own radio, his own music, his own noises and smells: it's not much, just a few cubic feet bumper to bumper with the next guy, but it's his. So he drives and they drive, and in this world neither will stop.

He creeps along in the outside collector lane and gets off at the first exit, Victoria Park Avenue. The traffic eases;

he doesn't. He is so aware of everything. North on Victoria Park, east on Sheppard, he slides easily around every winter pothole. He approaches every intersection as if a reflex test. His eyes on the traffic light, green turns to amber, he hits his brakes and watches; cars on either side roar through.

"Did you see that?!"

She nods.

Pedestrians rush anxiously in front of him for a bus. He watches them, the nose of his van centimetres behind the stop line. They are about two metres from the curb when the light turns red, "All right you guys, my turn!" he yells, and again he has his answer.

He drives in the right lane. Nearing the next light, he shifts to the middle lane to allow other cars to turn right on the light. The light changes, he jumps into motion. Glancing in his rear-view mirror, he angles to the curb for no apparent reason. Then he hears the siren of the ambulance he saw, and cars around him scrambling to get out of the way. The ambulance slows. He shakes his head.

"Look at that," he points. A sign at a gas station reads "49.9" cents a litre. "That was 50.4 this morning." He looks at his gas gauge and shakes his head, "It always goes down when I've got a full tank." She nods.

Another car speeds by. He is going nearly ten kilometres per hour over the speed limit, this rusting Ford Tempo twenty or more. It darts in and out of lanes without signalling, and races through the next intersection as the light turns red.

"Look at him!" he snarls. There are no police around, there is nothing to stop him. And the way he controls his car, in all the ways that things might even out, probably they won't. He seems even to be having fun. Frank is angry.

A stoplight makes *him* stop. Some people can live on the other side of wrong; he can't. They find it exhilarating; they don't care. He can't live with that kind of risk. Faced with an almost-certain something better that might be worse, he prefers things as they are. He can learn to handle almost anything God gives him. It's surprise that does him in. And shame. So if the stoplight doesn't stop him, with God at his shoulder and a mother there too, something will. Then he sees all those drivers rewarded for their wrong, and it drives him crazy.

There is no voice in their heads. They do what they want, they believe in *their own* rightness not in someone else's. They *do*, and suckers like him always find a reason and *don't.* And who makes it in this world? So go through a red light, dump garbage on a public walkway because it's easier and faster; because *why not?*

He doesn't like that game. He's no good at it. There *were* rules the way he learned it. Play by them and get rewarded, violate them and pay the price. And that's what he has done all his life. And he has been rewarded: a nice family, a house, a good job, a van. If others have been rewarded more, they have played the game better; and if they've broken the rules and been better rewarded, they will get theirs. For if there isn't some elemental justice, what is there? Why have red lights at all? To the strongest and smartest, to the fastest car, goes every reward? He needs rules. He is good at rules. Take them away and he's lost.

Yet more and more, he feels like a Marquis of Queensbury fighter in a back-alley brawl, getting his brains beaten out. *This isn't right.* Doing good now may have its reward in heaven, but if everyone else doesn't believe the same, and doesn't try, it doesn't work. There is nothing holding *them* back the way he's being held back. He has no chance in their game. He can't and he won't throw in with them, but he can't stop his anger. He wants everyone, he needs everyone, to live the same way.

It was so much better as a kid in Whitby and Don Mills. Everybody thought the same way, everyone believed in something bigger and more powerful than themselves, or feared it. Eternity, the future, the system, all were to be respected, not challenged. But some time between then and now they've lost their hold. Why *should* I believe? I'm going to do what *I* want to do. If you don't like it, make me.

Am I the fool in this piece? the snarl in his voice is asking. Does everyone else know something I don't? Did I miss another clue? It can't be this way. I won't let it. So he sees wrongdoing if no one else does, casts judgment if no one else will. And now every time someone goes through a red light or tries to push into line, he looks at the driver's face. And more and more it seems, that face is black or brown or yellow.

He doesn't like seeing things this way, and so he tries to understand. Life was hard where they came from, he thinks. They had so little, there were so many of them. "To grab whatever scraps of food, whatever money or job they could get, they had to fight. They had to be the way they are just to survive." So he sympathizes. "But they aren't there any more."

If they chose to come here, it was to be Canadians, he says. Not just to respect the laws of Canada but to do as Canadians do. That was the bargain. Surely we have the right to ask and expect that, surely that's what they expect us to ask and expect. But from what he sees, that bargain, their bargain with him, has been broken. And now he wonders, did they come here really to be here, or to live a safer, more prosperous *there* here?

He has no quarrel with them, but why should he have to change because they don't? This is *his* country, it's been his country all his life, the country of his father and mother, of their fathers and mothers, for most of their lives. He liked it the way it was. He knew how to be a Canadian, he was good at it. Sure, his people had also once come from somewhere else, just as the aboriginals had crossed from Asia. Sure, Canada would have changed anyway, from automobiles, airplanes, computers, from external forces if nothing else. But just as surely, at some moment Canada had become *a something*. There was about it some bundle of expectations and ways of doing things that met no surprise and were done, some things that people from the outside coming in could see and learn and adapt to, that reinforced and made stronger what was and is. That's what his grandparents had done coming from Ireland and Delaware. There *is* something called Canada. There *is* a Canadian way. There may be no words on paper to express it, but just as indelibly it is there in hearts and minds and souls. It's in him. But that's not what he sees in them. So why do they do that? And why do we let them?

Not long ago, he heard on his radio that immigration would soon be increased to more than 200,000 a year. Canadians like living in a multiracial society, he has heard the polls say. But what he hasn't heard, because in three minutes of news there isn't time, is that higher-educated, higher-income people like diversity far more than people like him. And the polls say that too. Maybe it's because people like them know more, or know better how life *should* be. Maybe it's because they live in different neighbourhoods, work in different offices, in greater control of their lives maybe they can do more often as they like. Maybe living side by side, as immigrants and lower-income people do, is harder.

Canada may be a "community of communities" from the top down, but at the bottom it is nothing so tidy. It isn't tiny western towns eight comfortable miles apart, Ukrainians here, Icelanders there, Ruthenians, Galicians. It's not economic ghettos, Toronto's Forest Hill, Montreal's Westmount, Vancouver's Shaughnessy. It's the modern city, people living cheek by jowl in a churning, swirling mix. Here, people collide. Just last week he and Carolyn were doing their grocery shopping at Franklin's, a frozen-food store. Another husband and wife, each with a grocery cart, had left their carts side by side as they went to gather things from the shelves, blocking the aisle. When finally they returned, they started yammering to each other in a language he didn't understand. Meanwhile, nobody could get by. When he and Carolyn were walking towards the one open cashier, a small, older woman behind them surged past and got there first. She was Chinese.

He doesn't want to be prejudiced, he's never thought of himself that way. But again and again Orientals or blacks are the bad guys in his stories. Maybe it has to do with the area, he thinks. More than 20 per cent of Scarborough's people, about 125,000, are Asian-Canadians. And to those like him, used to Anglo-Saxon homogeneity, every unfamiliar face and colour counts like two. The Chinese population of Scarborough has more than doubled in the past ten years. So a smattering has become a core and a core a community, which has come to serve its own needs as communities do. Chinese movie theatres, grocery stores, banks; a stretch of shops on Sheppard Avenue has become the Dragon Centre Mall. Store signs have gone up in Chinese, even street signs. And the area, once mostly Anglo-Saxon, called Agincourt, to the outsider has become "Asiancourt."

He can feel the world dividing. He remembers in some of his science fiction books how alien worlds attacked the earth and our various, antagonistic parts united against them. How ironic, he thinks; those books going one way, his world another.

"I feel like a stranger in my own country," he likes to say. "But I'm going to stay right here. They can have the rest, but this is mine. Here I can do what I want and not worry about them taking it from me." He stops, and shakes his head. "But even that's wrong. Look at the robbery we just had."

Maybe what he sees has little to do with immigrants and their different ways. Maybe it has more to do with time and urgency and survival of a different kind. Maybe crimes are perpetrated by big BMWs as often as rusty Ford Tempos, by downtown yuppies with cellular phones to their ears. Maybe it's happening everywhere; but he's not everywhere.

He crosses Warden, Birchmount and Kennedy, traffic is moving well. He points out another gas station whose price has dropped since the morning; he passes Dragon Centre Mall. Though Double D is still giving his airborne reports, he doesn't hear them.

"I think I'm going to pay some bills tonight," he says suddenly. She nods. He seems pleased with the thought. This is music night but Janine's teacher can't make it again, the chiropractor isn't until the third Wednesday of the month, it's bill time again, so, yes, that's what he will do. He'll go to Scarborough Hydro, the cable TV building, then Consumers Gas, it won't take long. It saves him a little in stamps and this way he knows his cheques arrive (there's nothing he can do about the post office, after all). But mostly it's for something to do. An excuse to get out of the house and have some time on his own, it's something to think about on his way home. He doesn't often go in winter, but the weather is fine, there's no reason not to. Yes, he thinks, it's a good idea.

"I'll go right after dinner, be home by seven-thirty. What're you doing?"

"Oh, I've still got some sewing to do."

"I hope Matt's done the fish," he says, on to the next thought. There is pain on his face. It is Matt's week to start the dinners and tonight is fish night but he doesn't like doing fish. "I bet he'll have the pizza." She nods.

They know it's going to be pizza. *And he's supposed to do the fish.* That's what he was told, that's what he knows he should do. But so often lately, he's just done what he wants, with no regard to anyone else. He doesn't listen or doesn't care, it's hard to know which and after awhile it doesn't matter. He is old enough to do things his way, he thinks, but they've been doing things *their* way so long, they just end up butting heads. He is testing them, and they are testing him. "I just know it's going to be the pizza," he repeats, and they both shake their heads. And a part of them *wants* it to be the pizza.

"Hello!"

"Helloo!"

"What's for dinner?" he yells. Matt has no idea what's coming.

"Fish," he says.

Frank takes off his shoes, puts on his slippers and turns the corner to the kitchen. "Ya got a salad goin'? What's this, corn? You don't need corn if ya got a salad."

He and Carolyn change into their blue jeans. He fixes them each a glass of brandy. She helps Matt with the rest of dinner; he oversees. Here, his posture is different. Here he wants to be noticed.

They sit down at the table.

"For what we are about to receive, may the Lord make us truly thankful."

Stephanie is half-done the grace before the others are ready. Matt and Janine drop their forks from their mouths.

"Well, I'm starved," he enthuses, and digs right in. "But if anyone's going to get a [fish] bone, it's going to be me." He laughs and shakes his head.

"You always get them, Dad."

"Well, what happened at school today?"

Stephanie starts right in. She tells a complicated story about how one of the girls in her class did this and her teacher did that, which was really unfair, so all the girls were going to see the teacher after lunch, but they didn't, but she thought she'd see her tomorrow anyway. Matt and Janine, their eyes never leaving their plates, keep eating.

"What about you, Matt?"

He knew it was coming. "Oh, nothing."

"Ya get your science back yet?" He has been asking the same question for a week and is getting suspicious.

"No."

"Not yet? How long can it take to mark a science test?"

Matt shrugs.

Stephanie isn't unhappy where the conversation is going, except she can't say much, so she changes the subject,

"Dad, why are all your shirts brown?"

Startled, everyone looks up. "They're not all *brown*," he growls.

"They all look brown. You should get some blue ones, maybe a pink one."

"Well, isn't that interesting," he says, trying to look exasperated. "Why just today at work, I don't know how many people commented on my shirt."

"Dad," she shakes her head, "they just feel sorry for you."

He glances at Carolyn. "I could put that one up for adoption," he smiles.

"Oh that reminds me," he says, interrupting himself, "you'll never guess what I found in my drawer this morning." He likes wearing white socks with coloured bands at the top. Matt wears white socks with coloured bands too, which wasn't a problem until his feet grew and their socks began appearing in the wrong drawers. Which would have been OK except Matt's socks are tubed and his are fitted and he hates tube socks; and because Matt wears his socks seven days at a time, twenty-four hours a day or so it seems to him, so they get all dirty and crusty and end up in *his* drawer, and his clean, soft, fitted ones in Matt's; which Matt then wears until *they* get dirty and crusty. So last month, he bought some new white fitted ones with *no* colour band at the top. Now there could be no confusion. Then this morning in the dark, he put on one of his new white socks, and it was dirty and crusty. How could that happen?

"I've got some all-white ones too," Matt insists.

"Yeah, mine," he thunders.

Janine is next.

"What about you, Janine?" She had hoped to be forgotten.

This is a big year for her. She is in grade 8 and still in her special-education class, and next year is looming. He and

Carolyn don't want her to be streamed into technical or commercial, they want her to go to a regular high school. But she's having trouble. She was fine in grade 5, grade 6 was harder, in grade 7 she picked up again, so much so that this year she has just one special class a week, but it hasn't seemed enough. Her marks are poor. He and Carolyn think if she is held back this year that next year would be fine, and the year after she might be placed in a regular high school. They're not looking for miracles. They just want her to do as well as her friends. Her dyslexia isn't that bad; she has to learn to cope with it. He doesn't want her to have to trail behind her labels that just confirm what she fears, for her to be what she doesn't have to be just because she, her teachers and the other kids think different.

"Oh, nothing," Janine says, and he lets her comment pass.

Stephanie has eaten as much as she wants and is picking price tags off jars and sticking them on again. Bored of that, she is ready to tell another story about *her* and *her* school because she likes school and is doing just fine. Instead, the phone rings. It is for her. She pulls the cord around the corner of the doorway and disappears into the dining room.

"Not too long now," he yells. "We're still at dinner." He looks at Carolyn, "I don't know why they always call at dinner."

Stephanie returns, none too soon, and he shoots her a look. "Sit up straight; elbows off the table," and they all straighten up. She pushes too far sometimes, he thinks. He likes that about her and it bothers him; she gets away with it and that bothers him; and he envies her. Carolyn's mom exclaimed to them once, "Well, if she isn't Margaret Bloye." And he had to agree she was right.

They are nearly done. He takes another bite, and again it happens.

"Can you believe it," he sputters through a mouth half-full of food. "If somebody's going to get a bone, it's going to be me." They shake their heads.

Matt looks like he wants to leave; the others aren't quite done. He has been eyeing him. Why is he in such a hurry? He's just going to go downstairs and sit in front of that TV set, or play computer games. Or disappear behind that door of his, doing who knows what. Certainly not his homework. He never does that. He doesn't have any, he says. It's the strangest school he has ever seen. Every year, Matt starts out poorly, he and Carolyn get on him, they tell him his TV time is at risk, he does a little more, suddenly he's getting 60s and 70s, well enough that he doesn't even have to write his final exams. And because he knows that by this time of year, or thinks he does, he stops working, which is probably why every year he has such trouble at the start.

Yet if he pushes him, Matt resists. Why am I being punished, he wants to know? I'm doing fine, as well as all my friends, and he is. So he just stands there like a stone, taking it, giving none back, doing nothing about it, wearing him and Carolyn down until the way things were seems a lot more livable than how they want them to be. If he can't watch TV until his homework is done, fine, he says, he won't study either. He'll do something else behind that closed door. They're tired, they're not going to stand over him. They don't want to fight him day after day. If they're going to be unfair, he'll be unfair.

"Ya call Athlete's World yet Matt?"

"No."

Pause.

"Did you call Bob?" His sister Sue's husband, Bob, is the comptroller of an aluminum siding business.

"No."

"Why not?"

Pause.

He tries again. "Why don't you go and call him right now? They've got to need summer help at least. If you don't, they're going to have all their hiring done." In his voice is pleading and anger, accusation and reconciliation.

Matt says nothing.

His voice changes again. "You've gotta go out and pound the pavement." He has said this too many times before, and immediately he wishes he had said nothing. Again the moment loses its energy and dies. He knows enough not to ask Matt for another commitment; Matt knows enough not to give one.

Lately, he has come upon a new weapon, Matt's driver's licence. Matt turned sixteen a month ago. Two days later, he had his temporary licence, a day after that he drove for the first time. On his birthday, Frank wrote this to himself:

"I'm the father of a sixteen-year-old. Sixteen years of happiness, excitement, turmoil and surprises. They flew by so fast. Now Matthew is ready for his next step toward manhood, his driver's licence, the piece of paper that spells freedom and independence. I know how he feels.

"I can still remember getting my licence. It was the most important thing in the world. It didn't matter that your dad wouldn't let you drive the car, you still had to have it. In Matthew's case, it will be different. He will be allowed to drive the car. I will add the insurance once he has completed the 'Driver's Ed' course at school. Unfortunately, this won't happen until next September."

But maybe I won't add the insurance at all, he is beginning to think. Why is insurance any different from high-priced sneakers? Why should I spend my hard-earned money putting a kid behind the wheel who just wants to lie in front of a TV set, when he could just as easily get a job and pay for some of the insurance himself?

He hasn't said anything to him yet, but at dinner last night Matt said he'd like to do some driving this weekend, and would he go with him? This time *he* said nothing. Before Matt can get his licence he must take a course and pay some of his own insurance, for which he must have some money, which he doesn't have, and a job he's in no hurry to get. So he's in no hurry either, he's decided. As for this weekend, he told him, we'll see.

"Can I be excused?" Stephanie chirps. No one else asks. They all get up; dinner is over.

He cleans up the plates and loads the dishwasher; she puts things away. The kids did their work preparing dinner, and now go their separate ways. When he returns from paying the bills, he goes downstairs, past the open door to Matt's room. Taped to it is a computer-printed sign with a giant fist, its index finger pointed like a gun at anyone who comes near:

Hey you!
Keep moving!

Matt is playing "Space Quest" on the computer. At his friends' he plays Nintendo which he much prefers, but at "sixty bucks a game!" his dad refuses to buy it. "Besides, all these games are all the same," Frank says. For him, they have to be. Here, a space ship has been blown up and its only survivor is a caretaker; an alien has stolen a bomb that can destroy the universe. The caretaker/Matt, now he too, has to find it. He wanders the screen solving puzzles, avoiding traps, collecting points as he does. A wrong step and he dies but there aren't many clues to tell him what to do.

Matt works skilfully around the traps, once or twice Frank offers advice; the caretaker dies, they begin again. Quickly they get back to the same spot, Matt moves a different way, the caretaker lives, the pattern of the game comes back to him, he piles up points. "Save it, Matt. You should save it," he says gently; Matt, absorbed in the screen, carries on; the caretaker dies. They start again, sometimes Matt remembers to save, often he doesn't. His reminders remain gentle. Matt knows what he is doing. They get to the end but missed a few points on their way. They will try again another night.

It's eight o'clock and time for "Who's the Boss?" Stephanie and Janine run from upstairs and join them; Carolyn has some things still to do in the kitchen and will be down later. The TV room is dark and cozy. Matt grabs the easy chair opposite the TV, resting his slippered feet against the edge of the pine coffee table which runs the length of the sofa. Janine takes the end of the sofa nearest the TV, leaving the rest for her mom. He and Stephanie sit opposite Janine in side-by-side director's chairs.

Not more than thirty seconds pass, "That's a ree-peat!" he growls; the kids murmur agreement. Yet their pleasure seems undiminished. They remember the story but the laughs still surprise them, and soon they are all chuckling loudly.

At eight-thirty it's "Growing Pains" and the laughter continues. Carolyn joins them. She sits beside Janine propped against two pillows, her legs extended, her glasses on, sewing, occasionally glancing up at the set. She has a bag of frozen peas in her lap, her right forearm rests on it. Her arm has been bothering her, and for some time she hasn't been able to lift more than a few pounds. He thinks it is from all her keying at work; she isn't so sure.

"Move your chair out from the wall," he says suddenly to Stephanie who is so absorbed in Mike's problems at school that she does.

The phone rings. Interrupting the TV lull, it sounds like a fire bell. Matt moves forward in his chair,

"Get that Matt please and by the second ring." His words run together. At Superior Propane, every phone had to be answered by the second ring, so what began as Carolyn's instinct, has become his mission. Matt returns to the room, nods to Stephanie, who gets up and leaves.

Stephanie has to go to bed at nine, so she can watch TV after dinner while the others must wait until eight. For if TV is a treat, why should the others be more favoured? But on Tuesdays, she is allowed to stay up to nine-thirty to watch "Roseanne." The Conners, Roseanne and Dan, live at the corner of Third and Delaware in Lanford, Illinois with their three kids, a boy, D.J., and his two older sisters, Darlene and Becky. Darlene *is* Stephanie. Quick, smart-alecky and able to deliver the most awful zinger with the most angelic look. Me? Me?! So they call Darlene

"Stephanie," and Stephanie loves it. So Becky has become "Janine." "Janine, don't you do that," they say when Becky gets into trouble, and Janine seems to enjoy that too. Unfortunately, D.J. is the youngest and Matt the oldest. Of all of them, Matt seems to like the show least.

Carolyn likes Roseanne. The way she can stomp through the muck of every day and have none of it stick. The kids complain, dinner gets burnt, and *zing*, she spits out the line that everyone wishes they had said, that goes farther than they'd ever have the guts to go. And she gets away with it, because it's TV, because it's so true. In her house, nothing is where it should be and she doesn't care. They don't have enough money for a lot of things, they eat hamburger and meatloaf, they fight, sometimes they don't like each other and admit it, but laughter is always there. Her "I don't give a shit" attitude which she delivers with such delicious conviction, because she knows, and the audience knows, everything is going to be fine. Life's not bad. We're going to make it.

Tonight, it's another "ree-peat." It has too much to do with Roseanne for Stephanie's liking and she gets bored, the others laugh steadily. Then as the show's final credits begin to roll, the voice from the side sings out, "OK, girls . . ." with just a little too much pleasure, and Stephanie and Janine shuffle off to bed.

Matt settles even more contentedly into his chair. The three of them watch "Doogie Howser, M.D." At ten, Matt goes to bed, Frank takes the chair and he and Carolyn watch "Law & Order." Carolyn sews and dozes, more than once he nudges her, "Carolyn, why don't you go up to bed?" but this time is their time just as before it was their time with the kids, so she stays. Every so often, he reacts to something on the screen, otherwise nothing is said. He holds the flipper in his hand yet even during commercials it stays idle. They don't watch "The Wizard of Oz," "The Handmaid's Tale," two episodes of "Civil War" on PBS, an old movie with Lena Horne and Cab Calloway, the CBC news at ten, even bits and pieces of them. They know what they want to watch, and watch it.

This isn't their preferred TV night. Matt likes "Cheers," "The Fresh Prince of Bel-Air" and movies most of all, especially pay-TV movies regular TV wouldn't permit. The girls like "sitcoms," Carolyn made-for-TV movies, kidnappings, wife batterings, childhood cancers, anything based on real-life stories. He likes nature shows, car races and monster truck pulls, "Diaries of the Rich and Famous." He likes gardening shows, and James Bond movies best of all. He also likes horror movies, always careful to stand outside their action as others, absorbed in it, squirm. He likes the effects. His mother was the same. In *The Godfather*, when the horse's head was found in the bed, she sat bolt upright, "That's ridiculous," she said. "There's not that much blood in a horse's head."

Partly because they thought they should, he and Carolyn have also found shows they both like. "Knots Landing," "L.A. Law," the characters live such utterly different lives from the Conners of Lanford, Illinois, yet in the money, power, violence, physical beauty of the people and their surroundings, the hint of sex, stew of action and consequences, they find something repelling, compelling and impossible not to watch. All these "real-life" Houdinis escaping the bounds of their deeds to do again another week. (And *we* think living on $35,000 a year is hard!) Everything so unreal, and maybe not. Lives too much on the other side for them, too fast, too bad, too complicated: I sure am glad that isn't me; they sure are fun to watch.

They have two TVs, but they are a family. What is the point in being home if three of them watch in the basement, two in the bedroom? They are apart enough, at school, with friends, listening to their own music in their own headsets or rooms. Watching TV together might not seem much, but week after week, sharing the same shows and episodes, they build reference points, they share the same experiences.

But why not more? Why does their TV act like some gigantic drain, catching them in its swirl, sucking them into the basement the moment they step in their door? Keeping them there 23.3 hours a week, statistics say, many more hours a year than the kids spend in their classrooms, about two-thirds what he and Carolyn spend at work.

It is the poor man's night out. It is habit. But mostly, it is a break. They don't want anything else to do. They have enough trying to keep up in the rest of their day. He doesn't want to be engaged, engrossed or stirred to action. He's not looking for information. Ottawa welcoming home Canadian troops from the Gulf War, on opposite "Law & Order": what does TV's information have to do with the rest of his life? Technology has given us more to do when the sun goes down, yet still we need to sleep. So night after night he's not in his chair in the basement just to watch TV, but *to do nothing*, to sleep with his eyes open. Take away "Roseanne" and "L.A. Law" and he'd still be there. He is no weak, addicted member of the "entertain-me" generation, he is tired.

The kids are asleep, Carolyn has gone upstairs, he can hear her in the bathroom. He turns off the TV and climbs the stairs. His day is not quite done. He continues to the kitchen, empties the undrunk coffee of the day into a pot on the stove as his mother always did, and opens the refrigerator door. A nearly empty orange-juice container stares back at him. "I don't know why they can't make up the juice themselves," he mutters, and shakes his head. When the family moved to Scarborough and he had to move quickly through the morning darkness for his 6:05 bus, he had time only for orange juice, and no time to make it up. So he began checking the night before. Usually, he takes a can from the freezer and leaves it in the refrigerator to thaw overnight. Tonight, he decides to make it up. He fills the can to a bubbly top, careful that nothing spills over, turning off the faucet between each filling. He adds most of a fourth can to the mix, more water than the directions say, stirs until every lump is gone, then leaves the juice to chill for the morning, seven hours away.

He goes to the bathroom, reads as Carolyn snoozes beside him, says his prayers, and with his head back, toes up, hands clasped on his belly and covers pulled up to his chest, he falls asleep.

14

Yesterday was the big day. They opened the pool for the fifth time. Finally, officially it's summer. Yeahhh! It's hard to believe it's been five years already, six since they moved to Scarborough. Anyway, no more being cooped up inside, unless it's a wet summer of course, which it could be. The weatherman said it should be unusually hot and dry but you can't believe him and last summer was so good maybe they'll get more rain this year. They probably deserve it. Anyway, there are lots of things to do in the garden.

He sits where he sat a year and a day ago, in the same lawn chair on the same brick patio, his hands snuggling the same nearly empty coffee mug which, one more year from his fortieth birthday, looks no more chipped or stained. He has on the same blue jeans, even after a year of wearings and washings still as dark and indigo-coloured as before, but a different T-shirt, white not pale blue, fitting just as snug, maybe a little snugger over his belly. He wears the same old beige Hush Puppies and white socks, his or Matt's, old or new, he knows for certain though no one else does.

His moustache is gone. One morning several months ago he just shaved it off, got tired of it, and the next morning and for a few mornings after that he was surprised by the much younger person he saw in his mirror. Now his same old face is there again. A little fleshier than a year ago, though he hasn't gained weight, perhaps a pound or two, his hair a little thinner, but he *looks* the same. He looks fine. He doesn't expect Kevin Costner staring back at him every morning so he's not disappointed. That fat, dumb little kid is still there, but now he sees him only when things go very wrong, which they don't seem to as much, though he isn't sure why.

And yesterday went pretty well. There was the usual fight getting the kids up and fed and out to help. Matt decided he had to have a shower first, which no matter the time or circumstance always lasts five minutes longer than his best, most patient mood. Janine, after a year's worth of sleep, was still too tired; and Stephanie, anxious to please especially because her brother and sister were not, was suddenly called to the phone where she took her own sweet time planning out the rest of her day when nothing should have mattered until the pool cover was off. Anyway, he had to admit, they did just fine. Matt even managed not to have to slink into the pool to rescue the cover. He was pleased about that, Janine and Stephanie less so. But Matt did a good job, and he told him that. When he puts his mind to something, it's amazing what he can do. He told him that too. Then, his train of thought this far from the station and picking up steam, he said some other things as well. He probably shouldn't have. Anyway, Matt got the message, he thinks.

He loves today. It's the day after, when all the pressure is off. Anything that could have gone wrong would have gone wrong yesterday, today is for piddling around, doing the odd jobs that still need to be done with more time than he needs to do them. And today it's just him. He likes having the kids around, likes it when they do things together as a family. Sharing the work, sharing the fun, that's what a family is supposed to be. But it's hard. Different ages, different personalities, stages and needs, yet the work still has to be done. So they test each other and him, and he tests them, and nothing is ever simple or easy on the nerves. And all they're doing is taking a bloody cover off the pool. Why can't it just be that? He shakes his head.

He feels good today. One full day into the weekend and he's so much more relaxed. Saturday night is a bad TV night so last night he rented a video as he often does on Saturdays. He cooked hamburgers on the barbecue, then sat down early to the movie with Carolyn, Matt and Janine; Stephanie was at a sleep-over at a friend's; they were in bed by eleven. This morning, he got Janine up and collected Stephanie; the girls had their papers to do which they couldn't get out of the house to do until they had argued and everyone but Matt was awake. It will be the same next week. They argue to argue. Stephanie to remind Janine that three years older or not, no one's going to push her around; Janine to fight back.

He has a lot ahead of him this summer, just as he likes it. The tomato plants are in, the right ones this year, he hopes. The cherry tomatoes really weren't so bad. They were good on salads, and the rest they mashed up and added to the spaghetti sauce which gave them a few extra meals. Next door, John got in his plants a little sooner this year, so they are further along, which makes him harder to live with. But all the big jobs of summer are still ahead. The front walkway hasn't been moved, the patios are still uneven, his small wooden table still wobbles. They are all, as Carolyn puts it, "still in the wish jar."

But all in all, it's been a pretty good year. He doesn't think in terms like that very often. Day to day is challenge enough; look, and you never know what you might find. Lots of things may not have gone the way he wanted, but together everything added up to something good. He got his van, they kept their jobs, got promotions and raises, Janine got her keyboard, all the kids passed, Stephanie into grade 6, Janine to a regular high school, Matt into grade 11 (without writing his final exams).

They are all healthy. He is hardly ever sick, a cold once a year he can count on, but nothing that keeps him home from work. He hasn't missed a day in three years. He does get tired more often. His body metabolism seems to be slowing just as the metabolism of his work speeds up; his biological and social/economic clocks have collided. Not a good sign. But with his trips to the chiropractor, his back feels better. He still needs to lose a few pounds, his cholesterol level is high. Carolyn says it's their dinners. The kids get the meals started, they prepare to their tastes, skill and time, so nearly every night they have french fries and meat of some sort. Not much he can do about that.

He's having a little trouble with his teeth. His gums are receding, some nerves have been exposed and the enamel the dentist puts over them keeps chipping off. He needs bifocals now, but twenty years ago he tried them and tripped over curbs and things, so "I hate bifocals, I can't wear bifocals, etc., etc.," and he won't try them again. He has a large lump on his left temple, as if he was once hit by a baseball, and the lump has been there for years. It grew slowly, but hasn't grown since his last physical three years ago. The doctor advised him to have it removed, but an old guy at work told him he had the same thing done with his, and it just grew back. So he has left it.

But none of these are big problems, and most don't flare up unless he pushes himself, which he doesn't do often. Last winter, he was picking up Stephanie from school, the car got stuck and he tried to push it out. When he got home, he had to shovel the driveway. It was too much. Now whenever it snows, Carolyn yells to the kids, "Don't let your dad shovel the driveway," and he hates that. In his mind, he can do everything he ever could, unless he tries or someone doubts. When he is cutting the grass in back, when it's hot and sweat is pouring from him and Carolyn is yelling at him to take it easy, every so often he actually sees himself having a heart attack. His face, his body, the whole anguished scene. Sometimes he gets pains in his chest; but they go away. One of his supervisors at work had a heart attack and he was only forty-five. So now when Carolyn yells, he protests; and slows down a little.

In his father's or mother's history he doesn't see anything that makes him worry. His mother died of old age

and the body fatigue of bearing and raising eight kids. His
dad was a smoker and he doesn't smoke. His sisters and
brothers are all alive and well. Ann is nearly fifty-seven,
Mary Jean fifty-six, which he can't quite believe. Forty-three
isn't old, he knows, because he is forty-three; fifty-seven *is*,
but can't be, because Ann is his sister. But he has no great
physical ambitions, in his future no Boston Marathons to
run. For what he asks of his body, it still works fine.

And he doesn't think about age much. He is getting
older; people get old. Did he think he wouldn't? He won't
be Prime Minister. Did he think he would? Others may
have hidden themselves from themselves in youth and
ambition; he always knew. Not knowing hurt too much. At
forty-three, others may be seeing their pasts for the first
time, no longer just a series of stories, but *a story*, all its
paths, physical, emotional, intellectual, job, family, character, personality, coming together in one central path,
into the present, into *them*. And out the other side, also for
the first time, seeing a suddenly imaginable future gallop-
ing towards them. A mid-life crisis. Not him. His past is his
present is his future, and always has been.

His job is fine too. He complains about it, but who
doesn't? Yet at Imperial, complaining has become so much
the natural order of things that no one would know
enough to stop even if things were better, which they are,
or good, which they're not. Enough has changed that the
essence of the company now seems changed. The angle
through which all new information is taken in has shifted.
There is now an "old Imperial" and a "new Imperial," "B.T."
and "A.T.," before and after Texaco, and for the thousands
who remain, that is the story they will pass along. From now
on, the past will only improve, the present will not.

Management has been hit hardest. They are the myth-
makers and storytellers, the keepers and bearers of the
Imperial legacy. To them, it was always the guys on the floor
who got it. They weren't too smart; they did things
machines could do better if only machines could do them.

And someday would. They were different. Not like me. They were bodies and were replaceable, interchangeable. Of the firing sort. Bosses were minds and weren't. Bosses had been trained to be special all their lives; at home and school, the apple of every eye. They were "changers"; others changed. They stayed until *they* decided to leave. Now they're the ones "encouraged" to pick up the packages and go. And they don't know what to do.

They are like animals raised in captivity suddenly set loose. They have no idea what the outside looks like. Their competition has been inside, their network is inside. They have every educational skill they need to change, psychologically they're lost. The movers are being shaken.

But for him, how he feels mostly has to do with whether things are better than they were last week, the rest he can live with. And now, he is beginning to think it won't be long until everything is on an even keel again. What that even keel will be he doesn't know, nor really does it matter. He is used to change. Whatever it is will allow new routines to be set, surprises minimized, expectations remade. Then everything will be OK.

In his credit-card section, they have reorganized and reorganized again, broken into teams, worked in their teams until the bugs were out, then broke the teams up and tried something new. Nothing could be quite good enough. Some people had taken their packages and were gone, their work needed to be done, reduced, or taken over by technology in some new mix of ways for "premier" status to be achieved. But the equation wasn't balancing. But it had to balance.

They have automatic dialling now. He can be doing other work; if "the thing" gets "a live one," it buzzes his phone and switches his screen to the customer's account. They have automatic answering, "Push 0 if you want this, push 1 if you want that . . ." but many callers still push the wrong button and have to try again, which doesn't exactly put them in the mood to resolve matters quickly once they reach him. Average wait time on the lines has ranged from two to thirty minutes. This for busier people with less time to wait; for a company needing to offer premier service to earn a premier return in a more competitive marketplace.

Manage up, squeeze down. So directives have come forth: wait times will be cut to 120 seconds; to 60 seconds a month from now. Correspondence to be done after hours, phone lines kept open until 8:00 p.m. to handle B.C. "You won't find any of us staying until 8:00," he blurted gracelessly in one recent meeting. "I guess we'll just have to hire people who will," his supervisor said.

But he's not really concerned. He knows what Imperial is like. When Arden Haynes talked about Imperial's work-ers being its "most valued resource," he was listening. He has faith in the company. It will do right. It is going through hard times, struggling to be both what it was and now must be; he will go through them with it. There will be changes, and he will change because he must. But they will be grad-ual, manageable, humane, because that's how Imperial does things.

He knows the effect change can have, however, even on him. A few days ago, Gord Beddome, manager of the credit-card section, was passing his cubicle. "How's it going, Frank?" he said, as he must say a hundred times a week, not expecting a real answer. But Frank looked at him in a way that Beddome knew he was trapped.

"Yeah, really, how's it going?"

"You want the truth?" he asked.

"Yeah."

It rushed out.

"It's time you guys back off and leave us alone."

"What do you mean?" Beddome asked, not as ready as he thought.

"Well, Jesus Murphy, you got our noses to the grindstone already and now you're pushing harder. We're all adults, we're loyal to the company, we all need jobs. Back off, leave us alone, let us do them. Give up this 'premier company' stuff until we're through the merger. It's too much. One step at a time. We'll all get there."

He couldn't believe what he had said.

Yet that's the way things have been lately. In January, he got another good appraisal as well as his raise. Two years ago his supervisor rated him "excellent," last year "outstanding." He was her best at this, her best at that, her source of instruction for every new employee, she said. Conscientious, dependable, able to handle responsibility, he could be too excitable at times, she also said, especially when he was first in the job and found the number of calls, the pace and anger, the newness of it, overwhelming. But he had grown a lot since then, she told him.

When his supervisor does his appraisal, he must also do his own. His are always much harsher. It is what he believes, it is also his way to bring his own expectations low enough that no matter what his supervisor says, he'll feel better or less bad. It also puts his supervisor in the psychological corner of having to be his booster in order to balance the record. And it works, unless her words are *too* nice, because he can't handle that either. He isn't that good, has never been that good and whatever she says shouldn't be taken seriously; or, having "pulled the wool so badly over her eyes," it just goes to show he isn't as nice as she thinks, she'll soon find out and there will be hell to pay. Or if she doesn't, worse, he'll have new expectations to live up to.

He can't live with being so good. It's not his story; he doesn't know how to live it, he doesn't want the pressure of its expectations. So he cross-examines every good story in the making. You think I make good arrangements? You should see me at the end of the day. I stop listening, my mind is a blank, I can't see any of the stuff on the screen I'm supposed to see, etc., etc.

It is a story that is changing a little, however, though he would never admit it. Too many people are saying too many nice things that he can't quite not take in. He can see it in the way he's behaving. He is so much more aggressive: the way he drives, telling everybody where to go; in meetings, he used to fade into an empty chair, now he's asking questions when the answers don't even matter to him. It is that trouble-making other self of his who asked Carolyn to marry him, who to his teachers was more impertinent than funny, who he had always kept under such good wraps. Now, he's back.

A company vice-president was talking to their credit-card group not long ago. The first thing he said was, I don't like using a mike. Anybody can't hear me? And Frank said, *I* can't hear you. And the vice-president started talking, and again he asked, and again Frank told him. So he said to come closer to the front, and Frank said to come closer to the back. And he couldn't believe what was happening.

He buys a van, nothing happens. He gets a raise, gets great appraisals, tells Beddome to "back off." Nothing happens. He does it all as if there are no consequences. Why isn't God slapping me down? Before he bought the van, he even thought about that, and went ahead anyway. It's as if he is testing Him, taunting Him, pushing Him further and further. Ooh, it's coming, he tells himself. It's coming and when it comes, it's going to be bad. Then nothing. Last summer, he misread his supervisor and said some things he shouldn't have. But the matter passed. It never used to pass. He feels more sure of himself, as if all his disasters can now be undone. That's what's really different. A lifetime of big and little things, added up, subtracted, have somehow left him a feeling he's never had and doesn't understand. Confidence. He can do his job and keep it and get another if he loses it. *He* can do it.

Maybe, the rest of him thinks.

There *is* one thing he would like to have happen someday. It's not a big wish, he won't be devastated if it never occurs. He'd like to be a supervisor. There would be something quite fitting about that, he thinks. Starting at the bottom in the mail room, ten years in the computer room, in customer relations, now collections, each time something a little better, nothing too much. It would be recognition of all he has learned; that he has matured. It's a good goal, he thinks, the closest he can come to having no goal at all and still have one. It would just be there, he wouldn't have to think about it, with forty years of hard, never-miss-a-day work it should just happen, or almost happen, which is almost as good.

He doesn't like to set goals. He wanted a house, and bought it; he wanted a pool. But goals put you too glaringly in your own spotlight. How are you doing, they always want to know. Why aren't you doing better? To be a supervisor, though, he would need only to be himself, no one would even notice his ambition. He would hardly notice himself. Nearly halfway to those forty years now, he might just get there. He has trained a lot of people and been told he is good at it. He knows the book. A few years ago, he might even have gone higher, if things had been a little different.

It isn't often in his job that a big chance comes, but it did then. The company announced it would make credit "a profession." It established a clear career path and what it would take each step of the way, from assistant collector to senior collector, eventually to credit manager. More than work experience would be necessary. Those interested would have to take two home-study courses as well, one from a university. No more maybes or hope-to-bes, this was it.

He was more than forty years old, he had long ago given up the thought that this might be possible. Yet here was a chance to stop the present and jump into a different future. To do the undoable, graduate from the University of Toronto, something none of his brothers and sisters had done.

In the cold, clear light of the next morning, however, he seemed further away than before. Before, there had been no clear path. Before, being good at his job, working hard, putting in a life, it could happen; might happen. Now there was no getting around what he had to get around. He had to go back to school.

He hated school. He had never felt anything but stupid in school. He couldn't learn from teachers or textbooks. Never could, never would. So why was he even thinking about this? Still, if somehow he could get through. Still, it would mean so much time away from Carolyn and the kids, and with no assurance he could do the work or be better off in the end. After that other course he had taken, nothing had happened. Four hard years of nights, and the next day he was still a clerk. What had been the point?

At Superior Propane, he had taken a bookkeeping course. After his third straight "A" he got suspicious. "Hey, I'm not that smart. They pay the markers for each paper they grade, they just write 'A.' " So he stopped doing his assignments. Maybe all these courses are the same, he thought. What would be the point?

He went to his supervisor. He told her he understood the opportunity offered, but wasn't sure he wanted to go back to school. She felt the same, she said, but had decided to take the preliminary course and had just received her books. He asked if he could borrow them to look them over. A week later, he signed up himself.

The course was harder. They discussed their answers at work before mailing them in. His first result came back: "A." Here we go again, he thought, and stopped doing them. He still has his books at home, on the shelf under the computer table, other things are piled on them. On rainy Saturdays when he complains of nothing to do, he thinks of going back to them, then the rain stops and he never has. He hasn't sent in for his course refund, if he ever did mail them another assignment he thinks they would have to mark it. He could still finish the course; but two years have passed. Besides, the company said credit would become a profession "down the road." That might be a very long road years away. By that time it might have changed its mind.

So he jumped back into the present. Better just to keep moving.

Besides, he wants really to be a supervisor. And more than that, more important than some destination point is how he feels along his way. He wants to feel confident. And that has nothing to do with taking courses, and a lot to do with not taking them.

More than work, how he feels any day has mostly to do with the kids. They are all alive and well, something he never takes for granted. His mother's brothers weren't at their ages; Eileen had lost a daughter. His sisters, Lee and Sue, each have a child with Down's Syndrome. His own kids have had no illnesses or injuries to affect their futures. They aren't anorexic or bulemic, they've suffered no great emotional traumas. In their lives has been no divorce, no separation, no suicide or premature death. In school, they are where they should be; by Matt's age, he had already failed once, Carolyn twice. They seem good kids, as respectful and polite as any self-absorbed teenager is. They aren't bullies, don't pick on people except each other, they don't cheat, steal or take drugs so far as he knows. They aren't alcoholics, they don't carry weapons. Matt wears his baseball cap when some of his teachers say he can't, but that's about as bad as their trouble seems to get.

They seem happy. They are loved and love; they are as safe and secure as any suburban kid in the 1990s. They have enough to meet most of their material needs, and some of their wants. There isn't much yet they cannot be.

Still, he is too much his mother's son not to notice the rest.

It is why he has such a hard time with Matt. He is the oldest, he is getting there fastest, he will be there first. He tries to tell him: son, don't you get it. This world doesn't reward the big dream or big dreamer, not in people like you and me. We have to work hard. No one is asking you to be the smartest or strongest, no one assumes you are. Just be what you can be. Whatever you were born with, whatever you were given, but whatever you make of them too. So why don't you do your homework? Why not get a job?

John, Jim, Ann, Lee, Trish, Sue, they all went to college, they became professionals. They have bigger and better houses, two cars, they go on trips. They've had things easier, or better at least. I've done OK, my life is fine. I like my life, but everything I do takes me ten years longer. I want their life for you.

But that doesn't just happen. You like Air Jordans and Lamborghini Countaches; where will they come from? How will you get them? I never wanted much; you want so much more. To live my life you can't dream too hard. It hurts too much. And you are writing a far different story. I can see it, I know where it's going; and I'm afraid.

I'm an average guy. I've been average all my life. My parents and brothers and sisters and friends and all the kids in the neighbourhood saw me as average and treated me that way. My teachers did too. And that was fine. I never saw myself as anything more, I never tried to be. You have to learn to be average. And you have to want to be what you are to be good at it. To be happy and content. I could be good at average. Anything more didn't feel right, wasn't me. And average never hurt.

A lot of the kids I grew up with wanted much more. They were smarter, they did better in school; they wanted too much. They thought of themselves as stars, they had the expectations of stars. They were .250 hitters who wanted only to hit home runs, and swung themselves out of the league. They never learned the relentless, keep-at-it, year-after-year skills of being average. They've spent their whole lives trying to be what they're not. I *am* something. I am good at it. Average is my story, and that's just fine.

He doesn't expect a lot of his kids, he thinks. He's not like so many parents, pushing them to do this, join that. Years ago, he and Carolyn decided if any of them asked to do something, fine, if not they wouldn't push. Every summer Janine says she wants to play soccer, she waits for registration day, she says no. Fine. She and Stephanie wanted to join Brownies, Matt tried Cubs; they decided no more. Fine. They wanted to learn piano so he bought the keyboard as a test. Now all but Matt are playing. But if they stop, that's fine.

He won't forget, of course. And the next time they want something he'll bring up the piano and Brownies and they'll have to want hard to win that first fight. But it can be won. He's not looking to create prodigies. He has no hunger to make them into something he needs them to be. His parents didn't push, he and his brothers and sisters turned out all right, why should he push?

It isn't his parental job to spin grand dreams, he thinks. To inspire and push. Home isn't meant as an incubator of great deeds. It's "a safe haven," he says, a port in life's storm. "It's where you feel absolutely secure, comfortable, warm. Where there's no danger. You can roam from one corner of it to another without ever being lost or frightened. You have no worries. All your food, your bed and clothes are taken care of," he says. "Everything else in life, school, work, is an adventure out. Home you can rely on."

But he also doesn't push them because he doesn't know in which direction to push, nor whether he is up to it, or they are. There are no doctors or lawyers in his family, no rich businessmen or Olympic gold medalists. There could be, he thinks, there's no reason why not, this is a free country, work hard and anybody can be anything. But there aren't any, and maybe there's a message there.

He's not complaining. There has never been anything in his life he *had* to be or have. Like every other kid, he wanted to be a cowboy, a fireman, a farmer. He wanted a racing bike, a motor bike. He'd like a Mercedes 450 SL and a bigger house, but not much else. He has what he needs, the rest is trouble. It was the same around his parents' house. Eight kids have a way of keeping one's feet squarely on the ground, and so does religion. In the presence of immensity: creation, commandments, history, a force far greater than all others, there isn't much room to be too impressed with yourself.

You inhabit a tiny space of time. You do your best and then you die. Anything else is the sheerest presumption. ("Who do you think you are?") Anything else is set up for the fall.

"I just don't want them to turn out bad," he says of his kids. It is his greatest fear and wish. Anything else he can live with and so can they; *bad* has to do with character, that would be *his* fault, and how could he explain that to God and his mother? His kids grow up to be Prime Minister? "If it happens, it happens," he says. "But I don't want to force them to be something they don't want to be." For which is the bigger burden: not being, or having to try? He didn't go to university. He'd be "disappointed" if Matt didn't go, "thoroughly surprised" if Stephanie didn't, he hopes Janine might. He talks to them about it, well not very much, but he will. They know they will need to help pay their own way; university costs about $60,000 a year, he has heard, but he'll do what he can.

Stepping into the future. One day, he tried to express his greatest hopes for them. In an age where parents try to control every outcome, "I wish them every success," was all he said.

Then there's Carolyn. In two months, they'll be married twenty years. It seems enough like forever and only yesterday that whenever he tells stories of another time, he thinks of her as always there, yet can't quite fathom the sweep of the years. Time through both ends of the telescope. From the very beginning, they were comfortable together, and really, of course, they had to be. Her blonde hair and shy, gentle smile may have sparked his interest, but given his previous misadventures (and mostly non-adventures) with girls, he would never have asked her out, certainly never have gone out more than once, unless he had felt that instant ease. They liked each other, felt good around each other, and inhabiting the same space, they didn't need even to be doing the same things; breathing the same air seemed enough. This was no quivering, trembling collision of magnet and metal. They were two small streams running almost parallel, lapping at each others edges, coming together, blending into one. People who needed each other.

They see the world so much the same way. They laugh at how different they are, how opposites must attract, but beyond the obvious — he is Catholic, likes action movies and is cheap, she is Protestant, likes melodrama and is cheaper — they are soulmates. The lives given them more than forty years ago came with lots of sturdy strings attached. Obligations, responsibilities, and whether those came from the church or the religious-based values of the culture, they were understood. You were to be a good person, honest and fair, kind, decent, helpful to others. In big ways or small, to leave behind a better place than you found. Mostly, this would be done through the family. A spouse, kids, a home, the work would be hard and never-ending. If sometimes there was pain, pain was part of life and not to be avoided. A bed of roses, a bowl of cherries, the flower, fruit, thorn and pit, life was the whole package. And it was good.

The two of them may be rooted in the challenge of every day, but their focus has always been future. Children, family, tradition; the long-haul qualities of future: patience, dependability, consistency, caution, humility, respect, fear, faith, hope, trust, loyalty. At home or at work, *being there*. Life to them isn't a series of sprints with gold medals at the end of every race. It is a marathon, and only when you near the end do you know how you're doing. Nearly twenty years ago, they committed themselves to sharing that life. In good times and bad, for better and worse, in sickness and health, till death do them part. Without that belief in future, they know that everything seems a crisis, a disaster, a tragedy, nothing is just a bad stretch, a cycle, something to be lived with and gotten through. So they fight like everyone else, but living in the context of forever, things pass.

She was thinking about that recently. "I know he'd never waver," she said. Sounding too serious, she began to laugh. "He'll look, mind you. I tell him he can look as long as he doesn't touch," and she laughed again. "But there's no way. I'd be the most shocked person in the world if he told me he'd found someone else." He has seen the complications of breakup in her brother's life, but it's more than that. It wouldn't be right. Marriage is about more than him and her; it's about kids, their families and friends. Their stories. It's about the future, and no one has the right to mess with that.

His is a cranky generation. Born after World War II, the first raised on the dream of university, rich enough to be nurtured on space, on clean and new, on the scientific mind; on the corporate and political fast track, too smart not to hire and move ahead, able as no generation before to find answers to history's puzzles with the power of their trained minds. And who now, finally in positions of power, find these answers elusive. It's not how it was supposed to be. If religion is the opiate of the masses, politics, science and economics are the opiates of the élite.

Except the real opiates are faith, hope and busyness.

Like his parents, he is one generation out of synch. He believes in eternal life as those around him only hope. Yet now they are reaching an age where, having found no future in religion, they see none in science. Time is running out too fast. They will die before science will find a way to keep them alive. Death, divorce, layoffs, globalism, the bomb, etc., etc., now the future cannot be counted on. What is there now to bind generations together and hold them back? To make later seem more important than now?

And if there is nothing, why not now, why not me? Why not rob Peter to pay Paul, to pay Pamela and Patrick forever and ever? Why not reap more than we sow, run emotional, psychological, social, environmental, financial deficits? What is to stop us? Like soldiers on the eve of the final battle, eat, drink and be merry, for tomorrow we are earthly dust.

The loss of futureness. But not for them.

"The mass of men lead lives of quiet desperation." According to whom? Is that how it's supposed to feel when day after day life is the same? Riding the same route to work, eating the same food, watching the same TV shows, talking to the same people about the same things, sleeping under the same roof year after year? Thinking the same unexamined thoughts or no thoughts at all, without big dreams to lift you out of the mundane and average? Apparently. A car, a house in the suburbs, a TV, to the postwar critic that was conformity, to the postwar suburbanite a new and better life.

Who needs to dwell on the bad of life? What is the point? He has no stake in doom and gloom. This is his life, his only life, why should he let it feel that way? Life is tragic because he'll die? It doesn't feel tragic. He has lived more than forty years, he may have thirty more years ahead of him. That's a lot of time to wallow in something he can't change. Besides, the kids must be fed, the work-lists done. It's only the purposely tragic, or those with round-trip skills, talented enough to move in and out of bad whenever they please, that have a stake in bad. For everyone else, him and Carolyn included, you avoid bad, don't get bogged down in bad, you see what others see, but differently. You find people like you, make yourselves invisible, create your own kinder, more rewarding world. You avoid the bullies and kill yourselves off in every gunfight, just to feel what you feel when you open your eyes and life goes on.

The Hollywood ending is no Hollywood creation. It's how people feel and want to feel. What seems right and real to them. What has to. Things end happily because they do or because you shift your angle, zoom in, edit out, until everything looks that way. And why not? It's your story. In good times and bad, people tell pollsters how fundamentally content they are, as journalistic interpreters lob incredulous shots. Content? Are you crazy, how can you be content? The economy, the environment, crime in the streets, drugs, the state of the schools?

But these are for writers, academics, intellectuals who have time to dwell and brood. Whose job it is to see inside life, expose what others deny, show things as they are and shouldn't be. Feel life as life should be felt. And maybe it should feel that way. (We die, for God's sake!) Except the sun is still warm, the trees are green and someone still needs you. So he avoids the news, non-fiction and serious fiction, reads pulp fiction and autobiographies, watches TV and movies, because that's what his life feels like.

And he doesn't want that life to change. Those who want change control change, or think they do. To them, change is fun; interesting, stimulating, challenging. A game. It's no game for him. Those from reform-minded political parties go after his vote; we are your chance, they say. Don't take it any longer. What have you got to lose?

What have I got to lose?! I have *everything* to lose!! Don't you understand? You run things in your world — campaigns, canvasses, small businesses, charities; you think you can run the country; I get dragged around by my nose. I don't like that a lot, but after all these years I'm almost used to it. I know the tricks of it. I can roll with its worst punches. Change everything and I've got to learn everything again. I don't learn that easy. I might not be able to do it. And all those feelings coming back. Why would I want to go through that again?

But you wouldn't understand. You may have grown up in a house like mine, maybe you were poor. But there was something about you, in you, that made you and allowed you to take control. You're a star, I'm not. That's the difference. That's the real division in this world. Not money, not education or gender. It's those who move and shake and those who don't. It's an attitude, a style, a way of thinking and being. And you can't understand me and I don't understand you. I horrify you. I'm everything you set out in your life not to be, everything your parents weren't going to create. You can't even say the word, "average," without whispering it, apologizing for it, cringing. The sameness of my life; I am your worst nightmare. You think you can rise above everything, that everything's so bad, that everything should be so much better. I can't rise. For me, everything has to be fine. So it is fine. You want to represent me? The biggest favour you can do me is leave me alone; don't change a thing.

It was in high school, he thinks, that he read a book about an élite club. The club had in it ten or twelve members, Americans, Europeans, Arabs, Chinese, all very wealthy, none a political leader, yet together they controlled the world. Except no one else knew, for theirs was a secret club. Years before, they had worked up a plan, set it in motion, then slowly manipulated events their way. Bribing, terrorizing, assassinating, more often acting in subtle ways that seemed to every other eye accidental, coincidental or normal. Someone is planted in one place, others unconnected to the plan get pushed a little one way or another, still others are pushed by them, and others, until years later everything is as the plan set out.

He had never seen things work like that in his life. To him, it seemed entirely plausible. All the things he never understood; the stories on his radio. Even recently, why Mulroney, why Bush? Why free trade and no capital punishment? Nobody likes them, nobody *he* knows anyway, yet they happen. When he was a boy, why Kennedy and Martin Luther King? They were trying to do good. Who would want to stop them? Why did one Pope die so suddenly, why was another shot? He doesn't know, and knows he will never know. So unable to find sense in the normal sense of things, why *not* an élite club?

This is a scientific age. For every question there is an answer we must find, for only then are we truly in control. Able to change, to improve, at least to understand; everything subject to *our* powers, *our* free will. At the centre of *our* universe. So if we have no answer, we look until we create one, for one is expected. One is needed. One kid gets hit by a car, another does not, we explain, we blame. It's his fault, or hers. (Maybe the élite club did it.) A part of him wants and expects answers too. In movies and books, he enjoys the intricate web of conspiracy theories; the dark drama of paranoia. In real life, he wants nothing of the sort.

Most things in his life he doesn't know and isn't going to know. Over lots more he has no power. There is a force beyond him, he believes, and he accepts it and his own powerlessness before it because he trusts that force and has no choice. Better to be in merciful and forgiving hands than selfish ones; to be subject to some higher order than someone like him. If he can't understand everything, it's better that no one can. And if that force exists, better he never understands it nor spends his life trying; anguishing on why things are as they are, on what he cannot answer. (We live long enough to get things wrong and learn, and not long enough to get them right, and pass them on to others. God's joke.) Better to assume there *is* an answer, that somebody somewhere knows why, that things just are, that life just is.

That's all he has to know, all he wants to know, all that will do him any good anyway. Then he can set his eyes straight ahead on what he is doing, and everything will be fine.

Bloye luck. It's not bad.

At forty-three, nothing seems so great to him, everything/everyone is small, everything/everyone matters. It isn't an attitude that inspires great deeds, generates great wealth and power, transforms lives. He will never be Einstein or Churchill or Hitler or Rockefeller or Marx or Oppenheimer. His footprints on this earth will be faint, slight, shallow, and except in a "look," a phrase, a family photograph, in not many years they will be gone almost without trace. He has asked little, taken little, added and subtracted little except in his own little world. Outside it, not much will have changed for his being born. He is one, with Carolyn they will leave three behind; from his deeds, the world's clock will be no closer to its final midnight. He is part of life's continuity.

He's not sure where things will go from here. He hasn't thought about that much, though he knows he should. It isn't fair to Carolyn and the kids, they depend on him. It's not being mature. Yet it seems only weeks ago he was in high school, never going to get married, never to have kids. He's just now nicely settling in. It can't be that time yet.

It's not as if he has any ambitious retirement in mind that needs much planning. He owes about $35,000 on the house; it cost $87,900 six years ago. In Toronto's market he could probably sell it for $200,000, though he isn't sure. They would need to find another place to live. In the country, he imagines; in the city, she imagines. Sell the house, take back a mortgage for monthly income as his mother did, put the down payment in the bank and live off the interest. Then get a part-time job, pumping gas, or even better, and he laughs when he thinks of it, in a supermarket. Maybe he could get his old aisle back.

Instead of a house or apartment, he would get another trailer. Two actually. One in a small town somewhere, not far away, work his supermarket job there in the summer, have another trailer down south, in Florida maybe. He has never been to Florida; Carolyn has. She doesn't like trailers, she likes her house, but she could get used to it.

He'd like to travel more. He went to Expo '67 in Montreal, to the Maritimes a year later, Cape Cod on their honeymoon, that's about all. He'd like to go back to the Maritimes, drive out west, maybe go to Alaska, to England or Australia. He has never been on a plane, but he would enjoy flying, he thinks.

And maybe before all this, get a bigger house, though he knows that won't happen. Any real dreams he has, it seems, have to do with houses. Go to university, get a better job, win the lottery: buy a bigger house. It's always the punch line. To him, it's how money changes a life. It would be in the country, at the end of a long curving driveway; two-storeys high, with a pool in the back, and a proper garden with proper soil and sun, all on a big piece of land. The master bedroom would have a bathroom ensuite, the kids would each have a room. He'd have a spiral staircase; a TV room in the basement and a nice, big workshop with all the tools and wood he needed. He'd make furniture to fill all their rooms, do all expansions and renovations himself, and finally with the proper equipment and space, learn to do them right.

Or maybe he'd put an addition on their house. He has been thinking of that lately. He'd add a second storey, hire a professional to frame the outside and do all the inside himself. He'd have three or four bedrooms upstairs, a large master bedroom with an ensuite and a deck overlooking the pool. Downstairs, he'd turn the two back bedrooms into a family room, with French doors leading onto a patio and out to the pool. Stephanie's room would become Carolyn's sewing room. The outside would be in aluminum siding; Sue's husband is in the business. It would all cost about $100,000, he has been told. Oh well. As Carolyn said, "By the time we'd get around to it, the kids would be grown up anyway."

Soon it will just be the two of them. He is a little worried about that. He has heard of other couples who when it came to living their lives again, found nothing there. That's why he tells Carolyn they have to start doing more things together. They go on walks, have their drives to work and back, their time around the pool and watching TV. But sometimes they seem to wander through the house like two phantoms, past each other, no words, no recognition, as if the other isn't there.

Or maybe that's the comfort they feel. They get along so well. They seem so in tune. One will say something, the other will say, "I was just thinking that," and laugh. They rarely fight any more. After all the years of whose mother knows best, whose is butting in, and which of them, he or Carolyn, can pile a bigger history of wrongdoing on the other faster, none of that seems to matter as much. During the week, he does the bed his way, on the weekends she does it hers, on Monday when she is in the shower, he redoes it. No big deal. Even this morning. Half asleep in the bathroom, he picked up the toothpaste and squeezed from the bottom as he has taught them all to do. Whoever had last used the tube had forgotten to put on the cap and the toothpaste went all over him. He was not pleased. And when they're all together at lunch, he will make a point of that. Probably, a big point. But that was the kids. He and they *are* still competing. As for him and Carolyn, everything is easier, nicer. They have become partners in this life.

And really, of course, it could be no other way. He cannot leave Imperial, pick up a package and start his own business. He can't sell his house, move to another neighbourhood, send his kids to private school, leave the country and live somewhere else. He is where he is and here he must stay. He goes as Blackwater Crescent goes, as "Asiancourt" and Scarborough and Toronto and Canada and Imperial Oil, as the world around him goes. What is to others a front-page issue, is to him a *fact*. He cannot buy his way out, or skill his way out of the circumstances of his life, his marriage included. He must face them, deal with them, make the best of them, find a way.

He doesn't want to think too much about the future now. That time will come. He should be concentrating on now, he thinks, for these are the good times. This is what all those other years were for. To be good in his job, to provide for his family as his father had done for them, to feel secure and confident; to feel mature. And he's done that. They're there.

In the first forty years, you struggle, he likes to say. You try to be what you can be. Now you *are*, and for the rest of your life that's what you will be. For him, the struggle is over. He knows how to do what he needs to do, he has what he wants. "It's all downhill from here," he says. "It's time to smell the roses."

He shifts in his lawn chair and looks deeper into the late morning sky. Back from delivering her papers, Stephanie peeks from behind the curtains in their bedroom. She watches him. He nods to himself and smiles a tiny smile.

EPILOGUE

"Hello, my name is Frank Bloye, and I understand you'd like to talk to me." It was September, 1988, and it was the first time I heard his voice.

I knew only that someone would be calling. I didn't know his name, but from notes I had at the time I knew it would be a male, forty years old with a wife and three kids, a high-school education and an income of about thirty to thirty-five thousand dollars a year. A few months before, I had contacted a friend at Imperial Oil and a co-worker of his had been given permission to conduct a computer search for me. This information had come from his screen. What he had also been able to learn was that this person was "very nice but excitable," quiet but not necessarily shy, liked to read and, from a letter of complaint he had written to the company to protest a job promise not fulfilled, "wrote well." I also knew that he had been with Imperial since 1972, lived or had lived in Oshawa, had just bought a house, and had gone about as far as he could go with the company.

Not long before, I had worked briefly with the Ontario government. Very early in that job, I had come to realize that the people I was supposed to be acting for I didn't know. I also had the feeling that the politicians and bureaucrats around me didn't know them either. These weren't the "ordinary" achievers invited to be "the public" at government conferences and gatherings, or the "ordinary" articulate people interviewed on TV. These were people who go unnoticed because they aren't very noticeable and who for the most part don't want to be noticed.

What about them? What did they think about? How did they spend their time? What mattered to them? What did they hope for, what did they dream? The workplace was changing, the neighbourhood, the city, the country, the family — how were they doing? What was life like for them? I thought if I was to do this work, I surely had an obligation to find out.

We first met in a coffee shop near his work. He wore a sports jacket and tie. I haven't seen him in a tie since. He had a lot of questions. I tried to describe how it would feel to be written about. I told him when he first read the manuscript he would probably hate it, that everything he liked and wanted to have written about him would fade from its pages, and left would be scattered words, phrases and paragraphs he didn't like in over-sized type, in red ink. He would be embarrassed, humiliated, angry until, if things went well, family and friends would approach him, even people he didn't know, those for whom the black type hadn't faded, who had read the black *with* the red, and understood.

We spent two or three months talking, getting to know each other, trying to guess at what would be ahead. We knew it would mean a lot of time, and a lot more. If we decided to do it with each other, he had to stick with me, and I had to stick with him. To see us through the tough spots, everyone, Carolyn and the kids included, would need to be not just cooperative but willing, enthusiastic. In the late winter of 1989, we decided to go ahead.

We started slowly. I had other projects to complete; I also wanted for time to pass, to experience more of his life with him, to get to know him slowly. What I couldn't do, above all, was get in the way of him living his life. I had to be as absent and invisible from it as possible. So talks needed to be irregular, infrequent, over years of time. Later, we had a series of long conversations, neither of us knowing what we would find, starting with a direction in mind, going as conversations do, where the last thought led us. We would talk in the evenings, when dinner and clean-up were done and the rest of the family had gone to the basement to watch TV. Once I began writing, we would also talk on the phone, usually when he was at work.

I lived with him for a week, sleeping on the couch in the TV room, driving with him and Carolyn to work and back. I sat beside him in his cubicle for two weeks as he worked, listening to the voices from across the country through an extra headset hooked up to his phone, seeing their life stories on his screen. I talked with his sisters and brothers, to co-workers and old friends, each of whom in a hushed voice wanted to know: "Why are you writing a book about *him*? He's so, so average."

Along the way, we discovered the kind of biographer-subject coincidences that emerge with proximity:

We were born in the same year, 1947 (he is ten days older);

Our mothers were both named Margaret; his was a nurse, mine a teacher, until marriage brought them both into the home;

Our fathers were grade 10 dropouts and construction business salesmen who could "sell anybody";

His father and my daughter share the same birthday (January 5);

One of his brother-in-law's brothers and my brother played on the same hockey team (Canadian junior champion, Memorial Cup winner, St. Michael's College Majors);

He was at Don Mills high school when I was playing basketball across the city at Etobicoke; Etobicoke played Don Mills in the Toronto district playoffs (and lost).

Until that phone call, however, so far as we know our paths had never crossed. From high school on, we had lived very different lives. Yet in the nearly five years I have come to know him, I have learned more about myself and my own life than at any other time.

I am grateful, first of all, to Frank for trusting me with his story. It was not easy for him to do. He took an enormous chance when chances taken in his life haven't often been rewarded. Also to Matt, Janine and Stephanie, and especially to Carolyn. To the rest of the Bloyes and their spouses for their time and patience. To Imperial Oil, Bill Moher, Zen Yarymowich and Betty Schill for their cooperation and assistance. To numerous archivists and librarians, most particularly Brian Winter, who love so much what they are doing to give so willingly to those who share their passion. To Peter Foster, Rick Salutin, Desmond Morton and others for their comments and criticisms of various parts of the manuscript; to Peter Pearson and Mary Adachi whose love of language detects and loosens every "bump" and "stick." To Morton Mint who six years ago understood what I was trying to do; to Janet Pawson who always believes. To Cynthia Good who stuck with me, prodding, pushing, encouraging, always with enthusiasm and spirit. To Lynda, Sarah and Michael who make life interesting.

Ken Dryden
Toronto
June 1, 1993